CONDUCTING CHORAL MUSIC

3rd edition

Conducting Choral Music

Robert L. Garretson

Colorado State University,
Fort Collins

Allyn and Bacon, Inc.
Boston

© Copyright 1970 by ALLYN AND BACON, Inc.

© Copyright 1961, 1965 by ALLYN AND BACON, Inc.

470 Atlantic Avenue, Boston. All rights re-
served. No part of this book may be reproduced
in any form, or by any means, without permission in writing from the publisher.

Library of Congress Catalog Card Number:
74-107623

Printed in the United States of America.

783.8
G192c
3d ed.

Contents

Preface

IN THIS THIRD EDITION of *Conducting Choral Music,* the contents have been rearranged to begin with the aspiring conductor's most immediate concerns and end with those topics more pertinent to specific teaching situations. The chapter on rehearsal techniques has been completely revised and considerable new material has been added, including a section on improving music reading. Careful editing has been done throughout—some material has been condensed, the unessential has been eliminated, and various points have been elaborated upon and illustrated with additional examples. The list of references at the end of each chapter has been updated. The source information in the Appendix has also been revised, with special attention being given to the inclusion of new choral octavo publications and extended choral works.

Results of a study by the author focus attention upon the inadequacy with which many choral conductors regard their professional training. It was the consensus of a large group of conductors, whose views were sought, that their training should have been of a more practical nature. With this guiding thought in mind, the author has endeavored to present an approach to the solution of particular problems that the conductor is likely to meet, especially during his first few years of conducting experience. Specific practices and techniques have been presented to give the reader the utmost assistance. Since few teaching situations are identical, the inclusion of basic principles will be found helpful in increasing the conductor's insight and in providing a general approach for meeting and solving problems as they arise.

This book is addressed to conductors of school choirs and choruses, to church choir directors, to leaders of community choral groups, and to students who wish to improve their understanding of the art of choral singing. It may also be of interest and help to administrators and other individuals seeking a knowledge of the aims and problems of the choral conductor. Its design and content are intended to deal with the principles and techniques studied in college and university courses in choral conducting, choral methods and materials, and secondary school music.

Areas of particular concern to the choral conductor and necessary in his professional training are: conducting techniques, tone and diction, style and interpretation, rehearsal techniques, programs and concerts, and planning and organization. A chapter, therefore, is devoted to each of these areas. It is hoped that this book, based upon the teaching needs of numerous choral conductors, will contribute to the betterment of choral singing.

Many persons have contributed to the author's concepts as presented in this book. Some of the ideas have been formulated through observation and discussion with choral conductors throughout the country. The techniques suggested have crystallized during the author's application of them while working with various groups: with school choirs and choruses, church choirs, and choral groups on the university level. To all concerned—conductors and singers—I express my gratitude.

For permission to use excerpts from their choral publications, I am indebted to the following music publishers: Galaxy Music Company, Oliver Ditson Company, Theodore Presser Company, Franco Columbo Publications, Neil A. Kjos Music Co., Shawnee Press, G. Schirmer and Chappell & Co., Inc., Boosey and Hawkes, Inc., and Verlag Friedrich Pustet (Regensburg, Germany).

For permission to quote from their publications, I express appreciation to Oxford University Press, W. W. Norton & Co., *The NATS Bulletin,* Harcourt, Brace and World, Inc., Macmillan & Company, Ltd. and St. Martin's Press, and Collegiate Cap and Gown Company.

To Film-Art, Inc., Keichi Nakamoto, and to William R. Whitteker, for special photographs, and to Joseph Sagmaster, Director of Broadcasting, University of Cincinnati, for the material on television hand signals, I express appreciation. For his suggestions concerning conducting diagrams, I also make grateful mention of Professor Ippocrates Pappoutsakis of the University of Vermont. I benefitted considerably from the late Dr. Harry R. Wilson, of Teachers College, Columbia University, who contributed substantially to my thinking, particularly in the area of choral tone and diction. To colleagues R. Robert Hornyak, for helpful suggestions with regard to the chapter on conducting techniques, to Ira C. Singleton and Simon V. Anderson, for editorial help, and to Scott Huston for helpful suggestions with regard to the chapter on style and interpretation, I am especially indebted. To Mary H. Swift, for valuable editorial assistance, and to my wife, Aretha, who typed the manuscript and offered considerable encouragement, I am particularly grateful.

R. L. G.

CONDUCTING CHORAL MUSIC

Introduction

DURING THE TWENTIETH CENTURY, particularly since World War I, choral singing has assumed a position of increasing importance and popularity in our society. School and college choirs and choruses, church choirs, community choruses, and choruses sponsored by industrial and commercial firms have increased in size and in quality. Individuals are quite naturally drawn to activities that they enjoy. Let us, however, examine some of the underlying reasons for this increase and development of choral singing.

Considerable credit should be given schools and colleges for this phenomenal growth. In the past several decades choral music has progressed from a largely extracurricular activity to an integral part of the school curriculum. This would not have occurred without at least some degree of recognition of the values of music participation. Without attempting an exhaustive consideration of these values, for our purpose they may be summarized as follows.

While the benefits of choral singing are many, the *aesthetic* and *expressive* values of music are considered to be the most important. All persons need to develop a sensitivity to beauty in music and other art forms, as understanding and appreciation of them may serve to refine and humanize their entire existence. As music is a significant and integral part of man's culture, it is the school's responsibility to help students become more intelligent consumers of music. Participation in musical activities can serve as a means through which individual musical taste may be improved. Through a study of the vast wealth of music literature, students may learn to discriminate between the musically trite and the rich musical heritage which is the right and privilege of every individual. Man also has a need for individual self-expression in as many varied ways as possible. While many concepts and ideas may be expressed through language, other aspects of man's experience can be best expressed through various other art forms. The aesthetic and expressive values of music are, therefore, the principal justifications for its inclusion in the school curriculum.

The *personal-social* values of choral singing also deserve consideration. All individuals need opportunity to engage in activities that promote physical development and that feeling of well-being which is characteristic of good mental health. Music participation can contribute to these ends. Correct posture and proper breathing techniques are emphasized as an adjunct of choral singing and are a necessary attainment of the well-trained choral group. Music also serves as a wholesome outlet and expression of individual emotions. Through music, individuals not only can express themselves, but also can release pent-up feelings of frustration so common in our present-day society.

Through contributing time and talent to various social organizations, and being accepted by other members of such groups, man fulfills his need "to belong": his social being finds expression. A characteristic of the adolescent, as he strives to become a social being, is the strong desire to belong to the "gang," inasmuch as membership in various groups usually results in satisfaction and acceptance by members of the peer group. Through cooperative group endeavor, the chorus or choir provides additional opportunity for the development of democratic attitudes and a wholesome channeling of interests toward members of the opposite sex. Students in music activities develop pride in being identified with a fine musical organization and make many social adjustments through the close association with their peers.

Finally, and not to be overlooked, are the *avocational* and *vocational* values that accrue from music participation. Changes in the attitudes of our society, coupled with many modern living improvements, have resulted in a greater amount of leisure time for most individuals. These changes are highly desirable and offer increased opportunity for individuals to explore many possible areas. As a result of improved educational programs, many persons have discovered music to be an area from which they may derive great personal enjoyment and satisfaction. If continuing programs of music instruction are to be maintained in our society, then vocational needs must also be met. In addition to pursuing a teaching career, opportunities also exist in the area of professional music. If one is to be eminently successful in these areas of endeavor, then knowledge and skills must be developed at a reasonably early age.

Many institutions in our society other than schools have also contributed to influencing the status of choral music. Increasing awareness of the importance of music as a force in religious worship has resulted in a resurgence of emphasis upon church music programs. An increasing number of churches have employed full-time persons to assume responsibility for the development of the music program. Often these individuals carry the title of Minister of Music, and in effect their duties reflect this title. Choirs for children of elementary school age, for junior and senior high school youth, and for adults are maintained to meet the musical and social needs of all age groups.

Industry's increasing awareness of the importance of rapport in a cohesive, closely knit organization has prompted the establishment of numerous company choruses and other related music activities. Under capable leadership, these organizations have improved employees' morale, developed a feeling of belonging, improved labor and management relationships, and through periodical concerts have strengthened community ties.

The media of radio, television, motion pictures, and recordings have considerably influenced the tastes of the listening public in recent years. Radio has promoted greater understanding and has brought various sections of the country closer together. Remote and isolated areas have reaped a particular benefit. Music of many varied types has been made available to interested listeners at a minimum cost. Many FM stations, in particular, continue to present music of a high quality.

The impact of television, yet in its infancy, has been overwhelming and its cumulative effects have yet to be evaluated. Although an increase in the quality and quantity of musical programs seems desirable and would appear destined for the future, a limited number of excellent programs have been produced. Forward-looking teachers have brought these programs to their students' attention and have utilized them as a valuable educational tool.

Some choirs and choruses have been fortunate enough to make periodic appearances on television. Such experiences, by motivating a choral organization toward maximum group effort, can contribute substantially to the attainment of higher musical standards. The increased use of video tape for such programs also provides a choral group with opportunities to observe and to evaluate the visual as well as the musical aspects of their performance. Educational television especially has utilized the talents of amateur choral groups, and has presented a number of other programs designed to promote musical understanding and appreciation. Since choral music programs may be televised with a minimum of staging and production costs, further possibilities will undoubtedly be explored in the future.

Music has served effectively to heighten the intensity of dramatic situations in motion pictures; and the public is currently experiencing a barrage of tonal sounds and effects associated with theatrical and television productions and the modern dance. Although choral music per se has been too infrequently featured, this background music has perhaps to some extent developed a general tonal awareness of a variety of vocal tone qualities and instrumental tone colors.

Recorded music, especially since the advent of the long-playing record, has made available to the listening public more music of a high quality than ever before. Numerous recordings of college and university choirs, church choirs, and professional choruses from the United States and Europe are presently available. Previously produced recordings of choral organizations number in the hundreds, and new recordings are being released periodically. Especially strong interest has been developed in recent years by "hi-fi" and stereophonic recordings. While some of this interest may stem from mechanical or engineering factors, rather than musical aspects, it is felt that this development has been generally beneficial to the improvement of musical tastes. Inherent in choral recordings are tremendous educational possibilities which, if effectively utilized in educational programs, may further improve the quality of choral singing in America.

Choral music has grown considerably and is still growing in America. However, the previously discussed influences are bound to reap a desirable cumulative harvest. Capable and inspired leadership—emphasizing wide participation and high musical standards—will ultimately place choral music in its proper sphere as a social and aesthetic art.

1

Conducting Techniques

THE BASIC FUNCTION OF the conductor is to interpret the music for the singers. Through varied means he endeavors to instill life and vitality into the music—the end result of which is a truly thrilling and genuinely aesthetic experience for both the participants and the listening audience.

The conductor must be more than a mere time-beater. His musical knowledge and interpretative wishes should be conveyed through his conducting technique. Of course, the value and importance of demonstrations and verbal explanations should not be minimized. During rehearsals, however, lengthy verbal explanations should be kept to a minimum, for through his technique[1] the experienced conductor can more quickly help the group achieve the desired interpretation.

FUNDAMENTAL CONDUCTING PATTERNS

Each conductor is likely to have his own methods, but the fundamental patterns are the same. Time should be devoted to practicing

---

[1] *Technique* in this context refers to the multitude of devices used by a conductor to convey the intent of the music and to achieve musical and artistic results. Fundamental conducting patterns, important as they are, are really subservient to the bodily and facial expressions that reflect the mood of the music. Nevertheless, they provide a necessary basis from which to start.

5

the basic movements until they become automatic. For the purpose of clarification, each of the following meter patterns is presented in at least two ways. The first illustrates the basic direction of the beats within the pattern. The subsequent patterns illustrate the manner in which the conductor may apply them in the interpretation of music. The dotted lines in these conducting diagrams are called "rebounds"

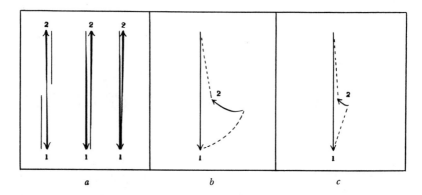

Fig. 1.   Duple meter (2/4, 2/2, 2/8)—(b) for slower tempi, (c) for faster tempi.

or "afterstrokes." Although they should be considered subordinate to the basic movements within the pattern, they serve as connecting motions between the various beats and as preparatory motions to each subsequent beat. A degree of tension should occur toward the end or point of each beat, which is followed by a degree of relaxation during the "rebound." Combined, these factors serve to give the conducting movements definiteness, clarity, and smoothness or flow—all of which are essential to artistic conducting.

In conducting fast tempi in triple meter (Figure 2c), the second and third beats are negated or omitted, and only the first or primary beat is utilized. In such instances, a slight pause generally occurs at the bottom of this beat; however, the faster the tempo, the less opportunity for pause.

Presented in Figures 4 and 5 are two basically different designs for conducting sextuple meter. Both patterns are utilized by present-day conductors, and one's selection is determined largely by personal taste. Although the pattern in Figure 4 is the one traditionally used by many conductors, the one in Figure 5 is increasing in popularity, especially among choral conductors, and offers a distinct advantage. A similarity will be noticed in the basic direction of the two patterns presented in Figure 5. In the last design, the secondary beats—that is, two, three, five, and six—are negated or omitted so that the pat-

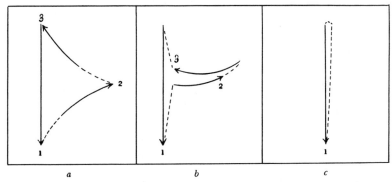

Fig. 2. *Triple meter (3/4, 3/8, 3/2)—(b) for medium and slower tempi, (c) for fast tempi.*

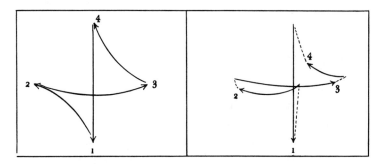

Fig. 3. *Quadruple meter (4/4, 4/2).*

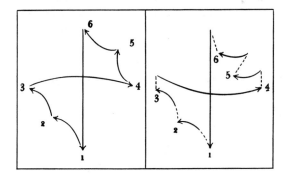

Fig. 4. *Sextuple meter (6/8, 6/4).*

tern may be adapted for use with faster tempi. Because of the similar direction of the primary beats (one and four), the conductor may more easily alternate from one pattern to the other. Because of this flexibility, the movements in Figure 5 are suggested for use with music involving changing tempi.

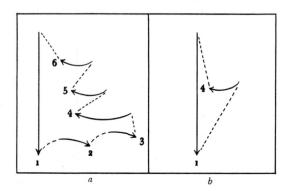

Fig. 5.   Sextuple meter (6/8, 6/4)—(a) for slower tempi, (b) for faster tempi.

IRREGULAR METER

Music in irregular meter, that is, 5/4, 7/4, etc., may be analyzed in combinations of two and three, or three and two; and three and four, or four and three. Irregular meter occurs rather infrequently in choral music; when it is encountered, however, it is suggested that the conductor utilize combinations of the duple, triple, and quadruple meters previously presented. For example, "Nachtens" ("Nightly") by Johannes Brahms, written in 5/4 meter, should be conducted throughout by combining duple and triple meter patterns. In "To Agni" (from the (*Rig Veda*) by Gustav Holst, also written in 5/4 meter, every other measure should be conducted with a triple and a duple meter pattern, and alternate measures with a duple and a triple pattern.

MUSIC IN FREE RHYTHM

Occasionally the conductor will encounter music without a time signature, measure bars, and seemingly without any regular or systematic rhythmic accent or pulsation. In such instances it is desirable to conduct all the beats downward with the exception of the last beat in the phrase, which generally should be upward. The beginning of

Fig. 6. The final measures of Gretchaninov's "Our Father"—with all but the last beat in the phrase conducted downward.

the phrase should receive a regular precise downbeat; the subsequent words should be treated with a slight downward movement, varying in length according to the relative importance of the words. In determining the frequency and the appropriate size of the downward movements, the conductor should carefully analyze the text of the music. The final measures of "Our Father" by Alexander Gretchaninov[2] necessitates this type of conducting treatment. The downward movements are indicated under the music.

---

[2] Text adaptation by Arthur S. Kimball, copyrighted in 1916 by the Oliver Ditson Company. Other examples of music in free rhythm are "Glory Be to God" by Rachmaninoff (Neil A. Kjos; H. W. Gray), "Gladsome Radiance" by Gretchaninov (H. W. Gray), and "To Thee We Sing," Russian Liturgy, arr. Tkach (Neil A. Kjos).

DIVIDED BEATS

In conducting music of a moderate tempo, the conductor may utilize effectively the patterns previously illustrated. However, as these patterns are applied to slower tempi, there comes a point where the precision of the beat may become lost and the pattern becomes relatively ineffective. The solution to this problem, therefore, is not simply to slow the beat down further, but to subdivide the beats within the pattern so that in effect they *consume more time by moving through more space.* Through this means, the rhythmic pulsations of the conductor's patterns become more marked and are distinguished by greater clarity, and as a result he is able to obtain a higher degree of precision from the group. When the music is of an exceptionally slow tempo, often indicated by the musical markings *largo* and *grave,* the conductor generally should employ the divided beat to clarify his intentions.

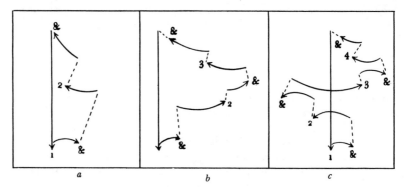

Fig. 7. (a) Divided duple meter, (b) divided triple meter, (c) divided quadruple meter.

Two well-known examples of choral music that necessitate use of the divided beat, as illustrated in Figure 7, are "Crucifixus" (from the *B Minor Mass* by Johann S. Bach), and "Surely He Hath Borne Our Griefs" (from *Messiah* by George F. Handel). An excerpt from the latter selection is shown on pages 11 and 12.

A subdivision of the conducting beat may also be desirable when the rhythmic movement of a particular passage needs to be emphasized or brought out, and during a *ritardando,* when the rhythmic precision of the group needs to be stabilized. Such instances are often likely to occur at the ends of phrases and in the final few measures of a composition. However, any of the beats within a given measure may be subdivided if the tempo of the selection allows sufficient time for the additional movements. The divided beat should not be utilized unless there is adequate time for the rebound of the divided or second half of the beat, as well as the rebound for the principal beat strokes. Figure 9, on page 12, offers a case in point, and the correct treatment depends upon the tempo being utilized. Thus, if the tempo were approximately M.M. ♩=54, then the use of the divided beat as illustrated in Figure 9*a* would be most appropriate. On the other hand, if the music were being conducted at approximately M.M. ♩=70, then the added motion of the divided beat would undoubtedly detract from the clarity of the conductor's movements. In this and similar cases involving moderate tempi, it is suggested that the conductor avoid the divided beat pattern and simply accentuate the rebound of beats one and two, as illustrated in Figure 9*b*. In this treatment a slight pause should occur at the end of each rebound prior to

Largo e staccato (♪ = 72)

Fig. 8. From the introduction to "Surely He Hath Borne Our Griefs" (from Messiah by G. F. Handel)—in which the divided quadruple meter pattern should be used.

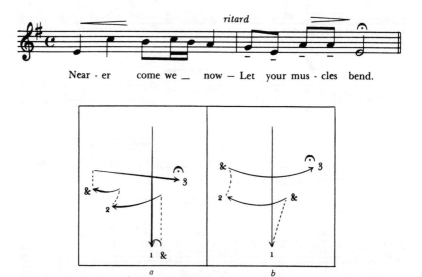

Near - er   come we _   now — Let   your mus - cles   bend.

Fig. 9. "Volga Boatmen" (folk song)—in conducting the final measure above, pattern (a) is utilized with very slow tempi, and pattern (b) with moderate tempi.

the stroke of the subsequent beat. This serves to accentuate the rhythmic movement of the divided beat.

Where he has a choice of the preceding alternatives, the conductor should thoughtfully consider the tempo of the music and the conducting pattern appropriate to the music's most effective interpretation.[3]

ATTACKS AND RELEASES

To be effective, attacks and releases must be executed by the entire ensemble at precisely the same time. To achieve this precision, the group must be alert, it must respond to the rhythmic pulsation of the music, and the conductor must give a clear and precise preparatory beat or movement for each attack or release.

The preparatory beat should always be given at the same rate of speed as that desired in the subsequent measures. Prior to beginning a selection, the conductor should thoughtfully consider his desired tempo and the appropriate preparatory movement. This is especially important to the beginning conductor, and is always important; however, as one gains experience, this process becomes somewhat more automatic in nature. In general, the preparatory beat should approximate the direction of the movement preceding the beat upon which the music begins. For example, if the music begins on the first beat of a measure in quadruple meter, the preparatory movement should occur in the fourth beat preceding, and should be made in the same general direction of the beat utilized for the standard conducting pattern for quadruple meter. Of course, when the music begins on the first beat of a measure in triple meter, the preparatory movement will occur on the third beat preceding the downbeat or actual attack (Figure 10).

One must also prepare adequately for releases if any degree of precision is to be achieved. A slight upward movement is usually sufficient as a preparatory motion to the actual release, which is generally a precise downward movement. The size of these movements (the preparation and the actual release) should coincide with the mood of the music and the general size of the conducting pattern being utilized. That is, the preparation and release of music of a soft,

---

[3] For further discussion of tempo, see pp. 18-22.

My coun-try, 'tis of thee, sweet land of lib - er - ty, Of thee I   sing.

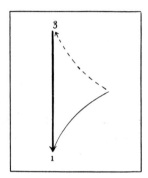

Fig. 10. "America" (Carey)—the preparatory beat for the attack is indicated by the dotted line preceding the first beat.

subdued nature will demand a shorter upward preparation and downstroke, while the release of a dramatic *fortissimo* passage will necessitate a larger upward movement and a longer, deeper downstroke for an effective and precise release.

The preceding general rules are particularly appropriate for a release at the end of a selection, for phrases with some degree of finality, or for those followed by a slight pause. The conductor, however, needs to utilize a modified technique for many of the phrases within the "heart" of a choral selection—particularly when the last note or chord in a phrase needs to be extended to its maximum value and quickly released, with the group "grabbing" a quick catch breath before the attack of the subsequent phrase. A suggested movement to utilize in such cases is to simply turn the palm of the hand over and close it. This movement has been likened to "turning off a water faucet." In certain musical selections one or more of the parts may need to be "cut off" while the others are sustained. When these voice parts are to the conductor's right, then this subtle release may be utilized with the right hand; when they are to his left, then the left hand may be used for the release, while the basic conducting pattern is continued with the right hand.

Attacks on Incomplete Measures

Problems in achieving precise, accurate attacks most frequently occur when dealing with *incomplete measures*. Following are several variants and suggested techniques for dealing with each.

1. When a composition begins on a full or complete beat, the conductor should prepare the group by conducting the preceding beat as a preparatory movement. For example, when in quadruple meter the music begins on the fourth beat, the conductor should utilize the third beat as the preparatory movement (Figure 11).
2. When a composition begins on the second half of the beat, the first half of the beat is given as the preparation (Figure 12).
3. When a composition begins after the second half of the beat and is closer to the following than to the preceding beat, then use a full or complete beat as the preparatory movement according to Rule 1 (Figure 13).

Oh   beau - ti - ful   for   spa - cious skies for   am - ber waves of   grain,

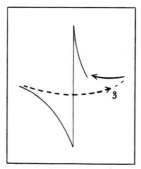

Fig. 11. "America, the Beautiful" (Samuel A. Ward)—preparatory beat is indicated by the dotted line preceding the fourth beat.

It will be noted that no special treatment is utilized in Figure 13 for the sixteenth-note preceding the fourth beat. As this note falls more closely to the following (fourth) beat than to the preceding (third) beat, the same preparatory movement is utilized as that for any music beginning on a full or complete beat (compare the diagram illustrated in Figure 13 with that suggested for use with "America, the Beautiful").

An exception to the treatment of a sixteenth-note occurs with the note following the *fermata* in Figure 14.

Fig. 12. "Dixie" (Daniel Emmett)—preparatory beat is indicated by the dotted line.

Fig. 13. "Marseillaise Hymn" (French National Anthem by Rouget de Lisle)—preparatory beat is indicated by the dotted line preceding the fourth beat.

De __ sun so hot I froze to death, Su- san-na don't you cry.

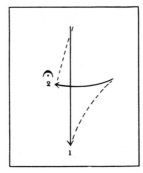

Fig. 14. Excerpt from "Oh! Susanna" (Stephen Foster)—the preparatory movement (following the fermata) is the upward motion that precedes the first beat of the following measure.

FERMATAS

One should prepare for all *fermatas* or holds if precision in perform- ance is to be expected; that is, the movements preceding the *fermata* should be especially clear, concise, and definite in character. When a slight *ritardando* precedes the *fermata,* as is often the case, the con- ductor should slightly enlarge the pattern of his beat as a means of gaining attention and preparing the group for the *fermata.* Raising the plane or height of the beat on which the *fermata* occurs is often helpful when the group is sustaining a *forte* passage. This is not always necessary, however, when the group is singing *piano.*

During the hold, the conductor should continue a slow, steady movement of the beat and avoid a stationary position in mid-air. Musical tone is continuing—not static—and this suggested slight movement will assist the singers in maintaining an even, steady flow of breath necessary for adequate tonal support.

The release of the *fermata* or hold is as important as the prep- aration, and either of two procedures may be utilized depending upon the interpretative effect desired. One procedure is to cut off com- pletely the tone following the hold; the alternative is to carry over the tone to the succeeding phrase without a break in the flow of the breath. The conducting patterns for these two procedures are illustrated in Figure 15.

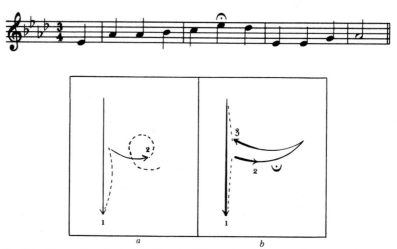

Fig. 15. "Flow Gently, Sweet Afton"—illustrating two procedures for releasing the fermata: *(a) complete release, and (b) carry-over.*

DETERMINING THE TEMPO

Performing a musical work in the proper tempo is an important aspect of artistic interpretation. In the process of determining a tempo, the conductor should consider a number of factors.

Style and Historical Period

Any consideration of tempo should begin with an analysis of the musical style and the characteristics of the historical period from which the music was an outgrowth. Artistic forms of expression are shaped by various social, economic, and political forces which influence a composer during his life. Tempo, therefore, as well as other interpretative considerations, should reflect the basic spirit of the times. (For a discussion of tempo during the various historical periods, see Chapter Three.)

Changes between historical periods were not abrupt, but slowly evolving. Within a given period, one may find unique differences among the styles of individual composers. With a concept of the general characteristics of particular periods as a starting point, the conductor should carefully analyze the style of the composer whose music he is preparing to perform. Although such a procedure may seem like a never-ending task, all efforts in this direction will contribute to a clearer understanding of the essential factors influencing interpretation.

Metronome Markings

Some music will contain metronome markings indicating the desired tempo of the composer and/or the arranger. The metronome marking indicates the number of beats occurring within the duration of a minute, and the type of note which receives this basic pulsation. For example, the abbreviation M.M. ♩=60 indicates that 60 quarter-notes may be sounded in the duration of a minute, or one quarter-note each second.[4] If the metronome marking were M.M. ♩=120, then the tempo would be double that of the previous tempo, and 120 quarter-notes would be sounded in the duration of a minute, or two quarter-notes each second. Prior to introducing a new selection to the group, it is desirable for the conductor to check his own tempo concept with that indicated by the metronome marking. Although such markings need not be slavishly followed, they can be helpful in providing the conductor with a basis for determining his ultimately desired tempo.

Tempo Markings

Although all composers do not include metronome markings on their music, many will indicate the approximate desired tempo through the use of appropriate words, sometimes in English, but usually in Italian. Following is a basic group of Italian terms that the conductor is most likely to encounter:

> Very slow: *Largo*—large, broad, stately
> *Grave*—heavy, slow, ponderous

---

[4] The metronome, a mechanical device used to indicate a particular desired tempo, was invented in 1816 by Mælzel, hence the name Mælzel Metronome, or the abbreviation M.M.

Slow:	*Larghetto*—slow (the diminutive of *largo*)
	Lento—slow
	Adagio—slow, leisurely
Moderate:	*Andante*—moderately slow, at a walking pace
	Moderato—moderate (tempo)
Moderately fast:	*Allegretto*—quite lively, moderately fast
Fast:	*Allegro*—lively, brisk, fast
	Vivace—brisk, spirited
Very fast:	*Presto*—very fast, rapid
	Prestissimo—as fast as possible

Although these Italian terms are only relative indications of tempo, they do provide the conductor with a general basis for determining the approximate tempo suggested by the composer or the editor. Equally important, however, are those terms indicating a change in the basic tempo. Some of the more common terms are:

> *Accelerando*—gradually increasing in tempo
> *Ritardando*—gradually decreasing in tempo
> *Rallentando*—gradually decreasing in tempo
> *Allargando*—gradual broadening of tempo, with
> slight increase in volume
> *Calando*—gradual decrease in tempo and volume
> *Stringendo*—gradually increasing in tempo and
> excitement
> *A poco a poco*—little by little, gradually
> *Poco meno mosso*—a little slower
> *Poco più mosso*—a little faster
> *A tempo*—return to the original tempo

In addition to the preceding terms, the conductor will encounter many others, particularly those pertaining to musical expression. Until the conductor becomes thoroughly acquainted with all such markings, it is suggested that he maintain, for quick and easy reference, a standard dictionary of musical terms.

Mood of Text

A thorough study of the mood of the text will provide additional insight in determining the most desirable tempo. An excerpt from the Christmas spiritual "Go Tell It on the Mountain" is included for illustrative purposes (Figure 16).

The author has heard this spiritual performed at various tempi, ranging from approximately M.M. ♩=60 to M.M. ♩=130. With such a wide variance in tempi, just what should be the conductor's guiding criterion? Although the mood of some spirituals is somber and serious, the text of this particular one describes the joyous, happy news that "Jesus Christ is born!" With this prevailing thought in mind, the author is inclined to select a beginning tempo of approximately M.M. ♩=100. The tempo of contrasting sections within the music,

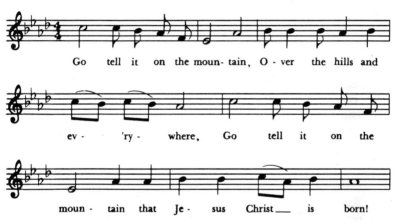

Fig. 16. "Go Tell It on the Mountain" (Christmas spiritual).

however, should be considered separately in light of the prevailing mood of the text.

Ability of the Singers

The complexity of various vocal lines and the harmonic aspects of the music are highly important factors in determining the correct tempo. Certainly the skill with which the singers can execute a difficult florid passage must be considered. For singers with limited technique, it is a far better practice to perform a selection at a slightly slower tempo than the metronome markings might indicate or one might wish, and to sing it *well,* rather than in a slovenly, unmusical manner. Folk-song arrangements that are straightforward in nature can often be sung at a more rapid tempo, without sacrificing tonal stability, than can music with an unusual harmonic treatment.

Acoustics of Performance Room

The acoustical properties of the rehearsal room or auditorium have a telling influence upon the total musical effectiveness of a selection. In comparison with instruments, the human voice—especially that of an inexperienced singer—has less sustaining quality. In rooms with little reverberation, a lifeless tonal quality with an insufficient connection between various tones within the musical phrase will often result. In such instances music may sound best at a slightly faster tempo than one would normally use in an auditorium or a room with reasonably good acoustics. Conversely, the conductor will find it desirable to employ restraint when rehearsing or performing in rooms with exceptionally live acoustical properties.

FACTORS IN EXPRESSIVE CONDUCTING

In developing one's conducting technique the fundamental patterns merely provide a necessary basis from which to begin. The conductor must also consider such matters as the conducting plane or height of the beat, the size of the beat in relationship to tempo and dynamics, the style of the beat in relationship to the manner of articulation, preparing for changes in tempo and dynamics, the length of the musical phrase, the use of the left hand, the cueing of entrances, and the modification of the basic patterns in relationship to varying rhythmic patterns.

The Conducting Plane

The level of the conducting beat is determined by the size of the musical organization and the eye level of the singers. If the size of the organization is reasonably small and if the group is seated on risers, the plane of the conductor's beat, for the most part, should be from the shoulder-level down to the waist. If the musical organization is exceptionally large, the conductor will find it desirable to raise the conducting plane slightly so that all singers may clearly see his beat.

Size of the Beat

The size of the conductor's beat should be determined by the dynamic level, the tempo of the music, and the style of articulation (discussed in the following section), as well as by the general mood or character of the music. The conductor should determine the appropriate dynamics of the music and adapt the size of his beat accordingly. Music of a high dynamic level generally necessitates a larger, broader beat, while music of a low dynamic level requires a relatively smaller movement. Particularly with music of a subdued nature, some conductors are inclined to utilize movements that are too large, and often, therefore, unprecise and unclear.[5] For example, in the choral selection "Since All Is Passing" by Paul Hindemith (Schott & Co.), the size of the conducting pattern that is appropriate to the first phrase—marked *piano* (*p*)—need not be more than 6 inches in height; for the second phrase—marked *pianissimo* (*pp*)—the pattern should necessarily be reduced slightly in height; the third phrase—marked *forte* (*f*)—should be prepared for vigorously and should be approximately 14 to 16 inches in height. The dynamic level of the final phrase is identical to the second and should be conducted accordingly.

Dynamic contrast is a problem of considerable concern to many directors, some of whom have often stated—somewhat in jest—that their choral groups seem to know only two dynamic levels—loud and louder. In view of this seeming dilemma, it behooves conductors to give careful consideration to the appropriate size of their conducting movements as they relate to the dynamic level of the music. This is essential if their groups are ever to sing in an expressive manner.

The tempo of the music is also an important factor influencing the size of the beat. Because of physical limitations, it is necessary for the conductor to limit the scope of his beat with music of a relatively fast tempo if any degree of precision is to be achieved. For example, in the well-known Ukrainian carol "Carol of the Bells" by Leontovich-Wilhousky (Carl Fischer), the tempo necessitates a relatively small beat. Although some parts of the music may be conducted one beat to a measure, the introductory section in particular requires a small, crisp three-beat pattern. And, to reiterate, if the pattern is to be clear and precise, it must be relatively small.

---

[5] The conducting movements for music of a low dynamic level should, for the most part, be immediately in front of the body; thus a more coordinated effort between the hand and arm movements and the facial expressions may be achieved.

Style of the Beat

It is highly important that the conductor's beat reflect the manner or style of articulation of the music, *i.e., legato, staccato, or marcato.*[6] In conducting music in a *legato* style, the director should maintain a continuous movement to his beat, for when it stops, the natural tendency is for the singers to stop also, or at least to lessen the flow of the breath. One of the difficulties involved, especially in slow, sustained passages, is maintaining control of the arm movement. When the arm moves too quickly and the end of the beat is reached too soon, the conducting will appear jerky and the smooth *legato* effect will be lost. To eliminate this fault, the conductor should imagine a definite resistance to his movements. Pretending to move one's hand through a pool of water often will produce the desired feeling.

Music in a *staccato* style must be conducted in a crisp, detached manner to indicate the desired articulation of the music. To do so effectively, however, the conductor should use a relatively small beat. As singing in a *marcato* style necessitates a sharp inward movement of the abdominal muscles on each note marked ($>$), this action should be reflected in the conductor's motions. Thus, music in a *marcato* style demands a vigorous movement, with a precise and definite point to each beat. Whereas many compositions may be found in either *legato* or *staccato* styles throughout, this is seldom if ever the case with *marcato* style.[7] Phrases indicating *marcato* are so marked for special effect and, to be effective, should be in contrast to other sections. "Glory to God" (J. S. Bach) is an excellent example for analysis and performance, that alternates between *marcato* and *legato* styles. An example combining all three styles—*legato, staccato,* and *marcato*—is "When Love Is Kind" (English Folk Song) —arr. Salli Terri (Lawson-Gould).

Changes in Tempi and Dynamics

Effective changes in tempo are not achieved merely by slowing down or speeding up the beat. The beat must be modified in some way that will attract the attention of the performers. A variation in the style or size of the beat is a suggested means of calling attention to changes

---

[6] For a discussion of the relationship of diction to these basic styles of articulation, see pp. 66-68.

[7] For examples of music in *legato, staccato,* and *marcato* styles, see pp. 66-68.

in tempo. Changes in dynamics may be handled in a similar manner. In all cases, the conductor should prepare the group for the changes prior to the time they occur.

Extending the Musical Phrase

Some singers are inclined to take unnecessary breaths between short phrases or in the middle of phrases. The conductor can eliminate some of this difficulty by making a circular movement toward the group—indicating that a breath is not to be taken and that the musical phrase is to be extended. This circular movement should commence at least one beat, and in faster tempi, two beats, prior to the end of the phrase that is to be carried over.

The Left Hand

Conductors, as a general rule, are inclined to overuse the left hand. Some fall into the habit of allowing the left hand to follow the pattern of the right. As overuse of the left hand renders it relatively ineffective for special situations, it should, for the most part, be held near the waistline. Conductors may then more effectively use the left hand for special emphasis, such as sudden accents, abrupt changes in tempo, cueing entrances of certain sections, *crescendo* and *decrescendo,* and to assist in effecting clear, precise attacks and releases.

Cueing

Cueing has been referred to as effective phrasing with a timely look in the proper direction. Several methods of cueing currently are utilized. The conductor may employ any of the following approaches, depending upon the tempo of the music, the style of the music, and the frequency of the entering parts:

1. through the use of the *hands,* providing there is adequate time to execute the movements;
2. through the use of the *head,* when a multiplicity of entrances occur in the music;
3. through *facial expressions,* appropriate in dealing with more subtle and delicate entrances;
4. through a *combination* of two or more of the preceding methods.

Cueing entrances of various parts is essential to rhythmic security and should be given the same careful treatment and preparation as the entire ensemble is given at the beginning of a choral selection.

Modification of the Basic Conducting Patterns

It is often desirable to modify the basic conducting patterns in an effort to reflect the character of the music and to elicit the proper musical response from the group. As previously suggested, the experienced conductor often adds a slight flourish or rebound to each beat, thus providing a symmetry and expressiveness to the movements. In addition, however, the following modifications are suggested:

1. *Notes of unequal duration.*
   In conducting certain figures or patterns containing notes of unequal duration, it is often desirable, particularly in *legato* music, to reduce the size or scope of the beat on unaccented pulses (Figure 17). For example, in conducting the Negro spiritual "My Lord, What a Mornin'," it is desirable to minimize the movements for the second and third beats in measures one, three, and four (Figure 17*a*), and to minimize the movements for all beats except the first in measure two (Figure 17*b*). This modification is more expressive of the music, it serves to lessen the singers' physical response on unaccented pulses, and it facilitates a more *legato* effect. Although this example is but one, the principle is basic and may be applied in numerous rhythmic patterns as a means of eliciting a more musical response.

2. *Syncopated figures.*
   The conducting of certain syncopated figures may be made more effective by utilizing a vigorous rebound to the beat preceding each accented or syncopated note in the figure, and shortening or reducing the size of the following beat (Figure 18).

3. *Off-beat accents.*
   Accents on the second half of each beat or pulse may be conducted more effectively by utilizing a slight downward movement of the hands and arm on the first half of the beat, followed by a definite and precise upward movement on the second half of the beat. The pattern should be entirely up and down, with the rebound retracing the path of the downbeat (Figure 19).

4. *Displaced rhythmic accents.*

The use of accents on beats other than those expected, *i.e.*, the strong beats of a measure, is a rhythmic device used by various contemporary composers. One means is the use of traditional rhythmic patterns in non-symmetrical forms. For example, in the

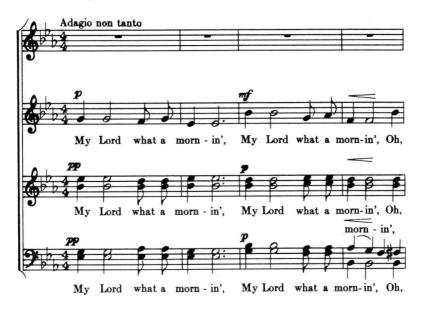

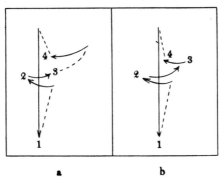

Fig. 17. *Excerpt from "My Lord, What a Mornin'" (Negro Spiritual), arr. H. T. Burleigh (© 1924 by G. Ricordi & Co., New York; used by permission of Franco Colombo Publications, a division of Belwin, Inc., N.Y.), in which the conducting patterns are modified—(a) for the rhythmic pattern (⁴₄ ♩♩♫), and (b) for the rhythmic pattern (⁴₄ ♩ ♩.). Note the rebound of the first beat and the relatively short strokes of the following beats. Compare these patterns with Figure 3, p. 7.*

composition "It Is Good to Be Merry" by Jean Berger, the traditional 9/8 pattern of 3+3+3 is altered to 2+2+2+3. In
Leonard Bernstein's "America" (from *West Side Story*), the 6/8

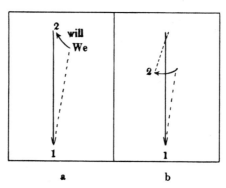

Fig. 18. Excerpt from "Ching-A-Ring Chaw" (minstrel song), from Old American Songs, *adapted by Aaron Copland, arranged for SATB by Irving Fine, in
which a modified conducting pattern is used for the syncopated figure
($\frac{2}{4}$ ♩ ♪ | ♩ ♪ |)—(a) for faster tempi, as in the example, and (b) for
music with slower tempi. A slight pause occurs at the top of the rebound,
especially in conducting faster tempi.* © *1954, 1955 by Boosey & Hawkes Inc.
Copyright assigned to Aaron Copland. Reprinted by permission of Aaron
Copland, Copyright Owner, and Boosey & Hawkes Inc., Sole Agents.*

way, way,— way, way, way in the mid-dle of the air

way, way,— way, way, way in the mid-dle of the air

way, way,— way, way, way, in the mid - dle of the way

way, way, way, way, way in the mid-dle of the way

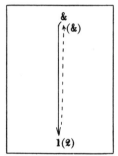

Fig. 19. Excerpt from "Ezekiel Saw the Wheel" (spiritual), arr. Simeone, in which the modified pattern above is used for conducting the off-beat accents (♩). From the Fred Waring choral arrangement. © 1950, Shawnee Press, Inc., Delaware Water Gap, Pennsylvania. Used by permission.

pattern of 3+3 is altered to 3+3+2+2+2. In the "Ballad of Green Broom" by Benjamin Britten, the 6/8 pattern of 3+3 is altered to 3+1½+1½ and 1½+1½+3.

In conducting such patterns, the director must first analyze the music for the shift of accents and then determine the most appropriate movements to convey clarity and evoke rhythmic precision from the group. The conducting pattern should not be too large if precision is to be achieved. Following the downbeat, it is suggested that the subsequent movements (beats) be made

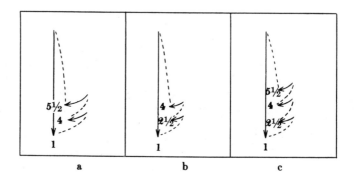

Fig. 20. Excerpt from "Ballad of Green Broom" from Five Flower Songs, *Op. 47, No. 5 (Benjamin Britten; Words anonymous). Conducting pattern (a) for measure one* 𝄞 ♩ ♪ ♪.|, *pattern (b) for measure two* 𝄞 ♪.♪.♪.♪♪♩, *and pattern (c) for measure three* 𝄞 ♪.♪.♪.♪.|. © *1951 by Boosey & Co., Ltd. Reprinted by permission.*

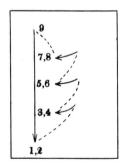

Fig. 21. Excerpt from "It Is Good to Be Merry" (Jean Berger) and a conducting pattern for the nonsymmetrical figure ♩ ♪♪♩ ♪♩ | (2+2+2+3).
Used by permission of Neil A. Kjos Music Co., Park Ridge, Ill.

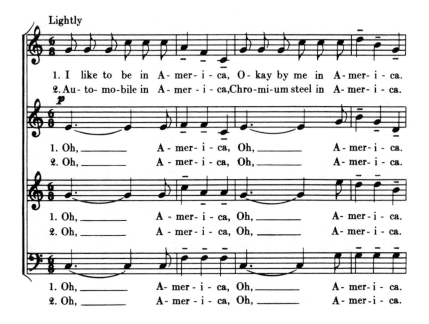

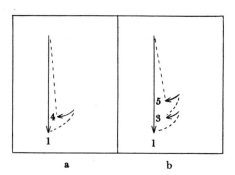

a   b

Fig. 22. Excerpt from "America" from West Side Story *(Leonard Bernstein) and patterns for conducting the nonsymmetrical figure* ⁶⁄₈ ♪♪♪♪♪♪♪♩ ♩ ♩ *| (3+3+2+2+2) (a) for measures one and three, and (b) for measures two and four. © 1957, 1959, by Leonard Bernstein and Stephen Sondheim. Used by permission.*

from right to left in a crisp, short, decisive manner (see Figures 20, 21, and 22).

Bodily Attitudes

Appropriate bodily attitudes are highly important to an effective conducting technique. The director should maintain good posture —that is, an alert stance—and his facial expressions should reflect the mood or character of the music. In short, the best advice that could be given is to endeavor to "look like the music." Regular practice before a full-length mirror will reap vast dividends for the conductor desirous of improving his conducting technique. Try it!

Topics for Discussion

1. Recall and identify the personality attributes of successful conductors you have known. With this information as a basis, discuss the factors that you believe are important to conducting success.

2. Recall and identify the facets of effective conducting technique that you have observed in various conductors.

3. Describe in class some of the conducting problems not usually encountered. Discuss the most appropriate means of handling these problems.

4. Discuss the differences in interpretation of a choral composition as illustrated in two or more recordings. Which interpretation do you believe is most effective, and why?

5. What effect do tempo, dynamics, accent, rhythm, phrasing, style, and mood of the music have upon the basic conducting patterns?

References

Cain, Noble, *Choral Music and Its Practice.* New York: M. Witmark & Sons, 1942. (Chapter 14.)

Christy, Van A., *Glee Club and Chorus.* New York: G. Schirmer, Inc., 1940. (Chapter 1.)

Davison, Archibald T., *Choral Conducting.* Cambridge: Harvard University Press, 1945. (Chapters 1 and 2.)

Finn, William J., *The Conductor Raises His Baton.* New York: Harper & Row, Publishers, 1944.

Jones, Archie N., *Techniques in Choral Conducting.* New York: Carl Fischer, Inc., 1948.

Krone, Max T., *Expressive Conducting.* Chicago: Neil A. Kjos Music Co., 1949.

McElheran, Brock, *Conducting Techniques: For Beginners and Professionals.* New York: Oxford University Press, 1966.

Rudolf, Max, *The Grammar of Conducting.* New York: G. Schirmer, Inc., 1950.

Sunderman, Lloyd F., *Some Techniques for Choral Success.* Rockville Center, L.I., N.Y.: Belwin, Inc., 1952. (Chapter 5.)

2

Tone and Diction

TONE QUALITY IS THE very substance of choral singing. Without properly produced tones, coupled with correct diction, effective choral singing is impossible to attain. Dynamic contrasts, proper blend and balance, accurate pitch and intonation, and effective phrasing are all dependent upon correct vocal production. Furthermore, projection of the mood or spirit of the music is dependent upon correct diction, as well as proper tone quality. Since good tone quality and correct diction are fundamental considerations in the training of choral groups, the conductor should develop a well-defined concept of all factors influencing tone and diction. Because choral groups react in varying ways, he should also develop a wide variety of techniques for achieving his objectives.

THE VOCAL INSTRUMENT

The human vocal instrument possesses the three components that are essential to the functioning of all musical instruments: an *actuator,* a *vibrator,* and a *resonator.* In addition, it has a component unique only to the human voice—an *articulator.* Generally, the components of the vocal instrument may be identified as follows:

1. The respiratory or breathing muscles and the lungs serve as an actuator.

35

2. The vocal cords (sometimes referred to as vocal folds) serve as a vibrator and are the source of the sound.
3. The pharynx, mouth, and nasal cavity serve as a resonator which amplifies the sound.[1]
4. The tongue, lips, teeth, palate, and the lower jaw serve as an articulator.

The principal muscles utilized in normal breathing are the diaphragm, the abdominal muscles, and the intercostal muscles. Although there is still some difference of opinion concerning the action of these muscles, the following is generally accepted. During inspiration, the diaphragm contracts and pushes downward, while the contraction of the intercostal muscles lifts or raises the ribs. The combined action of these muscles enlarges the thorax, which allows the lungs to fill with air. During normal expiration there is supposedly no muscle contraction necessary; the chest is decreased in size by the elastic recoil of the thoracic wall. In prolonged expiration, such as in singing a sustained note, the abdominal muscles gradually contract while the diaphragm slowly relaxes, and the intercostal muscles maintain enough tension to prevent bulging of the intercostal spaces. During the act of singing, breath control is of the essence; therefore, a delicate interplay or balance must exist between these opposing sets of muscles. When one set contracts, the other set should relax—but not completely—as their mutual activity provides for the best utilization of the air in the lungs.

The larynx functions somewhat like a valve—when open it allows the singer to inhale and exhale air to and from the lungs. The vocal cords or folds are the vibrating edge of the thyroarytenoid muscles, the posterior ends of which are attached to the arytenoid cartilages. The anterior or front ends of the vocal cords are attached to the thyroid cartilage, commonly known as the "Adam's Apple." The vocal cords are tensed by the contraction of the cricothyroid muscles. The tension of the vocal cords is decreased by the contraction of the thyroarytenoid muscles of which they are a part. The vocal cords are approximated or brought together by muscles controlling the position of the arytenoid cartilages, and are set into vibration by the flow or pressure of the breath during exhalation. The fissure or opening between the vocal cords is referred to as the glottis. During deep inspiration, the glottis assumes a somewhat round shape, but during quiet or normal breathing it assumes a V-shaped position.

---

[1] Some authorities also consider the paranasal sinuses, the trachea, the bronchi, and the chest cavity to be part of the resonating system.

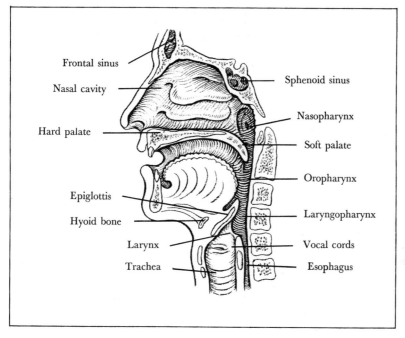

Fig. 23. *Relative locations of the larynx, the resonating cavities (pharynx, mouth, and the nasal cavity), and the articulating organs (tongue, lips, teeth, palate, and the lower jaw). Note the divisions of the palate (hard palate and the velum or soft palate), and the pharynx (laryngopharynx, oropharynx, and the nasopharynx).*

When one sings a high pitch the vocal cords come very close together and the glottis becomes a thin, narrow slit or opening. (See Figure 24.)

The pitch of the tone is determined by the tension of the vocal cords and the pressure of the breath against the vocal cords. If this

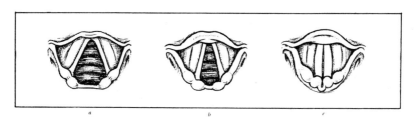

Fig. 24. *The larynx as observed through a laryngoscope—illustrating differences in the size of the glottis (a) while taking a deep breath, (b) during quiet or normal breathing, and (c) during phonation.*

pressure or breath support is inadequate, the laryngeal muscles often function incorrectly in their effort to obtain the correct pitch. This induces fatigue and undue strain on the voice.

In general, the resonating cavities may be divided into two types—fixed and adjustable. The nasal cavity is fixed, while the pharynx and mouth are capable of special utilization. On each side and above the vocal cords are cavities that amplify the vibrations produced by the vocal cords and increase their intensity as they are projected from the larynx. These cavities are fully utilized as resonance chambers only when the throat is relaxed and kept open. Similarly, the mouth is best utilized as a resonance chamber when all the muscles, including the tongue, are relaxed and the cavity of the mouth is enlarged—thus allowing for an increased resonance chamber. The nasopharynx and the nasal cavity are most effectively utilized as resonance chambers when a slight opening between the oropharynx and the nasopharynx is maintained, thus allowing for an extension of the vibrating column of air emanating from the larynx.

Flexibility of the articulating organs—the tongue, lips, velum (soft palate), and the lower jaw is highly important if the vocal mechanism is to function at optimum efficiency. Procedures for co-ordinating the various components of the vocal instrument are discussed in the following sections.

DEVELOPING CHORAL TONE

In the process of developing the tonal quality of a choral group, the conductor should take into consideration a number of factors: correct singing posture, proper breath control, the function and value of particular vocalises, and the development of deep-set vowels and high-forward resonance. Development of the high range, particularly in male voices, and the achievement of vocal flexibility are also areas of special importance and concern.

Achieving Correct Posture

Correct posture is necessary to the development of good tone production. Since vocal tone is affected by all of the muscles of the body, an alert bodily position must be maintained while singing, whether the individual is standing or sitting.

When in a standing position, one should place his feet approximately 6 inches apart and the left foot preferably should be several inches in front of the right. This stance affords the singer better balance and lays the foundation for the proper use of the breathing muscles. The weight of the body should rest to a great extent on the balls of the feet—not on the heels. The abdomen should be drawn in and the spine should be kept as straight as possible. The singer's upper back should feel as wide as possible and the chest should be held relatively high, but without strain or excess tension. Since the throat functions as an organ pipe, the head must be kept perpendicular to the shoulders in order that this "pipe" be kept clear and open. The music must be held in such a position that the director may be easily seen without the singers lowering or raising their heads, since any deviation in the position of the head is likely to affect the tone quality.

Fig. 25.   Correct posture for standing and sitting.

When seated, the correct posture from the waist up will be almost identical with the standing posture. The only basic difference is that the legs assume a bent position. While in a sitting position, the singers must keep both feet on the floor and lean slightly forward, away from the back of the chair, if they are to maintain adequate breath support. Some of the bodily weight must be distributed to the lower limbs and the feet. The proper coordination between the breathing muscles and the vocal apparatus will result only if this correct posture is maintained while singing.

Improving Breath Control

The next consideration in developing good choral tone is the establishment of correct breathing habits. This is necessary to insure the steady flow of the breath to the vocal cords and is fundamental to both tone quality and tone control.

Clavicular or collarbone breathing does not fill the lungs to capacity and, in breathing, the tension in the upper chest and shoulder muscles affects the muscles around the larynx and inhibits the proper action of the vocal cords.[2] Improper breathing habits that have developed over a period of years are not always easily corrected. First, the individual must thoroughly understand the effect of poor breathing habits upon his own tone production and upon the tone quality and blend of the choir. He must achieve a conception of the correct method of breathing.

In singing, it is necessary to use the muscles around the entire mid-section of the body, not just the diaphragm. The muscles of the upper chest and shoulders should be relaxed, with the greater amount of work being done by the intercostal muscles, the diaphragm, and the abdominal muscles. These are the muscles used in correct breathing technique (see p. 36).

The director should continually emphasize the formula, *breathe deeply, expand around the entire mid-section—in the back and around the sides, as well as in front.* Have the choir members bend over, from a standing position, until the upper part of the body is parallel to the floor. In this position clavicular breathing is difficult and somewhat unnatural. By pressing the hands against the waist, with thumbs to the back, one gets the "feel" of correct breathing

---

[2] This type of incorrect breathing is exemplified in the inspiration movements utilized by a child in preparation for blowing out a candle.

from this position. Try it! Another procedure, which is more easily managed in a crowded rehearsal room, would have the group lean forward in their chairs, placing one elbow on the knee. Proper breath action may then be checked by pressing the other hand against the waist. After the singers learn how the muscles are utilized in correct breathing, they must strive toward the attainment of proper breath control until it becomes automatic. Proper breath support and control will improve only through continual emphasis.

Use of Vocalises

Choral directors generally employ vocalises as a part of the vocal training of their choir members. They are utilized specifically for the improvement of choral tone and blend. Some directors utilize vocal exercises only as a part of the warm-up period—as athletes use mild exercise to prepare themselves for the more strenuous rigors of competition. Other directors feel that exercises employed for such purposes are largely a waste of time, since they are not directly connected with the immediate problem of improving the performance of the choral music. This latter group will often take a troublesome portion of the music out of context and utilize it as a vocal exercise.

Some directors seem convinced that only one of the previously mentioned procedures should be followed. It seems reasonable, however, to assume that both practices have considerable merit and that each approach should be employed to some extent, if the desired results are to be achieved. To be effective, vocal exercises must be varied periodically. Continued concentration on particular devices or exercises will eventually lead to boredom, lack of concentration, and less than maximum physical effort. As a result, more harm than good may occur. Therefore, *variety* is the watchword—variety in vowel sounds utilized, in the types of exercises, and in the time of the rehearsal period during which they are utilized.

Vocal exercises should be employed discriminately, since each exercise, if performed correctly, will produce a different type of color or tone quality. It is important to realize, then, that the overuse of one exercise to the neglect of another will not always produce the best or desired results. For example, if the choir sings with an overly dark tone, then the director should avoid too much vocalization on the darker vowels, such as **aw** and **oh.** It might be well for the choir director or voice teacher to think of various vocal exercises as a physician might think of a prescription or a form of therapy—that is, as a remedy or treatment for a specific individual or group need. For choral blend, a uniformity of vowel production must be achieved. Although the director is definitely concerned with individual voices and needs, the problem in practice is, for the most part, one of dealing with the tone problems of a large group.

Let us first of all examine the type of tone quality desired for high school, college, and community choral groups. There are several schools of thought concerning the "ideal" quality, and in addition, certain choral selections require subtle changes in voice quality. Nevertheless, it is essential that the director develop his concept of tone through private voice study and by listening to numerous choral recordings, and then strive toward that goal. A word of caution, however! Sometimes the inexperienced high school choral director is overzealous in his attempts to achieve the mature quality found only in adult choirs, and in his eagerness develops a tenseness and rigidity in the youthful voices. High school choirs have characteristic qualities common to this age level. These qualities should be carefully nurtured and allowed to develop slowly. Only in this way will the ultimate in high school choral singing be achieved.

Individuals participating for the first time in a choir generally display an abundance of technical faults. Some may sing with a throaty tone, others with white, nasal, or colorless tones. Without uniformity in tone production, blend is practically unattainable.

Just what type of voices are we endeavoring to develop? There are two characteristics that the director should strive to develop in voices at the outset—(*a*) a deep-set vowel, and (*b*) a high-forward resonance. When these two characteristics are present, the tone quality is rich and beautiful, and capable of lending itself to the wide gamut of emotions found in choral literature. Various exercises contribute to the development of these qualities and will be presented on the following pages.

Achieving Deep-Set Vowels

The deep-set vowel is usually associated with maturity and roundness of tone and with naturalness of production. It is achieved through minimizing unnecessary tension in the vocal apparatus and by correctly utilizing the resonance cavities of the mouth and throat. As has been previously discussed, correct posture and breath control are essential conditions. Clavicular breathing should be avoided, since the resultant tension in the shoulder muscles and upper regions of the chest is oftentimes reflected in the muscles surrounding the larynx, thus inhibiting the proper functioning of the vocal mechanism.[3]

The writer has observed high school and adult choral groups in various sections of the country. One of the most objectionable faults is that many teen-age youths, as well as adults, sing with a tight, rigid jaw. Some individuals believe that this condition is a reflection of environmental tensions. More likely, the condition results from lack of proper vocal training and individual awareness of the problem. Whatever the exact cause, the effect is disastrous upon choral singing. Tenseness in the jaw and facial muscles results in strident, pinched, and colorless tones. Depth of tone and subsequent choral blend is impossible to attain until the condition is alleviated. Following are suggested devices, techniques, and exercises to help eliminate this problem.

1. Singers should be instructed to concentrate upon relaxing their facial muscles. Gently stroking the face with the fingertips is one means of eliminating excessive tension that may be utilized in rehearsals. To develop further the singers' understanding of the importance of this relaxation, choir members should be asked to observe the facial expressions of an outstanding concert singer on television. In addition, they should compare their mental picture of this singer and their own facial expressions by checking in a mirror. (Enlargements of close-up group photographs taken during rehearsals provide a further objective means for the singers to analyze their difficulties.)

2. In addition to relaxing the lips and facial muscles, the jaw must be relaxed and the mouth opened wide if the deep-set vowel is to be achieved. The darker vowels, such as **oh, aw,** and **ah,** should have lots of depth and should be formed low in the throat. In order to make them round and full, one should think of singing the vowels up and down, rather than across. The jaw should be free from any rigidity. Exercise 1 is an excellent device for loosening the jaw and "rounding out" the tone.

---

[3] This is a particularly troublesome problem with high school boys, since large chest expansion seems to be associated with manliness. The problem here can be lessened somewhat by means of a frank and open discussion concerning athletes who employ deep abdominal breathing in order to increase their own breath control.

Exercise 1.

Yah, yah, yah, yah, yah,   Yah, yah, yah, yah, yah, *etc.*

1. Vocalize from low B♭ (below the staff) to E♭ (fourth space, treble clef). Much of the value of the exercise is lost if it is sung in the extreme high range of the voice.
2. In this exercise use lots of jaw action. A helpful physical device is for the singer to place the tips of each index finger on the approximate hinge position of the jaw. This procedure serves to increase one's awareness of the jaw movement.
3. In singing this exercise, there is an unconscious tendency for some singers to pull the upper lip downward over the upper front teeth. This practice should be discouraged since it is likely to darken the tone quality too much. Singers should be instructed to hold the upper lip stationary, with just a portion of the upper teeth remaining visible. A useful device is to have the singer check this position with a hand mirror. It should prove enlightening to him!
4. It has been found profitable for the singers to check one another's jaw movements on this exercise. This procedure seems to provide the proper motivation for the small percentage of singers who have a particular difficulty with the exercise.

    When the vowel **ah** is used, Exercise 2 is also helpful in developing the deep-set vowel. It has an added ear-training value, in that it provides an opportunity for the singers to hear more clearly their parts in relationship to the other tones in the chord.

Exercise 2.

1. Director should cue each entrance.
2. Singers should hold back the breath, explode the attack, and drop the jaw.

3. Crescendo, then decrescendo on final chord.
4. Proceed upward or downward by half-steps.
5. For the purpose of developing uniformity of vowel production, the exercise should also be sung on the various other vowels. Each vowel should be preceded by the consonant **M.**

Developing High-forward Resonance

The preceding exercises, if used consistently, develop depth in the voices and transform the thin, shallow voices of inexperienced singers into rounder and deeper voices. If used to the total exclusion of other exercises, however, they will make the voices dark and throaty, and as a result flatting sometimes occurs. To be most effective, these devices and exercises must be coupled with exercises designed to develop focus or high-forward resonance in the voices.

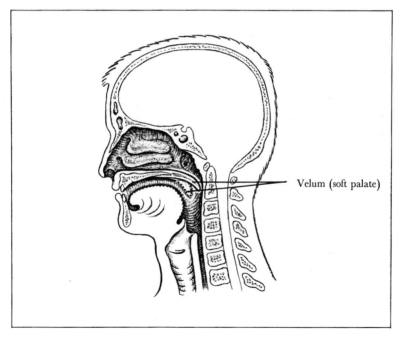

Velum (soft palate)

Fig. 26. The velum or soft palate—a controlling factor in the utilization of the nasopharyngeal cavity and the nasal cavity as resonance chambers. The dotted lines indicate the velum in its lowered or relaxed position.

When sound is produced by vibration of the vocal cords, it moves in many directions and is resonated and amplified in the various cavities of the body; that is, the chest, the pharynx, the mouth, and the nasal cavity. A sound, unrestricted by muscular tension, will seek and utilize *all* of these resonating areas. Muscular tension and interference, however, often limit the maximum use of these resonating chambers. Tension in the throat muscles prevents the most effective use of the pharynx as a resonator and, as previously mentioned, a tight, rigid jaw and an unruly tongue reduce the size of the oral cavity and lessen its effectiveness as a resonator.

Of particular concern to the choral conductor is the development of focus or high-forward resonance in the voice. By this is meant simply the maximum utilization of the resonating cavities or chambers above the oropharynx and the mouth, specifically the nasopharynx and the nasal cavity. The key to the most effective use of these resonating areas is to maintain a sensation of an opening between the oropharynx and the nasopharynx. The organ that regulates the size of the opening is the velum or soft palate. When swallowing food, the velum moves posterosuperiorly and maintains contact with the posterior wall of the pharynx. This muscular adjustment also occurs in the articulation of certain consonants. If this adjustment did not occur, air would escape through the nose and the precise articulation of these consonants could not be achieved. As the nasal consonants **m, n,** and **ng** are produced, the velum is in its relaxed or lowered position, the nasal port is widely open, and the nasopharynx and the nasal cavity serve as a more predominant center of tonal resonance. The velar opening or nasal port may be maintained, however, by a means other than relaxing or lowering the soft palate. It also may be opened by an upward and forward tension of the velum—as experienced in a deep yawn.[4] This suggested movement of the velum is contrary to the velopharyngeal contact utilized in articulating certain consonants.[5]

Choir members should strive to develop a high-forward arch to the velum or soft palate, so that the nasal port may remain slightly

----

[4] *Cf.* G. Oscar Russell, *Speech and Voice.* New York: The Macmillan Co., 1931, p. 18.

[5] *Cf.* Robert F. Hagerty and others, "Soft Palate Movement in Normals," *Journal of Speech and Hearing Research,* Vol. 1, No. 4, Dec., 1958, pp. 325-330.

[6] There is not complete agreement on the extent of the opening between the oropharynx and the nasopharynx. X-ray studies during phonation indicate a changing size, depending on the vowel produced, and variations on the same vowel among different singers. However, regardless of the size of the opening, the imagery of directing the tone through this space is helpful in achieving high-forward resonance.

open, thus allowing for an extension of the vibrating column of air emanating from the larynx and a more effective use of the upper resonating cavities.[6]

Thus singers should think of the nasopharynx as an extension of the oropharynx (which it actually is) and concentrate on drawing the breath "inward and upward." Many choral conductors recommend yawning as a means of developing a sensation of the high-forward arch of the velum. Other directors simply suggest singing with a sensation of a high arch in the back of the mouth. Both devices, however, achieve the same desired purpose and can be utilized to facilitate this necessary physical adjustment.

Muscles work in pairs throughout the body. When one set is in tension to effect a specific movement or action, the opposing set of muscles should be relaxed. When the opposing set of muscles is not relaxed, unnecessary tension occurs, resulting in wasted energy. The singer, therefore, must endeavor to relax the opposing muscles, so that the others may function at optimum efficiency. This is the singer's goal. However, until the correct vocal adjustment becomes automatic in nature, the singer must apply a degree of conscious effort toward arching the velum and opening the passage between the oropharynx and the nasopharynx.

Sagging facial muscles are also detrimental to the development of high-forward resonance. The feeling of a short upper lip and a lifting of the facial muscles directly above the upper lip will aid in the development of this resonance. When the correct singing sensation is achieved and the process becomes automatic, then the singer will be able to produce fully resonated tones with a minimum of effort. Exercises 3, 4, and 5, and the specific suggestions pertaining to their use, will be found helpful in developing high-forward resonance in the voice.

Exercise 3.

Hah,   hah,   hah,   hah,   hah,   hah,   hah,   hah.

1. Vocalize on the descending major scales, C, D♭ (C♯), D, and E♭. Sing each scale slowly—taking a "catch breath" between each scale step.
2. Sing with two fingers between the teeth. This insures an open mouth and a freer emission of the tone.

3. The feeling of the high arched roof of the mouth, as in yawning, is necessary for the proper adjustment of the velum or soft palate and the correct focus of the tone or voice. Strive to develop this sensation!

4. When yawning, notice the position of the lips! In their most relaxed position, they are extended away from the teeth; the upper lip is raised slightly and a portion of the upper teeth is visible.

5. Concentrate on the sensation of drawing the breath inward in a relatively narrow stream and focusing the tone in the resonating cavities behind the bridge of the nose. (Using various physical devices will assist the singer in achieving the correct tonal focus. Drawing the hand inward toward the body facilitates the singer's concept of the correct direction of the flow of the breath.[7] Placing the fingertips on the bridge of the nose is also a reminder of the correct point of tonal focus.)

6. Vocalize all voices to their lowest tones. Avoid forcing the voices in the lower register.

7. Avoid distorting and altering the vowel sound—a common pitfall is changing the vowel **ah** to **uh** when vocalizing in the lower register of the voice.

After a sufficient degree of progress has been made toward achieving correct resonance, the following two exercises may be alternated with the previous exercise.

Exercise 4.

Hah, _____   hah, _____

hah, _____   hah. _____

1. Sing each scale (C, D♭, D, E♭) slowly, taking a full breath between each descending scale.

2. Sing with two fingers between the teeth.

---

[7] The flow of the breath is actually from the lungs, through the larynx, and into the resonating chambers or cavities. The sensation of drawing the breath inward simply assists in directing the tone into the cavities above the pharynx and the oral cavity.

3. Vocalize all voices to their lowest tones. Avoid forcing the voices and distorting the vowel sounds in the lower register.
4. Concentrate on achieving correct tonal focus (see Suggestions 3, 4, and 5 in preceding exercise).

Exercise 5.

1. Start on middle C and vocalize an octave or more.
2. Vocalize with two fingers between the teeth—a freer emission of the tone is thus assured.
3. Raise the upper lip and extend away from the teeth.
4. The feeling of the high arched roof of the mouth, as in yawning, is necessary for the proper adjustment of the velum. Strive to attain the sensation!

In the preceding exercise, male singers quite often become easily discouraged when their voices crack or break in the upper range. Considerable benefit can accrue to the singers if they are encouraged to continue the exercise upward in a light head-voice or falsetto quality.

Another exercise that may contribute to the improvement of resonance, and is equally beneficial as a warm-up exercise, is as follows:

Exercise 6.

The exercise may be notated on the chalkboard, or introduced by means of syllables (all voices sing the interval of the octave—*do* to *do;* sopranos sustain *do,* altos descend to *mi,* tenors descend to *sol,* and basses descend to *do.*)

1. Singers should endeavor to maintain the forward placement of the **ee** vowel throughout the exercise; however, as the sound changes to **ah** the jaw should drop and be kept relaxed.
2. Singers should maintain adequate breath support and *crescendo* toward the end of the exercise.
3. Exercise may be repeated upward by half-steps (not to exceed four or five half-steps, depending on the maturity of the voices).

To afford variety, Exercises 7 and 8 may be alternated on subsequent days with Exercise 6.

Exercise 7.

1. Sing the exercise in unison.
2. Combine two parts together—SA, TB, ST, AB.
3. Sing in four parts.
4. Repeat upward or downward by half-steps.

Exercise 8.

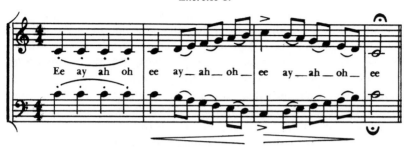

Ee ay ah oh   ee ay_ ah_ oh_   ee ay_ah_oh_   ee

The use of the nasal consonants (**m, n,** and **ng**) as a means of establishing a sensation for and a feeling of correct resonance is a somewhat disputed subject. One position stated is that "humming is not singing" and that the two acts require a different adjustment of the velum. In the broadest sense, this statement is true; that is, in humming the velum is in its relaxed or lowered position, while in singing this is seldom, if ever, the case.

The use of humming, prior to singing, the use of the consonants **m, n,** and **ng,** as a prefix to the vocalization of various vowels, and the vocalization of such words as **sing** and **hung** (immediately moving to and sustaining the **ng** sound) has become a rather prevalent practice. Proponents of the value of humming maintain that it provides the best muscular setting for the attainment of resonance. In this respect, the use of the nasal consonants has value, because during this act the vocal mechanism is well coordinated. Excessive tension in any aspect of the vocal mechanism will prevent the attainment of a fully resonated tone. Therefore, humming and the use of the other nasal consonants have value in that they facilitate the beginning of phonation without excessive muscular tension. Because of this "relaxing effect," choir members should endeavor to retain the humming sensation while singing.

The following humming exercise may be used for the above-mentioned purpose. In addition, it has a certain ear-training value,

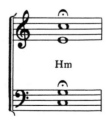

Hm

Figure 27.

if the group is instructed to listen carefully and to hold the chord until it is perfectly in tune. Instruct the singers to avoid gasping for breath; when a breath is needed they should drop out of the ensemble, take a full breath, and then re-enter as unobtrusively as possible. Some persons may hum incorrectly. To check, ask the group while humming to open their mouths at a given signal. If the tone changes into the vowel **ah,** then the group is humming incorrectly. When the mouth is opened, the correctly produced tone should change from **hm** to **ng.** It is wise to use this checking device frequently. The **ng** sound has greater intensity than the **hm** sound, and may be found preferable for use with certain selections calling for a humming background. Some high school directors have even found this exercise to be a profitable time-saver—when the students in the chorus enter the rehearsal room they immediately take their seats and commence humming their respective tones. After all the choir members have arrived, the director may immediately begin the rehearsal, since the group is in a more receptive frame of mind and less inclined toward verbal outbursts.

In striving for the development of deep-set vowels and a high-forward resonance, one could mistakenly get the idea that one vocal characteristic should purposely be developed prior to the other. In practice, both should be developed simultaneously.

If the utmost is to be gained from the previously mentioned exercises they should be sung with a free open throat. Excess tension in the muscles around the larynx should be eliminated insofar as possible. Vocalization on the vowel **oo** has been found to be helpful in opening the throat. When vocalizing on this vowel, it is suggested that the tips of two fingers be placed between the front teeth. This procedure assists in opening the throat and aids in a freer emission of the tone, substantially assisting in the development of the higher range of the voice.

Developing the Vocal Range

Voices with a limited vocal range make the performance of a considerable amount of choral literature prohibitive. If music with an extreme tessitura is used, the voices are likely to sound harsh, strained, and unmusical. Under such circumstances, blend, balance, and good intonation are impossible to attain. Therefore, developing the singers' vocal range is an important and essential task of the choral conductor.

The singing of correctly produced high tones is dependent upon an open throat (achieved through vocalization of the **oo** vowel) and a high-forward resonance (see Exercises 4 and 5). The heavy chest quality of the middle range is not easily produced in the upper limits of the voice and any attempt to do so will often result in unmusical sounds and breaks in the flow of the tone; therefore, the singers should try to lighten their voice quality in vocalizing Exercise 9, which is suggested for helping to develop the upper range.

Exercise 9.

1. Vocalize, in the beginning, on the vowel **oo**. This vowel opens the throat and facilitates a freer production of tone. As progress is made, however, it is desirable periodically to alternate the **oo** with the **ah** vowel. This latter vowel will give greater brilliance and "ring" to the voice.
2. Vocalize with two fingers between the teeth. This device facilitates the dropping of the jaw, which is an absolutely essential condition in singing the high tones.
3. When singing *high,* think *low,* and vice-versa. This thought facilitates the necessary muscular adjustment.
4. Vocalize all voices up to the extreme limits of their range. Sopranos and tenors should vocalize up to high C, and altos and basses at least up to high A♭.

Female voices will find Exercise 9 comparatively easy—that is, much easier than will the male voices. Treble voices are able to sing the higher notes without the unique muscular adjustment problem that occurs with male voices. With treble voices, the range simply needs strengthening and developing. The problem is not quite the same with the male voice. In vocalizing Exercise 9, male voices will quite naturally and normally change into a "falsetto" quality at a certain point. At first there may be some embarrassment on the part of the younger singers, but this should be expected. They should be told of the many fine singers who have extended their ranges by first learning how to use correctly their falsetto voice. Indeed, there may even be places in the literature where such a quality will be desired by the tenor voices.

There will exist, however, many other instances where it will be necessary and desirable for the male singers to sing with a full resonant quality in their high range. In order to do so, it will be necessary to develop the so-called *covered tone,* in which the vowel sound is slightly altered or modified toward one which is more easily produced in the upper register. It is full and resonant and is devoid of any falsetto characteristics. In singing the covered tone, a certain firming of the vocal mechanism occurs and the vowels are slightly modified—generally toward the **uh** sound. Exercise 10 is suggested as a means of obtaining the desired tone quality and placement.

Exercise 10.

Beginning on first line E (treble clef), slur up an octave, keeping the resonance high and forward. The sounds **ing** and **ay** are generally the best to begin with; however, eventually the other vowels should be used as well. Remember that the jaw must be dropped on all high tones. On the open vowels, sing with two fingers between the teeth. In singing the closed vowels **ee** and **ĭ,** the back sides of the tongue should be held against the upper back teeth. This device facilitates an easier and freer production of tone. Basses should eventually vocalize up to high A♭ and the tenors to high C.

In developing the lower range of the voice, it is suggested that the singers vocalize, using the vowel **ah,** on the descending five-tone scale (see Exercise 15, p. 185). The exercise should be begun on about first space F (treble clef) and should be sung slowly downward. The voice should not be forced, but should be produced with a naturally resonant quality. The greatest deterrent to developing the lower range in both male and female voices is that the singers often fail to drop the jaw. As a result, a considerable portion of the lower range of the voice frequently remains undeveloped. In addition, when the jaw is not dropped the vowel sound will often change from **ah** to **uh.** Singing the exercise with two fingers between the teeth will help to alleviate this problem.

Developing Flexibility

A flexible voice is usually a freely produced voice—one that is devoid of excessive strain and tension. A marked degree of flexibility is essential if desired interpretative effects are to be achieved in choral music.

Following are two exercises that should prove profitable in developing flexibility in voices.

Exercises 11a and 11b.

1. Vocalize only in the middle range of the voice. Proceed upward by half-steps.
2. Insert the tips of two fingers between the teeth. This assists in a free emission of the tone.
3. Avoid singing too loudly—excessive tension is sometimes created in this way, thus making the exercise more difficult and thereby decreasing the benefit from it.
4. At first, sing the exercise quite slowly—until the student becomes acquainted with it; then gradually increase the tempo.
5. Practice exercises in both a *legato* style and in a *half-staccato* style.

ACHIEVING CORRECT DICTION

Correct diction, necessary to the effective communication of the central thought of the text, is the over-all manner of vocal utterance as it pertains to the conveying of meanings and ideas. Pronunciation, enunciation, and articulation are all integral aspects of diction; these terms are often used rather loosely, and frequently their precise meanings are misunderstood.

Pronunciation is the manner of uttering the words, as regards the use of appropriate vowel and consonant sounds and the proper accent of words and phrases. "Sing as you speak" is a statement often heard. This advice would be worth-while providing everyone spoke correctly and there was a reasonable degree of uniformity in the speech mannerisms and habits of individuals. Careful analysis of words

Columbia College Library
Columbia, Missouri

spoken or sung by individuals will reveal a wide variety of similar, yet distinctly different, pronunciations of each vocal sound.

Vocal mannerisms characteristic of particular regional areas should be avoided and a standardized "general American" approach to pronunciation, as utilized by most radio and television announcers, should be adopted. In an attempt to become "educated," singers should avoid extreme alterations in pronunciation, lest they sound unnatural, affected, and ridiculous to local audiences. An exception to the use of a standardized general American approach to pronunciation in choral singing is readily evident in the performance of certain folk songs requiring a dialectal treatment. Pronunciation problems inherent in these choral selections should be carefully analyzed in regard to vowel and consonant sounds and accent or stress, and then diligently rehearsed. Careful attention must be given to all pronunciation problems if effective communication of the text is to be achieved.

Enunciation pertains to the manner of vocal utterance as regards distinctness and clarity of the various vowel and consonant sounds. Individuals who mumble their words, and who slur or omit consonants, have fallen into slovenly habits which are not conducive to good communication. The conductor should use every possible means to develop the singers' awareness of this problem. Demonstrating the singers' faults through imitation, and playing back tape recordings of rehearsals and performances, are suggested procedures for improving enunciation.[8] Only when effective enunciation is achieved will the central thought of the music be communicated to the listening audience.

Articulation pertains to the physical action of the articulating organs (tongue, lips, teeth, palate, and lower jaw) in forming and altering the channels and in projecting the various vocal sounds necessary to achieve intelligible communication. A further differentiation may be made between articulation and enunciation. When an individual is unable to speak distinctly because of lack of physical control, such as occurs with young children, he may be said to have poor articulation. When an individual's vocal utterance is indistinct because of slovenly diction and lack of concentrated effort, then it may be said that his speech or singing is poorly enunciated.

---

[8] Imitation of singers' faults always should be done in a spirit of joviality —never in a ridiculing manner. Imitation should be followed immediately by the conductor's demonstration of correct procedures, and the chorus's renewed efforts toward improvement.

Difference Between Vowels and Consonants

The vowels are utilized for sustaining the singing tone, and the breath flow is continuous. In sounding or articulating the consonants, the flow of the breath is momentarily interrupted. This is the basic difference between the vowels and consonants.

Vowels are the chief vehicle for sustaining the vocal tone, whereas the consonants have shorter sustaining qualities and in some instances may detract from the *legato* flow of the music. The vowels are all voiced sounds—that is, the vocal cords are set into vibration. However, approximately one-third of the consonants are voiceless. Intelligibility of the consonants is dependent upon the precise movements of the articulating organs, while the vowels are dependent more upon duration and resonance for their identity.[9] Singing a choral selection on the vowels only is a useful device for achieving uniformity of vowel production and improving tonal blend. Moreover, it demonstrates the fact that vowels have little meaning by themselves, and that intelligibility of the text is dependent primarily on the precise articulation of the consonants.

Vowels

If uniform tone production and tonal blend are to be achieved, the choral conductor must be cognizant of the precise differences of vowel sounds utilized in speaking and singing, and he must develop a similar awareness on the part of his choristers. Singers as a group are usually familiar with the primary vowels **(ee, ay, ah, oh, oo)**, since these are used rather extensively as a beginning point in vocalization. However, they are less familiar with the precise differences among the other vowel sounds. The vowel chart in Figure 28 illustrates the variety of vowel sounds that occur in the texts of choral literature. The International Phonetic Alphabet, with a specific symbol for each sound, was devised by phoneticians for the purpose of providing an accurate means of identifying and differentiating among the various vowel and consonant sounds. In the first column of this chart, the phonetic symbols for the different vowel sounds are listed. The diacritical markings for these vowels, as used in English dictionaries, are

---

[9] The formation of intelligible vowel sounds is, of course, dependent upon the adjustment of the articulating organs; however, the vowels are not so dependent upon such a rapid and precise adjustment as are the consonants.

Phonetic Symbols	Dia-critical Mark-ings	Illustra-tive Symbols	Examples
i (long e)	ē	ee	see, each, tree, Easter, free, glee, feet, sleep, deep, sheep, wheel
ɪ (short i)	ĭ	ĭ	sing, is, will, him, thing, ship, wish, April, similar, crib, been, king
e (long a)	ā	ay	say, faith, age, angel, rain, same, maiden, away, day, way, great
ɛ (short e)	ĕ	eh	yet, end, enter, help, never, every, let, men, said, then
æ (short a)	ă	ă	at, rang, mantle, ashes, agony, began, can, cat, that, than
a	ȧ	ȧ	ask, grass, laugh, bath, calf, craft, raft, chance, chaff
ɑ	ä	ah	father, Amen, alms, army, far, heart, calm, palm, psalm
ɒ (short o)	ŏ	ŏ	stop, hot, sorry, olive, God, watch, wander, John, yon
ɔ	ô	aw	law, all, awe, autumn, always, walk, warm, dawn
o (long o)	ō	oh	flow, old, road, hope, low, soul, snow, open, so, boat, home, cold
ʊ	o͝o	o͝o	look, bosom, took, foot, stood, should, would, book, full, brook
u	o͞o	oo	who, too, moon, whose, blue, true, through, flew, soon, tomb
ɝ	ûr	ur	birth, early, earth, world, worth, perfect, burden, were
ɚ	ẽr	er	ever, never, another, pleasure, mother, weather, measure
ə	ə,ȧ	uh	about, around, firmament, America, awhile, away, above
ʌ (short u)	ŭ	uh	but, sun, done, creation, other, until, wonder, thunder

Fig. 28. The single vowels frequently occurring in choral literature, with symbols and examples by which the conductor may illustrate and correct pronunciation difficulties.

listed in the second column. Both the phonetic symbols and the diacritical markings are presented primarily as a reference for the choral conductor. Because their precise meanings would not always be readily evident to a group of amateur singers, various illustrative symbols for each vowel are included in the third column, and are suggested for use with the choir members. When pronunciation difficulties occur in rehearsals, the conductor should identify and isolate particularly troublesome vowel sounds. These illustrative symbols may be written on the chalkboard, discussed, pronounced, and sung as a means of clarifying in the singers' minds the desired vowel sounds. Numerous examples of specific vowels as they occur in various words are also listed and may be used for illustrative or comparative purposes.

The formation of each vowel in Figure 28 requires distinctly different adjustments of the articulating organs, with the exception of the following: The vowel ɝ (ûr) is the counterpart of ɚ (ẽr) and the adjustment of the articulating organs is quite similar. The vowel ɝ (ûr) occurs only on stressed syllables and the sound ɚ (ẽr) occurs on unstressed syllables. Also, the vowel ʌ (ŭ) is the counterpart of ə and the position of the articulating organs is almost identical. The vowel ʌ (ŭ) occurs only on stressed syllables, while the vowel ə occurs only on unstressed syllables.

The various vowels are determined by the relative size and shape of the mouth and throat cavities. Specific determinants are the position of the tongue, the jaw, and the lips. As indicated in Figure 29, the vowels **ee** and **ĭ** are formed high and forward, while the vowel **oo** is formed lower in the throat. In singing the **ee** and **ĭ** vowels the tongue is relatively high, whereas in the **oo** vowel the tongue is back. In both cases the position of the jaw is high and the mouth is somewhat closed. Because of this condition, these sounds are often referred to as closed vowels. All other vowels are referred to as open vowels, even though the position of the tongue, lips, and jaw will vary to some extent. The tongue is most relaxed and the jaw at its lowest position while singing the vowel **ah,** as in the word **father.** Because of the lesser degree of tension, this vowel is the most freely produced and is therefore frequently used as a beginning point in vocalization.

In his exuberance, the novice chorister may tense the tongue too much and restrict the proper functioning of the vocal mechanism, and a thin, shallow tone quality is likely to result. A helpful device is for the conductor to suggest to the singers that, when singing the open vowels, the position of the tongue remain in the relaxed position of the **ah** vowel. There is a limit, of course, to the practicality of this suggestion as it affects pronunciation; however, the device does facilitate the reduction of excessive tension in the tongue muscle.

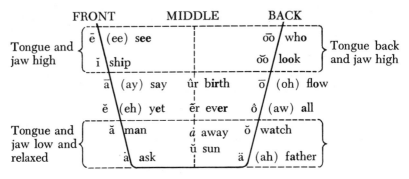

Fig. 29.   *Vowel formation from front to back placement.*

When singing the closed vowels **ee** and **ĭ**, it is suggested that the singers place the back sides of the tongue against the upper back teeth. When the position of the tongue is too high, this device serves to enlarge the oral cavity somewhat and allows for a freer emission of tone. It also prevents one from forming these vowels too low in the throat, which may cause throatiness and flatting especially in the upper range of the voice.

If a choral group sings with a nasal, white, or colorless tone, then vowels with extreme forward placement such as **ee** and **ĭ** should be utilized sparingly in vocalization, and the vowels formed lower in the throat, such as **aw, oh,** and **oo,** should be utilized. Conversely, if the group sings with an overly dark tone quality, then greater attention should be given the vowels formed high and forward. All the primary vowels (**ee, ay, ah, oh, oo**), however, should be utilized to some extent in vocalization, and concentration on any one group of vowels to the total exclusion of the others should be avoided.

Diphthongs

The diphthong may be defined as a compound vowel, or a syllable in which the sound changes from one vowel to another. In a simple or single vowel the articulating organs are held in a somewhat fixed position, whereas in a diphthong the articulating organs change position, thus altering the vowel sound. Figure 31 shows the diphthongs as they occur in English.

Except for **ju** or **Iu,** the durational stress should be given the primary vowel, and the secondary vowel should be sounded just prior

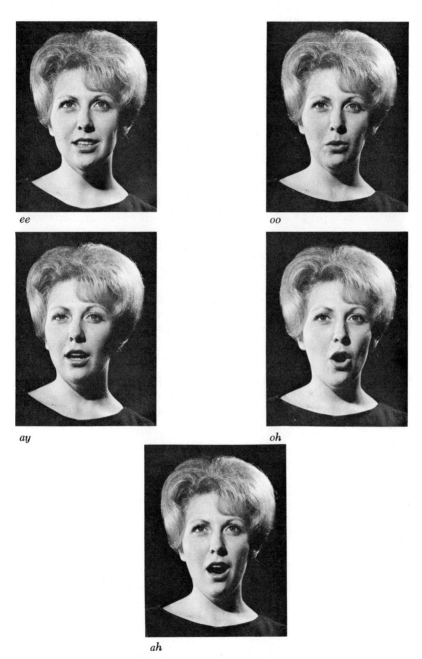

ee

oo

ay

oh

ah

Fig. 30. Relative positions of the lips and jaw in forming the primary vowels (**ee, ay, ah, oh, oo**). *Compare with Figure 29.*

Phonetic Symbols	Diacritical Markings	Illustrative Symbols	Examples
aɪ or ɑɪ	ī (long i)	ah—ĭ	night, high, light
aʊ or ɑʊ	ou	ah—o͝o	our, now, round
ɔɪ	oi	aw—ĭ	oil, rejoice, joy
eɪ	ā	ay—ĭ	day, faith, they
oʊ	ō	oh—o͝o	old, hope, low
ju or ɪu	ū	ĭ-o͞o—	beauty, few, view

Fig. 31. The diphthongs as they occur in English.

to the release of the diphthong. It is often helpful if the secondary vowels are thought of in terms of the same durational stress as are the consonants. This procedure should be followed whenever the musical notation and the tempo permit the *initial* vowel in the diphthong to be sustained for any reasonable length of time. Thus the word **night** if sustained would be sung as **nah——ĭt,** not **nah–eet,** and the word **round** would be sung **rah——o͝ond,** not **rah–o͞ond.**

The diphthong **ju** is actually a consonant-vowel combination. An example of this sound occurs in the word **beauty.** In this instance it is the secondary rather than the primary vowel that should receive the durational stress. The word should always be pronounced **bĭ-o͞o——ty,** rather than **bēe–o͞o–ty.**

In the treatment of all diphthongs, a smoother transition from the primary to the secondary vowel will be achieved if the diphthong is thought of as a single, composite sound, rather than as two separate and distinct vowel sounds.

Classification of Consonants

Generally the consonants may be classified into two types—the voiced and voiceless (non-voiced). The voiceless consonants include **k, p, t, f, h, s,** and **sh,** whereas the voiced consonants include **b, d, v, z, zh, l, g, j, w, r, y, m, n,** and **ng.** The consonant **th** is voiced in some words and voiceless in others. In producing the voiced consonants the vocal cords are drawn together, set into vibration, and the consonant is voiced as a result, whereas in the voiceless consonants there is no perceptible movement of the vocal cords. The voiced consonants are softer in character and less explosive than the voiceless (non-voiced) consonants. As the voiced consonants have a slight sustaining quality, they may be used effectively to bridge the gap between various vowel sounds, especially in *legato* singing. Developing the singers' awareness of the essential differences between these consonant sounds will result in improved enunciation.

For a number of consonants, the adjustment of the articulating organs is similar. Only one adjustment is necessary for the following paired consonants: **t-d, p-b, f-v, k-g, s-z,** and **sh-zh.** The first consonant in the pair is voiceless, while the second consonant is voiced.[10] The words in Figure 32 serve to illustrate further the similarities between the adjustment of the articulators and the differences in sound duration. Words are listed that include the use of an initial, a medial, and a final consonant.

Voiceless	*Voiced*
t—time, turtle, part	d—day, garden, afraid
p—pretty, happy, harp	b—bright, above, crib
f—faith, before, life	v—voices, ever, above
k—kind, because, music	g—garden, finger, flag
s—sing, asleep, peace	z—zenith, music, eyes
sh—sheep, ocean, wish	zh—Jacques, pleasure, rouge

Fig. 32. Paired consonants, with similar articulator adjustments.

Another means of classifying the consonants is by the manner in which the flow of the breath is released. The *explosive* consonants are **p, b, t, d, ch, j** (**dzh**)**, k,** and **g.** The *continuants* are **w, wh, f, v, th, s, z, sh, zh, r, j** (**y**)**, h, l, m, n,** and **ng.** In articulating the *explosive* consonants, the flow of the breath is momentarily interrupted by the contact between the articulating organs. An explosive sound is emitted as the articulating organs are separated precisely and the pressure of the breath is released. In producing the *continuants,* the articulating organs assume a relatively fixed position as the sound is emitted.

Still another means of classifying the consonants is by the position or placement of the articulating organs involved in producing the sounds. They are as follows:

Bilabial **(p, b, m, w)**.
Formed by the lower and upper lips. In forming the consonants

---

[10] Exceptions to the pairing of voiced and voiceless consonants are **h, r, y, w, l, m, n,** and **ng.** All of these consonants are voiced except the **h,** which is voiceless.

p and **b,** the flow of the breath is interrupted momentarily as the lips are drawn together, and the breath is released in an explosive manner as the lips are suddenly opened; **p** is voiceless and **b** is a voiced consonant. The consonant **m** is voiced and is formed by closing the lips, thus causing the flow of the breath to be emitted through the nasal passages. The consonant **w** is voiced and is referred to as a *bilabial glide.* It is produced by the lips forming a position similar to the **u** vowel and then moving or gliding quickly to the subsequent vowel sound.

Labio-dental **(f, v).**
Formed by the lower lips and the upper teeth. To form these consonants the lower lip and the upper teeth are brought together and the breath is forced audibly between the two articulating organs; **f** is a voiceless consonant and **v** is voiced.

Lingua-dental **(th).**
Formed by the tip of the tongue touching the back side of the upper front teeth. The breath is forced between these two articulators; **th,** as in the word **thousand,** is voiceless and the sound **th,** as in the word **there,** is voiced.

Lingua-alveolar **(t, d, n, l, s, z).**
Formed by the tip of the tongue and the upper teeth or gum ridge. In forming the consonants **t** and **d,** the flow of the breath is interrupted momentarily by the contact between these two articulating organs. The consonants are sounded and the breath is released in a slightly explosive manner as the contact between these organs is released; **t** is voiceless and **d** is voiced. The **n** is voiced and is formed by placing the tip of the tongue against the gum ridge and directing the sound through the nasal passages. In the consonant **l,** which is also voiced, the tongue is placed against the gum ridge and the sound is emitted over the sides of the tongue. In forming the consonants **s** and **z,** the sides of the tongue are kept in contact with the upper back teeth, and the tip of the tongue rests just behind the upper front teeth, although not touching directly. The flow of the breath is directed over the tongue where it strikes the back edge of the upper front teeth, thus causing the hissing sound descriptive of these two consonants. The **s** is voiceless and the **z** is voiced.

Lingua-palatal **(sh, zh, ch, dzh, j, r).**
Formed by the contact between the tongue and the hard palate.

In producing the consonants **sh** and **zh,** the sides of the tongue are placed against the upper back teeth, as in the position for the consonant **s,** except that the tongue is drawn slightly farther back; **sh** is voiceless and **zh** is voiced.

In sounding the consonant combinations **ch** and **dzh,** the tongue contacts the hard palate at a point slightly farther back than for the consonant **t.** The tongue comes in contact with the upper back teeth and the flow of the breath is interrupted momentarily. As the tongue is released, the breath is emitted in an explosive manner. The consonant **ch** is voiceless, but the **dzh** is voiced.

The consonant **j** as it occurs in certain words, is pronounced **dzh,** as in **judge, joy,** etc. In other words such as **hallelujah,** it assumes a softer, non-explosive quality as in the consonant **y,** and as occurring in words such as **yet, year,** and **beyond.** The **y** is considered by many authorities to be a voiced consonant; however, some writers classify it as a semi-vowel.

In pronouncing the consonant **r,** the sides of the tongue contact the upper back teeth. The tip of the tongue is curled or drawn back toward the hard palate and, as the sound is emitted, it glides smoothly to the adjustment necessary for the following vowel sound. This adjustment is common in such words as **run, around, read,** etc. In some words, however, the tongue assumes a much lower position in the mouth, and the glide occurs in reverse order. This action occurs in such words as **heard, her, creator,** etc., where the preceding vowel sound is stressed. In this case, the consonant is articulated as the syllable is released. The consonant **r** is a voiced consonant.

Velar **(k, g, ng).**
Formed by arching the back part of the tongue and pressing it lightly against the soft palate. In the **k** and **g** sounds, the flow of the breath is interrupted momentarily. As the contact is released and the tongue is lowered, the breath is exploded. The consonant **k** is voiceless, but the **g** is voiced. In forming the consonant **ng,** the position of the tongue is similar to that of the **k** and **g** sounds, except that the soft palate or velum is lowered slightly and the tongue is more relaxed, thus allowing the sound to be emitted through the nasal passages. The consonant **ng** is voiced.

Glottal **(h).**
Formed in the glottis or the opening between the vocal cords. The vocal cords come together in a position that restricts the flow of the breath slightly, but not enough to set the cords into vibration.

The consonant **h** is voiceless and is produced by forcing the breath between the non-vibrating vocal cords. This sound is often referred to as the *aspirate h.*

Styles of Diction

There are three basic styles of choral diction; namely, *legato, staccato,* and *marcato.* Each of these styles is distinctly different and each must be treated in a specific manner if effective interpretation is to be achieved.

Legato diction is smooth and connected. A minimum of emphasis should be given to the rhythmic stress or pulsation of the music in *legato* style. *Legato* phrases should be thought of in terms of long, soaring and descending musical lines. In addition, the explosive qualities of the consonants should be minimized if they are to be smoothly blended with the vowel sounds.[11] In achieving this effect, the singers should carry over the final consonants of one syllable or word to the following syllable or word. The following examples serve to illustrate this concept: **My Lord, what a mornin'** is sung **mah-ee law—rd hwah–tuh maw—rn–nĭn. Lost in the night** is sung **law—stĭ–n–thuh nah—ĭt. My love dwelt in a northern land** is sung **mah–ee luhv dweh–l–tĭn nuh naw–r–thern lă—nd.**

Any exception to this rule occurs as a result of the diction being unintelligible or creating a somewhat ludicrous effect. In the following examples, it is desirable to separate the sounds, as indicated by the diagonal lines, with a slight break in the flow of the breath.

"She's / like the Swallow" (from "She's Like the Swallow," Newfoundland folk song, Oxford University Press).

"Slumbers / not nor sleeps" (from "He Watching Over Israel"—by Felix Mendelssohn).

"We Three Kings of Orient / Are" (John H. Hopkins).

When the second syllable occurs on a stressed beat, one may further clarify the sound through careful articulation. *I.e.,* in the first example, articulate the word *like* with a "capital L."

Examples of octavo choral selections requiring a *legato* treatment of diction are included in the following list.[12]

---

[11] To achieve a smooth blending between the consonants and the vowels in *legato* diction, it will be helpful to request the singers to sustain the consonants as well as the vowels. This device, although seemingly quite unorthodox, lessens the explosive qualities of the consonants and contributes substantially to the desired *legato* effect.

[12] For complete names and addresses of the publishers referred to in this and subsequent lists, see the Appendix, pp. 302-306.

Ave Verum Corpus by Wolfgang A. Mozart. G. Schirmer, No. 5471.
Alleluia by Randall Thompson. E. C. Schirmer, No. 1786.
God So Loved the World (from *The Crucifixion*) by John Stainer.
    G. Schirmer, No. 3798.
How Lovely Is Thy Dwelling Place by Johannes Brahms, ed. H. R.
    Wilson. G. Ricordi, No. 1515.
I Wonder as I Wander (Appalachian carol) arr. John Jacob Niles
    and Lewis Henry Horton. G. Schirmer, No. 8708.
Lost in the Night (Finnish folk song) arr. F. Melius Christiansen.
    Augsburg, No. 119.
Mary Had a Baby by William L. Dawson. Tuskegee Institute Press,
    No. 118.
My Love Dwelt in a Northern Land by Edward Elgar. G. Schirmer,
    No. 2366.
O Divine Redeemer by Charles Gounod. Hall & McCreary, No. 1602.

In *staccato* diction, the words should be sung in a detached style as if there were a slight rest between each note. Good *staccato* diction depends upon distinct and precise articulation of the consonants. The lips should be flexible and devoid of excessive tension, and the lip movements should be exaggerated. The singers should refrain from singing too loudly, since excessive volume is likely to inhibit the precise articulation of the words. (Excessive volume tends to shift the focus from careful articulation to weighty tonal effects.) The vowels should be modified slightly and formed closer to the front of the mouth; words should be thought of as being formed on the lips, since sounds formed too far in the back of the mouth tend to become weighty, cumbersome, and difficult to articulate in a short, detached style. Exercise 12 will be found helpful in developing precise lip movements and in improving *staccato* diction.

Exercise 12.

Bah,   bah,   bah,   bah,   etc.   *(repeat one-half step higher, etc.).*

1. Use various consonants on this exercise (**b, p, t, f, d,** etc.).
2. Vocalize only in the middle register.
3. Work for clearness and precision of consonants and for flexibility.
   Flexibility will aid in developing freedom of voice production.

Examples of choral octavo publications requiring a *staccato* treatment of diction are included in the following list.

Cicirinella (Italian folk song) arr. Max Krone. M. Witmark, No. 5—
    W2952.
Hasten Swiftly, Hasten Softly by Richard Kountz. Galaxy, No. 1750.
I Saw Three Ships (traditional English) arr. Alice Parker and Robert
    Shaw. G. Schirmer, No. 10188.
Rock-A My Soul (spiritual) arr. Joseph De Vaux. Bourne, No. 667.
The Sleigh by Richard Kountz. G. Schirmer, No. 7459.
We Wish You a Merry Christmas (English folk song) arr. the Krones.
    Kjos, No. 4006.
Younger Generation by Aaron Copland. Boosey & Hawkes, No. 1723.

In *marcato* diction each note is sung with an accent and the
rhythm is quite pronounced. Effective *marcato* diction necessitates
correct muscular action, which is precisely a sharp inward movement of the abdominal muscles.[13] Perhaps the most effective means
of teaching this concept is to ask the singers to "grunt" each note in
the correct musical rhythm. By placing the hand on the abdomen,
singers are more likely to "feel" the movement, thus facilitating the
achievement of this concept. With attention focused upon this
muscular movement, it is helpful to have the group recite the text in
correct musical rhythm before attempting further to apply the concept to actual singing. A *marcato* treatment of diction is required in
sections of the following choral octavo publications, which are
included for study and analysis.

Hallelujah (from *Mount of Olives*) by Ludwig van Beethoven.
    G. Schirmer, No. 2215.
Hallelujah, Amen (from *Judas Maccabaeus*) by George F. Handel.
    M. Witmark, No. 5–W3026.
Let Their Celestial Concerts All Unite (from *Samson*) by George F.
    Handel. E. C. Schirmer, No. 312.
Psalm 150 by Louis Lewandowski, ed. H. R. Wilson. Hall &
    McCreary, No. 1640.
While by My Sheep (17th-century hymn) arr. Hugo Jungst. G. Schir-
    mer, No. 2532.

Although many choral compositions require only one specific
type of treatment as regards the style of diction, others will contain contrasting sections and phrases, each requiring a different
treatment. Prior to introducing a selection to the chorus, the conductor should analyze carefully the text and the music, giving particular
attention to the diction requirements. If in doubt about the style of
diction, one should always look to the text of the music. The mood

---

[13] For a discussion of the function of the abdominal muscles in the respiratory process, see p. 36.

and emotional content of the text will reveal many things to the conductor, including various shadings and nuances necessary for the most effective interpretation of the music.

The Sibilant S

Of the sibilants or hissing sounds in English (**s, z, sh, zh, ch,** and **j**), the most troublesome, especially in *legato* singing, is the consonant **s.** Unless handled correctly, the singing of this consonant may remind one of sounds emanating from a snake pit. An example of this may be found in the words "God so loved the world" from the chorus in John Stainer's *The Crucifixion.* Unless careful attention is given to the sibilant **s** in the word **so,** considerable difficulty may occur with amateur choral groups. Amateurs are often likely to sing the phrase as **Gaw——dssssssoh—luh——vd thuh wuh——rld.** The difficulty here lies primarily in the lack of the singers' accurate response to the rhythmic duration of the first measure. The **s** is anticipated with a resultant hissing sound. Tight, rigid jaws also contribute to the problem. If the jaw is not relaxed and the mouth kept open, the consonants **d** and **s** will inevitably follow too quickly the preceding vowel sound.

A solution to this specific problem, which also will apply to other problems of a similar nature, is first to concentrate upon the development of rhythmic accuracy in the chorus. The fact that the first measure has three beats must be understood and felt by all the singers. Having the group clap or tap the basic pulsation, or even conducting the traditional pattern for triple meter, will be found helpful. Next, have the group sing the phrase on a neutral syllable, such as **loo.** After rhythmic accuracy has been achieved, the group should endeavor to prefix the vowel sound **oh** in the second measure with the consonants **ds.** The final result should sound as shown in Figure 33.

Some directors have found it particularly helpful, in dealing with the hissing **s**'s, to assign the singing of them to only a particular portion of the chorus, with the remainder of the group singing

Gaw ____ dsoh - luh - vd thuh   wuh _____ rld.

Fig. 33. Excerpt from "God So Loved the World" (from John Stainer's The Crucifixion*).*

only the vowel sound. The use of this approach certainly depends upon the requirements of the musical situation, and its success depends upon a clear understanding on the part of the singers as to their particular specific assignments.

In certain choral selections it will be helpful to minimize the **s** sound by changing it to the shorter **z** sound. Certainly the obvious advantage of this procedure becomes apparent in singing the words "slumbers not" from Mendelssohn's *He Watching Over Israel.*

The Troublesome R

The consonant **r** is often the source of unmusical sounds in amateur choral groups. The difficulty usually encountered is the overanticipation of the consonant—often caused through the singer's inaccurate response to the rhythmic duration of the music. Words such as **ever** and **world** are particular examples of poor diction. How often has one heard the sound **eh–vuhrr** or the equally obnoxious sound of **wuhrrr–ld?** To alleviate the problem, singers must not only be made more conscious of rhythmic duration, but must also be instructed to sustain the vowel preceding the consonant **r** sound, and to add the **r** only briefly upon the release of the syllable. Thus **ever** should be sung as **eh–vuh——r,** and **world** as **wuh——rld.**

The Consonants M, N, and L

Although most of the consonants have a comparatively short duration, the consonants **m, n,** and **l** are particular exceptions and have a certain degree of sustaining power. As such they may be effectively used, especially in *legato* singing, to bridge more smoothly the gap between the various vowel sounds. For example, in singing the word **amen** the pronunciation **ah—mehn** contributes little to the smoothness of the *legato* phrase. A more effective procedure is to sing the word as **ah—m—mehn.** In this manner the consonant **m** serves to bridge the gap between the vowels **ah** and **eh,** thus creating an improved *legato* effect (Figure 34). To accomplish this successfully, the mouth must be closed momentarily upon the release of the first vowel and opened upon the attack of the second vowel sound. (Obviously, this treatment is appropriate only when dealing with *legato* diction. Utilizing this approach with a vigorous, Handelian chorus would be out of character and highly inappropriate. In most cases the approach used will be dictated by the demands of the musical situation.)

a   *b*

Fig. 34. *An example of bridging the gap between two vowel sounds. Note (a) how the word is written, and (b) how it is effectively sung.*

A similar treatment is suggested in dealing with the consonant **n.** In the words **mine eyes** the tongue should touch the back side of the upper front teeth as the **n** is sounded. The tongue should drop immediately before the first syllable of the word **eyes.** The phrase should be sung as **mah–een–nah–eez.**

In most cases, when dealing with the double consonants, the first of the two should be eliminated. Usually this procedure is dictated by common sense. For example, the word **better** is pronounced **beh—tuhr** and not **beht—tuhr**; the word **torrents** is pronounced **tŏ-rĕnts** and not **tŏr-rĕnts.** An exception to the rule, however, is the treatment of the double consonant **ll.** In the word **allelujah,** for example, both **l**'s should be sounded if *legato* diction is to be clear and connected. The word **allelujah** should be sung **ahl—lay—loo—jah,** rather than **ah—lay—loo—jah.** The initial **l** should be added upon the release of the first vowel and the second **l** should prefix the second vowel. Examples of this suggested treatment may be found in the following compositions:

Allelujah by W. A. Mozart. Carl Fischer, No. 541.
Alleluia by Randall Thompson. E. C. Schirmer, No. 1786.

The Aspirate H

The aspirate **h** is effected by means of a rapid flow of the breath, and when this condition does not prevail the sound is often strident and ineffective. For example, in the word **hallelujah** in the chorus "Hallelujah, Amen" from the oratorio *Judas Maccabaeus* by Handel, the initial consonant is often slighted, thus resulting in a poor attack and a tightening of the vocal mechanism. To avoid this pitfall, singers should be instructed to anticipate the attack and precede the initial vowel with a rapid push or flow of the breath. When singing in *marcato* style, a sharp inward movement of the abdominal muscles will help to activate the flow of the breath. Adequate preparation on the part of both the conductor and the chorus is essential. Singers should be poised, alert, and ready for the attack, and the conductor should provide a clear, precise preparatory beat.

The aspirate **h** will often cause difficulty when combined with another consonant. For example, the word **when** often is pronounced as **wehn** rather than **hwehn.** In addition to activating the flow of the breath, singers must strive for careful, precise lip action to ensure the correct articulation of this consonant combination.

Vowel-Consonant Balance

The concept of "singing on the vowel," important as it is, should not be stressed at the expense of the consonants. Overemphasis upon the vowel sounds to the neglect of the consonants may result in beautiful choral tone, but the singing will generally lack luster and the desirable expressive characteristics.

To achieve correct, understandable diction, a balance must be maintained between the vowels and the consonants. When given only equal stress, the vowel sounds usually predominate over the consonants because of their sustaining characteristics. Therefore, to achieve a desirable balance the consonants should be overexaggerated—not in duration, but in the degree of intensity.[14] Emphasis should be placed upon careful and precise articulation, rather than upon excessive duration of the consonants.

More effective results will be achieved by graphically illustrating on the chalkboard the relative degree of emphasis required in balancing the vowels and consonants, as in Figure 35.

Final Consonants

Amateur singing groups often do not finish their words, especially at the ends of phrases. The poetical qualities of the text are thereby lost and projection of the mood or spirit of the song becomes relatively ineffective. The conductor should be careful to provide a clear, precise release to the phrase so that the group may utilize

---

[14] A word of caution! An exception to this treatment occurs in dealing with music in a *legato* style. Too much emphasis upon the intensity of the consonants is likely to disturb the *legato* flow of the music. In this style, emphasis should be placed upon the smooth connection of vowels and consonants. For a further discussion of this treatment, see p. 66.

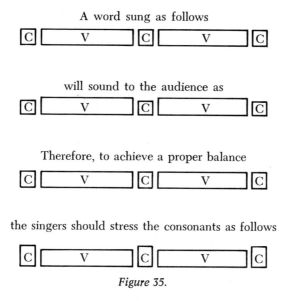

Figure 35.

this movement as a signal to add the final consonants. In addition, the conductor should endeavor to develop in his singers an increased consciousness of the problem. One effective approach is for the director to sing a series of words from which the final consonants are omitted; then ask the singers to identify the words. The variety of guesses will serve to illustrate the importance of including the final consonants of all words.

Tone and diction are the chief means of transmitting the poetic qualities of the music to the audience. Without properly produced and appropriate tone quality the effectiveness of the music is lessened considerably, and without correct diction choral tone becomes meaningless and little more than instrumental in character. Good tone quality and correct diction are essential to effective interpretation and, to be achieved, must receive the detailed, exacting attention of the choral conductor.

COMMONLY MISPRONOUNCED WORDS

Following is a brief list of some common errors in pronunciation.[15]

---

[15] This list, of course, does not pertain to songs necessitating a dialectal treatment.

This list, though incomplete, may serve as a starting point for the conductor who wishes to develop his own list of mispronounced words—or words that are troublesome in his particular locality.

Word	*Pronunciation*
angel	ayn-j*eh*l, not ayn-juhl
beautiful	bĭ-ōō-tĭ-foŏl (bū-tĭ-foŏl), not be-ōō-tee-fuhl
Bethlehem	Bĕth-lē-hĕm, not Bĕth-lē-ham
can	kăn, not kĭn
Christmas	Chrĭs-más, not Chrĭs-muhs
creation	kree-ay-sh*uh*n (kre-ā-shŭn), not kree-ay-shĭn
dew	dĭ-*oo* (dū), not dōō. (Other words containing this problem are: new, beauty, few, view, pure, and human.)
for	fór, not fûr
forget	fŏr-g*eh*t, not fŏr-gĭt
forgiveness	fŏr-gĭv-n*eh*s, not fŏr-gĭv-nuhs
Galilee	gă-lĭ-lē, not gă-luh-lē
get	g*eh*t, not gĭt
glory	gl*oh*-ree, not glaw-ree
government	guh-v*ern*-mehnt (gŭ-vērn-mĕnt), not guh-ver-mehnt
heaven	heh-v*eh*n, not heh-vuhn
judgment	jŭj-mĕnt, not jŭj-muhnt
kindness	kah-ĭnd-n*eh*s (kīnd-nĕs), not kah-ĭnd-nuhs
listen	lĭs-*eh*n, not lĭs-uhn
Lord	L*aw*rd (Lôrd), not Lahrd, or Lowrd
love	lu*h*v (lŭv), not lahv
manger	mayn-je*r* (mān-jēr), not mayn-jĭr
Mary	M*eh*-ree (Mâ-rē), not May-ree
mountain	moun-t*eh*n, not moun-uhn
night	na*h*-ĭt (nīt), not naht, or nah-eet. (Other words containing the long ī [a diphthong] include high, sigh, fly, etc.)
open	oh-p*eh*n, not oh-puhn
poor	poŏr, not pohr
pretty	prĭ-t*ē*, not prĭ-dē
roof	rōōf, not ruhf
silent	sah-ĭ-l*eh*nt (sī-lĕnt), not sah-ee-luhnt
spirit	spĭ-rĭt, not spĭ-ruht
the	th*ee* before words beginning with a vowel, or the silent *h* (th*ee* everlasting, th*ee* hour). th*uh* before words beginning with a consonant (th*uh* night, th*uh* heavens).
triumphant	trī-ŭm-fănt, not trī-ŭm-funt
virgin	vûr-jĭn, not vûr-juhn
wheel	*h*weel, not weel
when	hwĕn, not wĕn (wehn)
worship	wûr-shĭp, not wûr-shup
your	yoŏr, not yuhr

TERMS PERTAINING TO CHORAL TONE AND DICTION

Actuator—the part of the vocal mechanism which actuates or begins the flow of the breath, i.e., the lungs, the diaphragm, the intercostal muscles, and the abdominal muscles.

Articulation—the action or physical adjustment of the articulating organs in the formation of intelligible sounds.

Articulators—the part of the vocal mechanism which forms or shapes the various language sounds and which determines their particular distinguishable characteristics. Specific determiners are the tongue, lips, teeth, lower jaw, the hard palate, and the velum or soft palate.

Aspirate h—a vocal sound characterized by a slight constriction of the vocal cords; the cords are approximated, but not close enough to be set into vibration.

Bilabial—the consonants formed by the upper and lower lips **(p, b, m, w)**.

Breath support—the flow or pressure of the breath against the vocal cords in an amount sufficient to effect the vibration necessary for a given pitch; considered to be adequate when phonation occurs without unnecessary constriction or tension in the laryngeal muscles.

Closed vowels—the vowels **ee, ĭ,** and **oo,** classified as such because of the relatively small oral cavity caused by the high position of the tongue in the mouth.

Consonants—the vocal sounds formed by precise, articulate movements of the lips, tongue, and jaw and characterized by an interruption or restriction of the flow of the breath. Consonants give intelligibility to vocal expression.

Covered tone—a slightly modified or altered vowel sound utilized by male singers in the production of tones in the upper register. The covered tone is full and resonant and lacking in any falsetto characteristics. A firming of the vocal mechanism occurs and the vowel being sung is modified toward the **uh** vowel.

Deep set vowels—vowels characterized by a roundness and fullness of tone quality, and a naturalness of tone production, creating a sensation of being formed low in the throat. Essential physical conditions are a relaxed tongue and an open throat.

Diaphragm—a broad muscular partition located between the chest cavity and the abdomen. The diaphragm is one of the principal muscles used in inhalation. It is arched and dome-shaped in its relaxed state. As the diaphragm is tensed it contracts and flattens out, thus pushing downward against the organs in the abdominal

region. Coupled with the action of the rib muscles, the diaphragm contributes to the enlargement of the chest cavity, and
as a result the air pressure is lowered. The lower air pressure is
equalized by air entering the lungs. When the diaphragm
relaxes, it returns to its normal state and pressure is made upon
the small air-sacs in the lungs, thus effecting or causing exhalation, and completing the cycle of breathing.

Diphthong—a compound or double vowel, in which the vowel
sounds change smoothly from one to the other. For example, the
word **round** contains the diphthong **ou** (**ah** and **oo**) and is pronounced **rah-oond.**

Enunciation—the manner of vocal utterance as regards distinctness
and clarity of vowels and consonants.

Falsetto—a light, head voice, lying above the natural or normal range
of the male voice. In singing a falsetto tone, only the inner edges
of the vocal cords vibrate.

Final consonant—the last consonant in a word.

Glottal—relating to, or produced in, the glottis; the aspirate consonant **h,** formed in the glottis.

Glottis—the fissure or opening between the vocal cords or bands.

Hard palate—the portion of the roof of the mouth between the
alveoli and the velum or soft palate. The hard palate is a structure of bone with a layer or cover of tissue.

High-forward resonance—a focusing of the tone in the "mask," or
more specifically in the frontal cavities of the head. Essential
physical conditions are an open throat and an arched velum.

Hooty tones—a muffled tone quality lacking in correct tonal focus.

Initial consonant—a consonant situated at the beginning of a word.

Intercostal muscles—the muscles that lie between the ribs and partially control the process of respiration.

Labio-dental—the consonants formed by the lower lip and the upper
front teeth **(f, v).**

Laryngeal muscles—the muscles that regulate the size of the glottis,
control the degree of tension of the vocal cords, and close off
the larynx during swallowing.

Larynx—sometimes referred to as the voice box; a cartilage that
houses the vocal cords, situated at the upper part of the trachea
or windpipe.

Legato diction—a style of diction in which the vowels and consonants
are smoothly connected. The explosive qualities of the consonants are minimized, and the final consonants of most syllables
or words are carried over and prefix the following syllable. For
example, the words **night time** are sung **nah–ĭ taheem.**

Lingua-alveolar—the consonants **t, d, n, l, s,** and **z,** formed by the
tip of the tongue touching the alveoli (teeth or gum ridge;
portion of the jaw where the sockets for the upper teeth are
situated; area between the teeth and the hard palate).

Lingua-dental—the consonants formed by the tip of the tongue touching the upper front teeth (**th** as in **thousand,** and **th** as in **there**).

Lingua-palatal—the consonants formed by the contact between the tongue and the hard palate (**sh, zh, ch, dzh, j,** and **r**).

Marcato diction—a style of diction in which each note in the music receives an accent and the explosive qualities of the consonants are exaggerated.

Medial consonant—a consonant situated within a word.

Nasality—an undesirable, exaggerated nasal quality often arising from some obstruction in the nasal cavity. When the nasal cavity becomes infected and swollen, as with a headcold, this quality usually occurs.

Open throat—an expression used to describe the feeling of a relaxed throat; an essential condition to correct voice production.

Open vowels—all of the vowels with the exception of **ee, i,** and **oo.** They are classified as open vowels because of the relaxed tongue position and the relatively low position of the jaw. The basic open vowel is **ah,** as in the word **father.** This vowel is the most naturally produced and is widely used as a beginning point in vocalization.

Palate—the roof of the mouth (*see also* hard palate and velum).

Pharynx—cavity extending from the base of the skull to the esophagus.

Phonation—the act of uttering or producing vocal sounds in singing or speaking.

Pronunciation—the manner of pronouncing words as regards the selection of appropriate vowels and consonants, and the proper accent of words.

Registers—the compass or range of the voice in which the singer is able to sing without readjustment of the vocal cords. Principal classifications are the chest and head registers; however, some authorities consider the middle range of the voice as a third register. Certain other authorities emphatically deny the existence of vocal registers.

Resonance—the amplification and enrichment of a fundamental tone emanating from the larynx—by means of supplementary vibrations in the bodily resonance cavities.

Resonator—the part of the vocal mechanism which amplifies or resonates the tone and provides its characteristic timbre. Specifically, the pharynx, the mouth, the nasal cavity, and the sinuses. (Some authorities believe the trachea, the bronchi, and the chest cavity also contribute to vocal resonance.)

Respiration—the process of breathing, involving the alternate inhaling and expelling of the breath; inspiration followed by expiration.

Sibilants—the hissing sounds caused by the raised tongue position and the flow of the breath being directed at the back side of the upper teeth. The sibilants in English are **s, z, sh, zh, ch,** and **j.**

Soft palate— (*see* velum.)

Sonorous—a full, richly resonant tone quality.

Staccato diction—a style of diction in which the notes and the words are distinctly separated or detached.

Strident quality—a harsh, grating, unpleasant tonal quality.

Sustained consonants—consonants with a longer degree of sustaining power, such as **l, m,** and **n.**

Syllable—a single sound or a part of a word, which may be pronounced separately without interruption.

Tessitura—the average range of the melodic line or a voice part.

Throaty quality—an excessively dark tone quality sounded or resonated deep in the throat.

Tonal focus—direction of the vocal tone to a particular localized area of the frontal resonators.

Tremolo—an excessively wide and slow *vibrato* which detracts from the expressive qualities of the voice.

Velar—the consonants formed by arching the back part of the tongue and pressing it against the velum or soft palate (**k, g, ng**).

Velum or soft palate—a muscular membrane, continuous with and attached to the bone of the hard palate. It serves an important function in phonation in that it may be raised to prevent the breath from entering the nasal passages during the articulation of certain consonants.

Vibrato—a rapid fluctuation of vocal tone alternately above and below a given pitch level—for the purpose of adding beauty and warmth to the tone.

Vibrator—the part of the vocal mechanism in which the sound originates; the vocal cords or membranes that are attached to the inner portion of the larynx, and are set into motion or vibration by the flow of the breath.

Voiced consonant—a consonant phonated with a distinguishable movement of the vocal cords.

Voiceless consonant—a consonant phonated without movement of the vocal cords.

Vowels—the vocal sounds utilized for sustaining the tone and in which the flow of the breath is continuous. The primary vowels are **ee, ay, ah, oh,** and **oo.**

Topics for Discussion

1. What environmental factors cause a singer to utilize clavicular or high-chest breathing, when as a child one quite naturally employs abdominal breathing?

2. Discuss the tone quality of various choirs and choruses you have heard either in concert or in recordings. What tonal characteristics do you feel are desirable? What characteristics are undesirable?

3. What is the relationship between flexibility and good tonal quality?

4. Differentiate between the terms *pronunciation, enunciation,* and *articulation.*

5. What truths and what fallacies exist in the statement "sing as you speak"?

6. How may the choral conductor employ the concept of *front-to-back vowel placement* as a device for the improvement of tone quality?

7. Which consonants are likely to cause a choral group the most difficulties? Why? What procedures may be utilized to overcome these difficulties?

8. Why does each varying musical style require a distinct type of treatment in terms of diction? In terms of tone quality?

9. Why is it desirable for the choral conductor to have a *variety* of techniques for achieving good tonal quality and correct diction?

References

Adler, Kurt, *Phonetics and Diction in Singing: Italian, French, German, Spanish.* Minneapolis: University of Minnesota Press, 1967.

Cain, Noble, *Choral Music and Its Practice.* New York: M. Witmark & Sons, 1942. (Chapter 10.)

Christy, Van A., *Glee Club and Chorus.* New York: G. Schirmer, Inc., 1940. (Chapter 4.)

Dewey, Philip, *Bel Canto in Its Golden Age.* New York: King's Crown Press, 1950.

Dykema, Peter W., and Karl W. Gehrkens, *The Teaching and Administration of High School Music.* Boston: C. C. Birchard & Co., 1941, pp. 90–94. (Chapter 8.)

Fields, Victor A., *Training the Singing Voice.* New York: King's Crown Press, Columbia University, 1947.

Finn, William J., *The Art of the Choral Conductor.* Boston: C. C. Birchard & Co., 1939. (Chapters 2, 3, 4, 13, and 14.)

Frisell, Anthony, *The Tenor Voice.* Boston: Bruce Humphries, 1964.

Garretson, Robert L., *Ear Training Devices and Warm-up Exercises Successfully Used by Illinois Choral Directors* ("Music Extension Bulletin No. 28.") Urbana, Ill.: University of Illinois, 1952.

Howerton, George, *Technique and Style in Choral Singing.* New York: Carl Fischer, Inc., 1958. (Chapters 1–4.)

Huls, Helen Steen, *The Adolescent Voice: A Study.* New York: Vantage Press, 1957.

Jones, Archie N. (Ed.), *Music Education in Action: Basic Principles and Practical Methods.* Boston: Allyn and Bacon, Inc., 1960, pp. 150–167.

————, *Techniques in Choral Conducting.* New York: Carl Fischer, Inc., 1948. (Chapters 2 and 3.)

Kagen, Sergius, *On Studying Singing.* New York: Rinehart, 1950. (Also Dover edition.)

Krone, Max T., *The Chorus and Its Conductor.* Chicago: Neil A. Kjos Music Co., 1945. (Chapters 4 and 5.)

Marshall, Madeline, *The Singer's Manual of English Diction.* New York: G. Schirmer, 1953.

Reid, Cornelius L., *The Free Voice.* New York: Colman-Ross Co., Inc., 1965.

Stanley, Douglas, *Your Voice.* New York: Pitman Publishing Corp., 1945.

Strong, Leon H., "The Mechanism of Laryngeal Pitch," *The Anatomical Record,* Vol. 63, No. 1, 1935, pp. 13–28.

Sunderman, Lloyd F., *Some Techniques for Choral Success.* Rockville Centre, L.I., N.Y.: Belwin, Inc., 1952. (Chapters 2 and 3.)

Westerman, Kenneth N., *Emergent Voice* (2nd Ed.). Ann Arbor, Michigan: privately published, 1955.

Wilson, Harry R., *A Guide for Choral Conductors.* New York: Silver Burdett Co., 1950. (Chapter 3.)

————, "Artistic Choral Singing," *Educational Music Magazine,* Vol. 33, No. 2, Nov.–Dec., 1953.

————, *Artistic Choral Singing.* New York: G. Schirmer, Inc., 1959. (Chapters 6 and 7.)

The following references pertain primarily to the anatomy and physiology of the human vocal mechanism.

Appelman, D. Ralph, *The Science of Vocal Pedagogy.* Bloomington, Indiana: Indiana University Press, 1967.

Berg, Janwillem van den, "Calculations on a Model of the Vocal Tract for Vowel/i/ and on the Larynx," *Journal Acoustical Society of America,* Vol. 27, 1955, pp. 332–338.

————, "Myoelastic Aerodynamic Theory of Voice Production," *Journal of Speech and Hearing Research,* Vol. 1, No. 3, September, 1958, pp. 224–227.

————, "Transmission of the Vocal Cavities," *Journal Acoustical Society of America,* Vol. 27, 1955, pp. 161–168.

———— and A. Sporr, "Microphonic Effect of the Larynx," *Nature,* Vol. 179, 1957, pp. 525–626.

————, J. T. Zantema, and P. Doornenbal, Jr., "On the Air Resistance and the Bernoulli Effect of the Human Larynx," *Journal Acoustical Society of America,* Vol. 27, 1957, pp. 626–631.

Borchers, Orville J., "Practical Implications of Scientific Research for the Teaching of Voice," *Music Teachers National Association, Volume of Proceedings,* 1947, pp. 209–215.

————, "Vocal Timbre in Its Immediate and Successive Aspects," *Music Teachers National Association, Volume of Proceedings,* 1941, pp. 346–358.

Brody, Viola, *An Experimental Study of the Emergence of the Process Involved in the Production of Song.* Unpublished Ph.D. thesis, University of Michigan, 1947.

Denes, Peter B., and Elliot N. Pinson, *The Speech Chain, the Physics and Biology of Spoken Language.* Baltimore: Bell Telephone Laboratories, 1963.

Farnsworth, D. W., "High Speed Motion Pictures of the Human Vocal Cords," *Music Teachers National Association, Volume of Proceedings,* 1939, pp. 305–309.

Hagerty, Robert F., and others, "Soft Palate Movement in Normals," *Journal of Speech and Hearing Research,* Vol. 1, Number 4, December, 1958, pp. 325–330.

Hixon, E., *An X-ray Study Comparing Oral and Pharyngeal Structures of Individuals with Nasal Voices and Individuals with Superior Voices.* Unpublished M. S. thesis, State University of Iowa, 1949.

Husler, Frederick, and Yvonne Rodd-Marling, *Singing: The Physical Nature of the Vocal Organ; A Guide to the Unlocking of the Singing Voice.* London: Faber and Faber Limited, 1965.

Jones, David S., Richard J. Beargie, and John E. Pauly, "An Electromyographic Study of Some Muscles of Costal Respiration in Man," *The Anatomical Record,* Vol. 117, No. 1, December, 1953, pp. 17–24.

Lewis, Don, "Vocal Resonance," *Journal Acoustical Society of America,* Vol. 8, 1936, pp. 91–99.

Negus, V. E., *The Mechanism of the Larynx.* London: Wm. Heineman, Ltd., 1929.

Norris, M. A., *X-ray Studies of Vowel Production as It Is Related to Voice.* Unpublished M. A. thesis, State University of Iowa, 1934.

Russell, G. Oscar, *The Vowel.* Columbus: Ohio State University Press, 1928.

————, *Speech and Voice.* New York: The Macmillan Co., 1931.

————, "X-ray Photographs of the Tongue and Vocal Organ Positions of Madame Bori," *Music Teachers National Association, Volume of Proceedings,* Vol. 27, 1932, p. 137.

————, "First Preliminary X-ray Consonant Study," *Journal Acoustical Society of America,* Vol. 5, 1934, pp. 247–251.

Secord, Arthur E., *An X-ray Study of the Hyoid Bone, Thyroid Cartilage and Cricoid Cartilage in Relation to Pitch Change in the Human Larynx.* Unpublished Ph.D. thesis, University of Michigan, 1941.

Strong, Leon H., "The Mechanism of Laryngeal Pitch," *Anatomical Record,* Vol. 63, No. 1, August, 1935, pp. 13–28.

Vennard, William, *Singing: The Mechanism and the Technic.* Revised Edition. New York: Carl Fischer, Inc., 1967.

Westerman, Kenneth N., "Resonation," *Music Teachers National Association, Volume of Proceedings,* 1949, pp. 295–300.

Westlake, Harold, *The Mechanics of Phonation, An X-ray Study of the Larynx.* Unpublished Ph.D. thesis, University of Michigan, 1938.

Williams, R. L., "A Serial Radiographic Study of Velopharyngeal Closure and Tongue Positions in Certain Vowel Sounds," *Northwestern University Bulletin,* Vol. 52, No. 17, pp. 9–12.

Wolfe, W. G., *X-ray Study of Certain Structures and Movements Involved in Naso-Pharyngeal Closure.* Unpublished M.A. thesis, State University of Iowa, 1942.

were often distinctly different during the various periods, and can be controlled somewhat by the conductor in striving toward his interpretative goals.

THE RENAISSANCE PERIOD

Remembering that cultural change is a slowly moving process, and that ascribing particular dates to certain periods is an arbitrary matter, the approximate 200-year period that we call the *Renaissance* (c. 1400–1600) does have certain salient characteristics. In some circles of European society, the religious orientation declined before rising secular interests. Ultimately this shift of interest was to culminate in the development of the modern scientific inquiry of the seventeenth century. The Renaissance intellectual began to emphasize his destiny here on earth, rather than considering life only as a prelude to the hereafter. He developed new confidence in his ability to solve his own problems and to determine his own fate. The wisdom of the church usually was not denied, but, in addition, the claims of other sources of truth were staked out.

Considerable discussion has occurred as to the exact beginnings of the Renaissance period in music. There appears to be some uncertainty as to the beginning of the period; however, the year 1400 seems to be the most suitable date. Jeppesen concurs with this point and offers the following well-founded reasons:

> As far as can be discerned at present, there is a marked and very significant boundary line, especially in a musico-technical respect, at about the transition from the 14th to the 15th century. What happened at that time may be characterized as a change in the conception of consonance—the definite, practical recognition of the 3rd and 6th as not only having privileges in musical art equal to the 4th, 5th and 8th, but moreover as main consonants—tonal combinations decidedly preferred above all others, and regarded as fundamental factors in musical composition.[1]

Meter and Stress

Most of the music of the Renaissance period was unmetered, with stress occurring only through the emphasis of particular syllables in

---

[1] Knud Jeppesen, *The Style of Palestrina and the Dissonance,* Second Edition. Copenhagen: Ejnar Munksgaard, Publisher, 1946, p. 222.

important words. The barline, with the resultant stress on the first beat of the measure, was generally not used during this period. While the barline did come into being during the latter part of the period, it was utilized only as a "measure" of elapsed time and as a means of keeping the singers together.[2] When metrical stress is utilized for music of this period, the inherent beauties and flow of the vocal lines are destroyed.

In Figure 36*a*, an excerpt from Palestrina's *Missa Papae Marcelli* is shown illustrating the use of the traditional barlines. The normal syllabic accents occurring on the words *Ple*-ni sunt *coe*-li et *ter*-ra are obscured and the rhythmic counterpoint so necessary to the music does not occur with this manner of barring. Figure 36*b*, however, is barred according to the natural accent of the text, thus revealing the beauties of the rhythmic complexity of the music.

The conductor should be always alert to the tendency for singers to stress certain figures or rhythmic groupings in a manner that is inimical to the proper interpretation. For example, in the motet *Cantantibus Organis* by Marenzio, there often exists a tendency for some singers to stress, in a somewhat mechanical manner, the first and third of each group of four eighth-notes. This practice should be avoided, as stress should occur only through the natural accent of particular syllables in important words. The sacred music of this period, in particular, should be performed in a smooth, flowing manner, and phrases should be thought of in terms of long ascending and descending lines.

Tempo

The tempo of Renaissance music is determined largely by the syllabic setting of the text and the mood of the music. When one syllable is set to a melodic figure (melisma), then the tempo should be restrained so that the inherent beauty of the vocal line may be revealed. On the other hand, when each syllable is set to a different note, of a comparatively longer duration, then the tempo may be pushed slightly forward.

---

[2] As a convenience to the singers, modern-day publishers employ several means to facilitate the reading of Renaissance music. While some employ the use of regular barlines, others utilize dotted barlines as a means of minimizing the natural stress following the barline. Still other publishers use a short vertical line before certain words at regularly spaced intervals to serve as a guide to the singers.

Fig. 36.   Excerpt from Missa Papae Marcelli *by Palestrina. (a) illustrates the
use of traditional barlines, while (b) is barred according to the natural accent
of the text. From Homer Ulrich and Paul A. Pisk,* A History of Music and
Musical Style. *New York: Harcourt, Brace & World, Inc., 1963, p. 148. Used
by permission of Harcourt, Brace & World, Inc., and of Rupert Hart-Davis
Limited, Publishers.*

Fig. 37. *An excerpt from* Cantantibus Organis *by Marenzio, in which mechanical stress should be avoided in the eighth-note groupings in measures two, three, and four, and the music performed in a smooth, flowing manner. Used by permission of* Verlag Friedrich Pustet, *Regensburg, Germany, publisher.*

The tempo should remain relatively steady throughout the entire composition, or at least throughout a particular section. Any change in tempo should result only through a contrasting change in the mood of the text and a resultant change in the musical texture. Any changes in tempo within a given section should be extremely gradual and subtle, lest the symmetry of the music be destroyed.

Rallentando, as we know it today, did not exist in the music of the Renaissance period. Composers of the period were, however, aware of this effect and when it was felt desirable they made it a part of the music itself. That is, they achieved the effect by simply broadening or lengthening the musical notation. Therefore, conductors should avoid the deliberate use of *rallentando* as this would only distort the music interpretation.[3]

A somewhat greater freedom, however, may be said to exist in the performance of madrigals and related genre, than with the masses and motets of the Renaissance period. Madrigal composers were captivated by the expressive qualities of the words. The mood of the text, therefore, is an essential determining factor in the selection of the correct tempo (and the proper dynamics). Restraint and avoidance of extremes, however, should always be paramount in the conductor's mind.

Dynamics

The dynamics of the music of this period is related to and is dependent upon any changes in mood in the text. Changes in dynamics would occur only as with changes in tempo, *i.e.,* with a contrasting mood between sections of the music. Within the over-all framework of the music, however, dynamic levels should be moderate—extremes should seldom occur. Due to the high degree of consonance, the pervading imitation, the lack of harmonic complexity, and the restraints inherent in the style, a climax seldom occurred and was not even sought by composers of the period.[4]

Through the use of the "seamless" technique there existed an overlapping or dovetailing of cadences, *i.e.,* one phrase ended in two or more of the parts, while another began in the other parts. Through this technique many cadences were somewhat obscured and the tension of the cadence was minimized, thus lessening the necessity for dynamic changes. It should be added, however, that dynamics, especially in the madrigal, frottola, and canto carnascialesco, may be realized simply through the natural tessitura of the voices, as well as in the intensity of the word symbolism.

Texture

The music of the period was primarily contrapuntal in texture, *i.e.,* the various vocal lines were conceived as horizontal in nature. Com-

---

[3] *Cf.* Curt Sachs, *Rhythm and Tempo: A Study in Music History.* New York: W. W. Norton & Company, Inc., 1953, pp. 218–219.

[4] *Cf.* Robert Stevenson, *Music Before the Classic Era.* London: The Macmillan Co., Ltd., 1955, p. 42.

posers wrote using anywhere from three to six or more parts. Upon first examining music of the period, one might feel some compositions or portions of others were conceived harmonically rather than contrapuntally. Upon careful examination, however, one will often discover, for example, that the third in a particular part may be omitted in an effort to achieve the best movement in the various vocal lines.[5]

Imitation as a contrapuntal device was used by composers from Dufay throughout the remainder of the period. The term, "point of imitation," pertains to the introduction of a figure or motive in one part, which is taken up successively in the other parts. These points of imitation should be emphasized slightly. The entrances need to be definite and precise, but vigorous accents are out of place and should be avoided. These entering parts should be brought out slightly, but should never overshadow the other contrapuntal lines. As other parts enter they should then recede into the background.

Expressive Aspects

The sacred music of the Renaissance period sounds remote and restrained, primarily due to the large degree of consonance. There was a wide use of unisons, thirds, fifths, sixths, octaves, and triad sounds. Dissonance of the unprepared variety was used sparingly and was considered something "vehement and violent." Therefore, the objective was to conceal or muffle it in so far as was possible.[6]

Renaissance music possesses very subtle points of harmonic arrival. As previously mentioned, with the "seamless" technique there existed an overlapping or dovetailing of phrases, *i.e.,* one phrase ended in two or more parts, while another began in the other parts. Through this technique many cadences were somewhat obscured and the tension of the cadence was minimized. The conductor should search out all the suspensions in Renaissance music, mark them in his score, and have the chorus "lean" on them ever so slightly during performance.

The masses and motets of the Renaissance are impersonal in nature and should be performed with an atmosphere of quiet reflection and sincerity of feeling, *i.e.,* as a prayer unto God, and not as a concert. The tone quality, therefore, should be kept light. Heavy dramatic quality and excessive vibrato in the voices are both inimical to the expressive character of the music; both should be eliminated.

[5] See, for example, Jeppesen, *op. cit.,* p. 92.
[6] *Ibid.,* p. 108.

As previously mentioned, Renaissance music, when performed correctly, sounds remote and restrained. The resonance in the church or hall in which it was originally performed contributed substantially to this effect. The impersonal quality of Renaissance sacred music is comparable to the detachment that may be observed in certain paintings of the period in which the Madonna is not caressing her child, but is maintaining a distance between Him and herself.[7]

A somewhat greater freedom existed with the madrigals and related secular styles of the period. Composers were well aware of the expressive qualities of the text and often employed word painting in their music. That is, they used the music to portray, in a variety of ways, the character of certain words. For example, leaps in the melody were often used to depict joy, while the voices might ascend on such words as "heaven" and descend on words such as "earth." To depict grief and sadness, a diminished or augmented triad was often used, and dissonance was employed to represent such words as "sadness" and "pain."

The conductor should study his score and identify the various word-painting devices employed by the composer and, for an effective performance, the singers must be led to an understanding of them. The music must be sung with an emotional expressiveness that can result only through proper understanding of it. Secular music of the period, while light in texture, should never be sung in an insipid manner. While a firmness of approach is necessary to performance, the inherent emotion in the music should not be allowed to run rampant; rather, the music should be performed with a certain degree of restraint.[8]

THE BAROQUE PERIOD

The Baroque period began toward the end of the sixteenth century, and is generally considered to have ended by 1750—the year of the death of Johann Sebastian Bach. The word *baroque* is said to have originated from *barroco,* a Portuguese word meaning "a pearl of

---

[7] See, for example, the painting *The Cowper Maiden* by Raphael (1483–1520).

[8] For a further discussion on the interpretation of madrigals, see Charles Kennedy Smith, *Madrigal Singing.* London: Oxford University Press, 1931.

at $\quad \mathbf{\mathsf{J}} = \mathbf{60}$. He also, however, sometimes wrote notes of a larger or greater value as a means of achieving the desired intention of *largo,* i.e., simply broad. For the conductor to further slow down the pulse of the music would make the ending too slow and thus distort the desired effect.[20]

In the early Baroque monody, a considerable flexibility existed in the tempo so that the emotions in the text and the music might be fully expressed. In the late 1630's, however, a reversal of this trend occurred and the tempi of music became more strict and restrained.[21] The relative freedom of emotional expression gave way to rhythmical shifts within a stricter tempo.

According to Machlis, one of the most notable characteristics of Baroque music is its steady pulsation or unflagging rhythm.[22]

> The Baroque demanded a dynamic rhythm. The time was ripe for regular recurrence of accent and for clear-cut energetic movement. The bass part became the carrier of the new rhythm. Its relentless beat is one of the most arresting traits of the period. This steady pulsation, once underway, never slackens or deviates until the goal is reached. It imparts to Baroque music its singleness of purpose, its unflagging drive. It produces the same effect of turbulent yet controlled motion as animates Baroque painting, architecture, and sculpture.[23]

While a steady pulsating drive is important to proper interpretation, this does not mean that the tempo should be completely unyielding. For instance, at cadences immediately prior to subsequent sections, a slight holding back of the tempo is often desirable. The exact treatment of each cadence, however, will vary according to the music itself.[24] In reference to the handling of cadences *Grove's* states,

> Each needs its own natural flexibility, though this may vary according to circumstances from the merest easing scarcely consciously perceptible, at the one extreme, to a majestic broadening at the other. It is

---

[20] *Ibid.,* p. 157.

[21] Sachs, *op. cit.,* pp. 265–266.

[22] Exceptions to this general characteristic of Baroque music are the *recitative,* which is sung in a declamatory style with stress or accent occurring as a result of important words or particular syllables, and the *arioso,* which in style lies somewhere between the recitative and the aria and possesses some of the characteristics of each.

[23] Joseph Machlis, *The Enjoyment of Music,* Regular Rev. Ed. New York: W. W. Norton & Company, Inc., 1963, p. 397.

[24] For a discussion of conflicting viewpoints in regard to tempo changes, see Sachs, *op. cit.,* pp. 277–280.

for the performer to judge on the merits of each case between senti-
mental excess and self-conscious rigidity.[25]

   Accelerando and *ritardando* (*or rallentando*) are inappropriate
and out of place in Baroque music, principally because these concepts
of gradually increasing or gradually decreasing the tempo did not exist
in this period. These concepts grew out of the Mannheim school in the
latter part of the eighteenth century. Another concept, often misunderstood, is the treatment of the *fermata*. A *fermata* in Baroque music
simply indicates the end of a phrase and a point at which the singers
may take a breath. The concept of the *fermata* as an untimed hold
developed during the latter part of the eighteenth century, as did also
the modern concept of *accelerando* and *ritardando*.

Dynamics

The concept of *crescendo* and *decrescendo* did not widely exist during
the Baroque period, principally because the instruments of the period
did not have the necessary flexibility to achieve these ends. The organ,
for example, did not possess swell shutters, and the piano was not
invented until the latter part of the period. Therefore, contrast was
sought by other means.[26] Contrast in dynamics was achieved by adding or dropping out various instruments or voice parts. This was
referred to as *terraced dynamics,* meaning various levels or plateaus
of dynamics. Extremes in dynamics, therefore, should be avoided,
as the concept of terraced dynamics would render them undesirable.[27]
The conductor should utilize a dynamic range only from *piano* to
forte. Extending the dynamics above or below these levels is inappropriate and should generally be avoided except upon rare occasions.

Texture

The beginning of the Baroque period ushered in a change from a
texture of independent, but interrelated parts to a single melody or

---

[25] *Grove's Dictionary of Music and Musicians* (edited by Eric Blom),
Volume II. New York: St. Martin's Press, Inc., 1954, p. 986.

[26] According to *Grove's Dictionary of Music and Musicians, crescendo*
and *decrescendo* were not entirely unknown to Baroque composers, as written
indications of it are found in the mid-seventeenth-century music of the Italian
composer Mazzochi (*Grove's,* Vol. II, p. 988).

[27] Gore, *op. cit.,* pp. 157–158.

voice part supported by chords or chordal combinations. This change from modal polyphony to a homophonic style necessitated a change in the harmonic system—from the medieval church modes to a system of major and minor tonality. While the polyphony of the Renaissance symbolized the submissiveness of the individual, the new style fulfilled the need for greater individual expression. Secular music gained vastly in importance and the new style allowed for a greater emotional expression of the text. When polyphony returned, after a brief lapse, it did so within a different harmonic framework, *i.e.,* the system of major-minor tonality.[28]

Expressive Aspects

In contrast to the Renaissance composer, who expressed emotion with considerable restraint, the Baroque composer gave freer vent to his emotions. Nevertheless, his music was still somewhat impersonal, with the emotion stemming not from an individual struggle, as in the Romantic period, but from the tumultuous and dramatic forces affecting all mankind.[29]

Within the new system of major minor tonality each chord assumed a definite relationship to the others. Harmonic tension and repose were well understood by composers of the period and were used as devices in composition. There were fewer, but stronger cadences and the drive to the keynote was apparent. There was a considerable increase in the intensity of the music and in the amount of dissonance that was used for the purpose of achieving emotional intensity. Whereas in the Renaissance period dissonance was permissible only when prepared, *i.e.,* when first heard with a consonant interval and introduced through a suspension, the use of unprepared dissonance became accepted and widely used as an expressive device.[30]

Tone painting, or the way in which the music portrayed the words, was increasingly given attention by composers of the period. Bach, for example, advised his students to "play the chorale [pre-

---

[28] While polyphony was rejected by most composers during the early Baroque period, it was never abandoned by the famous three S's: Johann Herman Schein (1586–1630), Samuel Scheidt (1587–1654), and Heinrich Schütz (1585–1672).

[29] George Howerton, *Technique and Style in Choral Singing.* New York: Carl Fischer, Inc., 1957, p. 133.

[30] Claudio Monteverdi (1567–1643) is often credited with the first wide use of unprepared dissonance.

lude] according to the meaning of the words." It must be understood, however, that while the text gave birth to the musical idea, it was the music itself that ultimately reigned supreme.[31]

The Baroque period marked the first time in history that instrumental music assumed an equal position with vocal music. The spirit of the times prompted the development of new instruments and the improvements of the old. The new status of instrumental music has caused certain persons to say that some music was conceived instrumentally rather than vocally. The performance of Baroque music, therefore, necessitates a most exacting rhythmic precision. Singers, therefore, should be as exacting as instrumentalists. They should also maintain a steadiness and purity of vocal line, devoid of excessive vibrato, as this may adversely affect the intonation and thus blur the polyphonic structure. These qualities are especially important in singing contrapuntal music.

The matter of the proper pitch level at which to perform Baroque music should be given proper consideration. From the period between approximately 1600 to 1820, the standard accepted pitch level—although there were many deviations—was about a semi-tone lower than the present A-440. The implications of this fact are that, to perform Baroque music in as authentic a manner as possible, one ought to lower the pitch a half-step to return it to its original key. Of course, practical considerations such as the difficulty of transposing the orchestral parts, or even the piano or organ accompaniment, often make this practice unfeasible. Another argument, however, against this practice is the additional brilliance which is often achieved through performance in the higher key. On the other hand, when the tessitura of the various parts appears to be too high and thus negatively influences the tone quality, then the conductor may consider lowering the pitch. If he elects to do so, he then will have at least two justifications for his decision. By and large, however, the conductor will find his problems minimized if he performs the music in the key in which it is presently written.

THE CLASSIC PERIOD

While Bach and Handel were carrying the Baroque style to its culmination in the first half of the eighteenth century, forces were already at work leading toward the formulation of a new style. The

---

[31] Machlis, *op. cit.,* p. 392.

Classic era, generally considered to cover the period from 1750 to 1820, includes such diverse aesthetic trends as the Rococo (*Stile Galant*), *Empfindsamer Stil* (literally, "sensitive" style), Enlightenment, and *Sturm und Drang* (storm and stress). The Classic period thus lacked any unifying social and aesthetic philosophy, such as shaped artistic expression in the Baroque period. While each of these aesthetic trends had its proponents, it was the master composers of the period—Haydn, Mozart, and Beethoven—who were able to synthesize the elements of each into their music.

The Rococo style (c. 1720–c. 1770) repudiated the massive forms of the Baroque. The endless vistas gave way to intimate glimpses; the grandeur of Baroque decoration changed to delicate, often unnecessary, ornamentation; monumental sculpture decreased in size to figurines for the mantle; the center of life moved from the ballroom to the boudoir; and the grandiloquent language of the Baroque changed in manner and tone to witty, tête-à-tête conversations.[32] The expansiveness, grandeur, and impressiveness of Baroque music gave way to an expression of elegance in delicate proportions. The polyphony of the later Baroque was abandoned in favor of a homophonic style, with interest focused on the soprano line that often was adorned with a proliferation of ornamentation.

While the music of the Rococo was elegant and ornate, and written to please the aristocracy, the *Empfindsamer Stil* (or expressive style) was more the music of the middle class. This bourgeois style reflected the attitudes of honesty and goodness and often approached the borders of sentimentality. It is reflected, for example, in the title of a collection of songs by the German composer, J. F. Reichardt, "Lullabies for Good German Mothers."[33]

The eighteenth-century Enlightenment, or Age of Reason, began as a reaction against supernatural religions, formalism, and authority. The underlying philosophical belief was that man should be "natural" in all these respects; *i.e.,* natural religion, natural behavior as opposed to formality, and individual freedom as opposed to submission to authority.[34] Denis Diderot's *Encyclopedie,* or *Classified Dictionary of Sciences, Arts, and Trades,* was published serially beginning in 1751 and symbolizes rationalism and the spirit of scientific inquiry. Thomas Paine's book, *The Age of Reason,* also reflects such rationalism. The Marquis de Condorcet's book, *The Progress of the Human Spirit*

---

[32] William Fleming and Abraham Veinus, *Understanding Music: Style, Structure, and History.* New York: Holt, Rinehart & Winston, Inc., 1958, pp. 309–310.

[33] *Ibid.,* p. 312.

[34] Donald Jay Grout, *A History of Western Music.* New York: W. W. Norton & Company, Inc., 1960, p. 411.

(1774), set forth ten stages from which man had progressed from primitive life to nearly ultimate perfection. This philosophy expressed the belief that man, through the use of his rational and moral powers, could ultimately control his environment. Jean Rameau was an outstanding exponent of rationalism and sought to restore reason to musical thought. There is evidence of this philosophy in the optimism expressed in some of the music of Beethoven, who was the movement's most articulate spokesman.[35]

The *Sturm und Drang* (storm and stress) movement in Germany ran counter to the elegance of the Rococo, the optimism of the Enlightenment, and the restricted emotionalism of the *Empfindsamer Stil*. These aesthetic trends were rejected in favor of a search for emotional truth and a more flexible use of the imagination. This philosophy may be seen in the literary works of both Goethe and Schiller. The best-known literary example is Goethe's *Faust*. Faust rejects the tenets of the Age of Reason, ceases to search for nature's secrets in books, and seeks the ultimate truth in experiences and emotion. It is felt by some authorities that Haydn, Mozart, and Beethoven were all influenced by this philosophy, as indicated by the pathos and sometimes violent outbursts in some of their music.[36]

The center of cultural life in the Classic period was the palace. The ruling aristocracy surrounded itself with the arts, which it considered its privileged right. Beauty of expression and elegance of manner became formalized and permeated its existence. The artist of the period created for his patron, who was far above him in social rank. Composers were employed for what they could contribute to the aristocracy's "cultural" surroundings. In general, the patron was interested in the artist's creative products, rather than in him as an individual. In other words, a certain degree of reserve existed between employer and employee. In this social setting, where the emphasis was upon courtly manners, the artist avoided becoming too personal in his art, as this would have been considered in poor taste. Objectivity and reserve, therefore, became a necessary part of the artist's creative expression.

Meter and Stress

The art of the Classic era, the Rococo style in particular, strove for elegance and more delicate proportions. These general charac-

[35] Fleming and Veinus, *op. cit.*, p. 313.

[36] *Ibid.*, p. 314.

teristics were also reflected in the music of the period. Therefore, the pulsation of the music was more delicately marked than in the Baroque period. In order to convey clearly this style to his performers, the conductor should, therefore, utilize a lighter beat, yet with a definite or marked precision to delineate the crisp rhythmic patterns of the music.[37]

Tempo

Tempi in the Classic period were generally moderate and extremes were avoided. Beginning with the Classic period composers indicated to a much greater extent what they desired in their scores. Markings indicating the desired tempo, correct phrasing, and tonal quality were often included. Tempo was often indicated through the use of Italian words, *i.e., allegro, adagio,* etc., and signs indicating dynamic changes were written in.[38] In the waning years of the Classic period composers, Beethoven in particular, were able to prescribe the desired tempo of their compositions through the use of metronome markings (the metronome was invented by Maelzel in 1816).

Tempo rubato originated from the vocal art and eventually was utilized as a device in the interpretation of instrumental music. It was first discussed in a book on singing by Pier Francesco Tosi, published in 1723. The letters of Mozart reveal that he was well aware of the device and used it in his piano performances. In addition, Philipp Emanuel Bach (1714–1788) discussed *tempo rubato* in Volume Two of his *Versuch.*[39] It is reasonable to assume that other composers of the period were also aware of this interpretative device. It is suggested, however, in performing music of this period, that *tempo rubato* be used with discretion and restraint, and that its more exaggerated use, as in the subsequent Romantic period, be avoided. In general, the principle of strict time should be followed. The exceptions where *tempo rubato* seems desirable, will usually be dictated by the poetical aspects of the text.[40] The use of *ritardando* and *accelerando* became more frequent, especially during the latter part of the period. In accordance with the general

[37] Howerton, *op. cit.,* p. 142.

[38] Frederick Dorian, *The History of Music in Performance.* New York: W. W. Norton & Company, Inc., 1942, p. 155.

[39] *Ibid.,* pp. 186–193.

[40] For a further discussion of *tempo rubato,* see Sachs, *op. cit.,* pp. 306–310.

characteristics of the music of the period, such alterations in tempi should be slight and performed with restraint.

Dynamics

While dynamic contrast was an important part of the music of the period, composers did not seek the extremes that occurred during the later periods. One of the most significant developments growing out of the latter part of the eighteenth century was the *crescendo-decrescendo.* Such a concept was in marked contrast to the terraced dynamics of the earlier Baroque period. While the concept of *crescendo-decrescendo* was not entirely unknown and had been utilized to some degree in Italy from the beginning of the century, it had not been widely used elsewhere. Through the efforts of Stamitz, the precision of the orchestra at Mannheim was developed to such a high degree that this carefully controlled *crescendo* became known as the *Mannheim crescendo.* In choral performances the *crescendo-decrescendo* should be performed with some restraint, considering the general dynamic level of the passage. The *crescendo* should not begin from as low a dynamic level, nor reach as high a level, as it would during the Romantic period. Generally, in *crescendo* and *decrescendo,* the dynamic level should change gradually just one degree higher or lower, *e.g.,* from *p* ———— *mp;* and rarely from *p* ———— *f.*

The *forte-piano* contrast was an unwritten law of dynamic execution; *i.e.,* repeated phrases and/or periods should be performed *piano,* as in an echo. Periods performed *piano* the first time should be performed *forte* on the repetition.[41] The harmony itself will provide the conductor with further clues for the treatment of dynamics.

Philipp Emanuel Bach points out that every tone foreign to the key can very well stand a *forte,* regardless of whether it occurs in dissonance or consonance. . . . Quantz distinguishes clearly three classes of dissonances, to be played *mezzo forte, forte,* and *fortissimo,* respectively. He also explains that the theme of the composition calls for dynamic emphasis. Likewise, all other notes of importance (in a theme, in a contrapuntal passage, or in a harmonic structure) must be stressed by means of dynamics. The notes introducing the theme must be marked; the dissonance must be made stronger than its resolution.[42]

[41] Dorian, *op. cit.,* p. 166.

[42] From *The History of Music in Performance* by Frederick Dorian. By permission of W. W. Norton & Company, Inc. Copyright 1942 by W. W. Norton & Company, Inc. Page 168.

It is also often necessary and desirable to adjust the dynamics to the acoustical conditions of the performance hall. The conductor needs to consider the character of the music, the number and maturity of the performers, and the size and the acoustical conditions of the performance hall or auditorium. To maintain the classic proportions of the music, it should never become overbearing from the dynamic standpoint. An overly large musical organization, coupled with an auditorium with exceptionally live acoustical properties, can create a dynamic level that is much too high; to be effective, the dynamic level must be reduced in size and/or scope.

Texture

Composers sought for lightness and simplicity in their music. In place of the heavy Baroque texture, there was a combination of textures in which chordal patterns, running figures, unsupported melodies, and other devices were used alternately, depending upon the expressive intentions of the composer. Contrapuntal devices were also sometimes used, particularly in the masses; however, polyphony was generally not sought by composers of the period. During the Baroque period a polarity existed between the melody and the bass parts. The bass supported the melody, while the inner voices sometimes only completed the harmonies. During the Classic period, the inner voices assumed greater importance, and the previous supporting function of the bass part gave way to one of greater flexibility and interplay with the inner voices.[43]

Expressive Aspects

In contrast to the late Baroque period, where the cadences were relatively infrequent and somewhat inconspicuous, and the phrases were "spun-out," the composers of the Classic period utilized phrases of a regular two- or four-bar length that were shorter and more distinct. There were generally rather strong points of harmonic arrival and the period structure was well defined. While the harmonic vocabulary did not differ substantially from the late Baroque period, the harmonic progressions were certainly less weighty.[44] Melody reigned supreme, while the other parts served to support and enhance it, and were often subordinate to it. Ornamentation

---

[43] Homer Ulrich and Paul A. Pisk, *A History of Music and Musical Style.* New York: Harcourt, Brace & World, Inc., 1963, pp. 322–323.

[44] Grout, *op. cit.,* p. 417.

developed to its fullest bloom. This embellishment of the melodic line, however, was only reflective of the spirit of the times, where elegance and grace were considered so highly important, particularly to the patrons of the arts.

The music of the Classic period was generally abstract in nature and "discreet" in taste and was an integral part of a sophisticated mode of living. It was moderate in style, avoiding the extremes of the later Romantic period. Emotional content was less important and unity of design became the composer's goal. Form served to eliminate the personal qualities and universalized the style. Symmetry, balance, clarity, and restraint summarized the composer's artistic creations.

THE ROMANTIC PERIOD

The French Revolution, beginning in 1789, resulted in the breakdown of the aristocratic way of life and led to the development of nineteenth-century liberalism. In the world of the arts, it was paralleled by the rise of the Romantic movement, in essence a revolt against formality and authority. Previously, composers had for many centuries worked under the patronage of either the church or princely courts. Under this system, composers generally wrote music to please their patrons. They were careful not to let their music become too personal in nature. With the breakdown of the patronage system composers were free to express themselves individually. They were no longer inhibited or restricted by a patron's demands, and were able to please their equals—the general public. With their greater freedom, composers sought out new and unique means of expression. This led to a greater display of emotion, heretofore largely restrained.

While the composer, no longer bound to his patron, was able to express himself more freely, his financial insecurity, on the other hand, often caused him to withdraw from the world about him. He sometimes became preoccupied with his own inner problems and even pessimistic about the future.

The term "Romanticism," as it pertains to the nineteenth-century, is inexact and somewhat misleading. The Romantic period contained many diametrical differences, which seemingly run counter to its name. According to Machlis:

The nineteenth century included many opposites: liberalism and reaction, idealism and the crassest materialism, bourgeois sentimentality and stark realism, mysticism and scientific inquiry, democratic revolution and royalist restoration, romantic optimism and no less romantic despair.[45]

Meter and Stress

Composers in the Romantic period, in their seeking for freedom from rules, often sought to break the strictness of the rhythm, yet remain within the time-honored rules. A widely used device to achieve this objective was through the use of meter changes without changing the meter signature.[46] An outstanding example of this device may be found in the Brahms *Requiem.* Such metric alteration results in displaced accents, *i.e.,* accents where they are not normally expected, in a relatively short space of time. Whereas Romantic composers achieved these unique rhythmic effects within the boundaries of the accepted rules, the modern-day composer would normally utilize alternately different meter signatures (see page 114 for examples). Other varied means of syncopation also became widely used during this period as an expressive device and as a means of evoking interest. Intricate rhythmic patterns and rhythmic surprise were characteristic of the music of the period. Composers sometimes used a phrase structure that was irregular, that is, of varying lengths. Brahms in particular was noted for his elongated or extended phrases; in some cases they were absorbed into contrapuntal textures so that it is difficult to determine where they actually do end.[47]

Tempo

The restraint typical of the Classic period was abandoned during the Romantic era. It was a period of extremes—fast tempi were often performed exceptionally fast and slow tempi exceptionally slow. Tempo was closely aligned with mood, and as the composer was often expressing varying moods within a composition, extreme abrupt changes in tempo often occurred. *Accelerando* and *ritardando* became more frequently used than in the previous period. As an element of expressiveness *tempo rubato* was developed to its ultimate.

---

[45] Machlis, *op. cit.,* p. 85.

[46] Sachs, *op. cit.,* p. 344.

[47] Ulrich and Pisk, *op. cit.,* p. 485.

During the Romantic period two diametrically opposed schools of interpretative thought existed. One, represented by Mendelssohn, was based on classical principles; the other was the highly romantic, sometimes called "neo-German" type of interpretation, which was initiated by Liszt and exemplified by Wagner. The Mendelssohn school sought to preserve the Classical tradition and to eliminate some of the practices which they felt were extreme. Mendelssohn was an exponent of regularity of rhythm and fluency of tempo. Wagner, on the other hand, favored broad, singing melody, and considerable liberty in tempi.[48] He felt that the correct tempo could be determined only through "a proper understanding of the melos."[49]

While composers may be said to have had tendencies toward one or the other of the above positions, and certainly were influenced in one way or another, it would be unwise, as well as impossible, to categorize them all in either group. The music of each composer must be considered individually. Only through a thorough analysis and study of the music will a proper tempo be determined. For example, music with a light texture may be performed in a faster tempo than should music with a heavy, sonorous texture. The latter should be performed somewhat slower if it is to be effective. Relating to this point, the following statement by Robert Schumann in both interesting and revealing:

> You know how I dislike quarreling about tempo, and how for me only the inner measure of the movement is conclusive. Thus, an allegro of one who is cold by nature always sounds lazier than a slow tempo by one of sanguine temperament. With the orchestra, however, the proportions are decisive. Stronger and denser masses are capable of bringing out the detail as well as the whole with more emphasis and importance; whereas, with smaller and finer units, one must compensate for the lack of resonance by pushing forward in the tempo.[50]

Dynamics

In contrast to the restraint of the Classic period, composers of the Romantic period often used extremes in dynamics ranging from *fff* to *ppp,* but with a slight leaning toward the use of the lower dynamic

---

[48] Dorian, *op. cit.,* pp. 230–231.

[49] *Ibid.,* p. 281.

[50] From *The History of Music in Performance* by Frederick Dorian. By permission of W. W. Norton & Company, Inc. Copyright 1942 by W. W. Norton & Company, Inc. Page 227. *Cf.* Sachs, *op. cit.,* p. 379.

levels. Some editions of the Verdi *Requiem,* it may be noted, even contain dynamic markings of *ppppp.*

Crescendo and *decrescendo,* or the gradual swelling and diminishing of tone, became a widely used expressive device by nineteenth-century composers. In certain compositions it was used to create the illusion of distance, *i.e.,* of a group or object gradually coming closer and then receding into the distance.

Some composers employed a slight *accelerando* with a *crescendo* and a slight *ritardando* with a decrescendo. Rossini, in particular, was noted for his combining "a gradual dynamic increase with great rhythmic momentum."[51]

Composers in the nineteenth century endeavored to indicate more clearly on their scores their intentions through the use of a variety of tempo and dynamic markings. Some of these terms encompassed both tempo and dynamics. For example, *morendo* (dying away) indicates that the music should be both slower and softer, and *andante maestoso* (moderately slow and majestic) implies a moderate tempo yet with a full sonority.

In addition to *crescendo* and *decrescendo,* the use of more sudden climaxes also became a common practice. Grieg, for example, employs this device to a considerable extent in his *Psalms* (for mixed voices). The use of dynamic accents, such as *sforzando* (*sfz*) and *sforzato* (*sf*), occurred with much greater frequency. See, for example, the Choral Finale to the *Ninth Symphony* by Beethoven, *Elijah* by Mendelssohn, the *Requiem Mass* and the *Stabat Mater* by Dvořák, and the *29th Psalm* by Elgar. In contrast to the moderately sized ensembles utilized in the various princely courts of the Classic era, the combined forces of large orchestras and choirs became the ideal medium for the expression of the dynamic extremes of the Romantic period.

Texture

New harmonic relationships were explored by composers of the Romantic period. Dissonance became more widely used and an increasing use of melodic and harmonic chromaticism gave the composer a wider range of expressive devices. There was a lessening of harmonic drive, with an increased tendency toward the use of deceptive resolutions and obscured cadences. That is, cadences were sometimes

---

[51] Ulrich and Pisk, *op. cit.,* p. 455.

avoided, or resolved deceptively. In contrast to "wandering" chromaticism, composers sometimes utilized sudden harmonic and enharmonic changes, or shifts of tonal center.

While a balance between harmony and counterpoint is said to have existed during the late Baroque period, the nineteenth-century Romanticist altered the balance in favor of harmony. The Romantic composer, however, often alternated the texture within a short time-span. Counterpoint, when used, focused upon the opposition of masses, rather than upon vocal lines. In contrast to the light and clear texture of the Classic period, the texture of music in the Romantic period was often thick and heavy.

Expressive Aspects

The Romantic period was characterized by a revolt against formality, convention, authority, and tradition. Whereas the Classic composer was highly concerned with expression within a particular form, the Romanticist was not to be restricted by it. He both relaxed the previous forms and strove to develop a freer form through which he might better express himself.

Individual expression became the composer's principal goal. To express emotion freely, the composer drew on all the multitude of musical resources at his command. As a means of creating tension and expressing emotion, composers of this period experimented considerably in the field of harmony. Unusual harmonic effects, as well as unusual rhythmic effects, wide contrasts in dynamics, and changing moods with a resultant change in texture, were all used as expressive devices. Tone color, however, is considered one of the greatest achievements of the Romantic period. Through tone color composers sought to express sensuous beauty and tonal enchantment. Musical terms, such as *con amore* (with love), *con fuoco* (with fire), *con passione* (with passion), *dolce* (sweetly), *gioioso* (joyous), and *mesto* (sad) were increasingly used by composers as an indication of their intentions to the performers. These terms, in addition, indicate the frame of mind of the composers of the period. Music of this period, both vocal and instrumental, was influenced by the lyricism of the human voice. It is notable that many of the themes of instrumental music of the period have been adapted into popular songs. Their popularity is, in part, affected by their singability.[52]

---

[52] Machlis, *op. cit.*, pp. 86–88.

The center of musical life in the nineteenth century was in the concert hall, rather than in the palace or the church. Because of the lack of restrictions in regard to size of performance organizations, composers during the latter part of the period increasingly wrote for larger groups and in a more colorful and grandiose style than was characteristic of the earlier part of the period.[53]

THE MODERN PERIOD

Toward the end of the nineteenth century the subjective expression of Romanticism had run its course. Some composers, however, continued to write in a modified Romantic style. Among the more notable of this group of late Romanticists were: Sergei Taneyev (1856–1915), Edward Elgar (1857–1934), Gustav Mahler (1860–1911), Richard Strauss (1864–1949), Alexander Gretchaninov 1864–1956), Enrique Granados (1867—1916), Max Reger (1873–1916), and Sergei Rachmaninoff (1873–1943). Most composers, however, began to seek new means of expression. The main currents of musical expression in the Modern period are described below.

Impressionism

This movement developed as a reaction against the emotionalism and subjective aspects of Romanticism. It emerged during the last quarter of the nineteenth century and was exemplified in the music of Claude Debussy (1862–1918) and Maurice Ravel (1885–1937). Debussy was highly influenced by the Impressionist painters and the Symbolist poets, who avoided the exact and clear-cut representation of things, but rather sought to create a momentary impression of them. The painters often did not mix their paints, but juxtaposed daubs of pure color on the canvas, with the "mixing" left to the eye of the viewer. Also seeking new paths, the Symbolist poets rejected emotionalism and turned to nebulous suggestion and dreamlike evocation of mood.[54]

---

[53] *Ibid.*, p. 88.

[54] Joseph Machlis, *Introduction to Contemporary Music.* New York: W. W. Norton & Company, Inc., pp. 111–112.

Expressionism

Appearing about 1910 as a reaction against the "vagueness" of
Impressionism, this is sometimes referred to as the German answer
to French Impressionism. Expressionism also received its impetus
from painting and poetry. Artists, perhaps influenced by Sigmund
Freud's work in psychology, endeavored to capture on canvas the
myriad thoughts from the unconscious. Distorted images, expressing
the artist's inner self, took the place of the traditional concepts of
beauty. Composers also rejected older aesthetic concepts and sought
new means of expression.[55] Expressionistic music is characterized by
its continuous intensity, high level of dissonance, angular melodic
fragments, complex rhythms, and fluctuating tempi. The expressionist
composer utilized all the devices at his command to express the conflicts, fears, and anxieties of man's inner self. The outstanding ex-
ponents of expressionism are: Arnold Schoenberg (1874–1951),
Alban Berg (1885–1935), Anton von Webern (1883–1945), and
Ernst Krenek (1900–   ).

Neo-Classicism

In this phase of musical expression, which appeared after World
War I, composers sought to recapture the ideals of the eighteenth
century, where the emphasis was upon craftsmanship rather than on
emotional expression. They sought to restore the proper balance
between form and emotion and rejected the excesses of the Romantic
period. The return to form was a primary consideration in composition, with emotional expression being a secondary factor. The Neo-
Classicists decried the idea of program music and gave more stress to
the intellectual aspects of music. Composers who have written in
this style are: Igor Stravinsky (1882–   ), Paul Hindemith (1885–
1963), Darius Milhaud (1892–   ), Francis Poulenc (1899–1963),
William Schuman (1910–   ), Benjamin Britten (1913–   ),
Irving Fine (1914–1962), Vincent Persichetti (1915–   ), and
Lukas Foss (1922–   ).

Some musicologists have applied the labels of Neo-Classicism
and Neo-Romanticism to specific composers, most of whom have
written in various styles. It is impossible to categorize the works of
all composers in this manner. Each student will need to analyze each

---

[55] *Ibid.*, p. 335.

work under consideration to determine the "tag" that most appropriately applies.

Neo-Romanticism

Twentieth-century composers have not all found the styles of Impressionism, Expressionism, or Neo-Classicism to their liking. Some, therefore, have utilized means of expression more closely aligned with the ideals of the Romanticists. This group has been referred to as the Neo-Romanticists. Music in the Neo-Romantic style is usually rich in sonorities, contains frequent climaxes, and is comparatively easy for the non-musician to listen to. The Neo-Romantic composers utilize many of the tonal and rhythmic devices of the Neo-Classicist, but they convey it in a subjective manner—in such a way as to instill emotion and warmth in their music.

While, during the first part of the twentieth century, the majority of composers had rejected the ideals of the nineteenth century in favor of other modes of expression, the political and economic situation of the second quarter of the century led the way to a more emotional means of expression. World War II, in particular, created an atmosphere more receptive to romantic ideals and a need in some composers for a more personal means of expression, in which greater emphasis is placed upon the poetical and dramatic aspects of music.[56] Some representative composers of this style are: Ernst Toch (1887–1964), Carl Orff (1895–   ), Howard Hanson (1896–   ), William Walton (1902–   ), Paul Creston (1906–   ), Samuel Barber (1910–   ), Gian Carlo Menotti (1911–   ), Norman Dello Joio (1913–   ), and William Bergsma (1921–   ).

In addition to the styles of musical expression discussed above, separate consideration must be given to those composers who utilize folk material in their music. This group has often been referred to as the Nationalists. Among the more prominent are: Ernest Bloch (1880–1959), Zoltán Kodály (1882–1967), Ralph Vaughan Williams (1872–1958), Charles Ives (1874–1954), Randall Thompson (1899–   ), Aaron Copland (1900–   ), Heitor Villa-Lobos (1887–1959), Carlos Chávez (1899–   ), and Alan Hovhaness (1911–   ).

Whereas the nineteenth-century composer utilized folk material more for color effects and altered it when it did not fit his com-

---

[56] *Ibid.*, p. 314.

positional scheme, the twentieth-century Nationalist incorporated more of the flavor of the original folk idiom in his music. Modal music and material with asymetrical rhythms are often used to create fresh, new effects.[57]

Meter and Stress

Impressionistic music possesses less tension and rhythmic drive than does music in the Romantic period. Impressionist music, particularly that of Debussy, gives the impression of being "suspended in space." Accent or stress occurs rather infrequently; therefore, the conductor generally should avoid using too vigorous a beat.

In contrast to the rhythmic vagueness of Impressionism, Expressionistic music possesses considerable rhythmic incisiveness, *i.e.,* the rhythm is more clear-cut. The rhythm of the music is generally aligned with the durational values of the text; however, as a means of achieving tension, the Expressionists often distorted the normal accentuations of words. This alteration usually necessitated the use of changing meter to accommodate the resultant rhythm.

A particular characteristic of Neo-Classic music is its rhythm. As a means of avoiding the monotony of the regular stress following the barline, composers employ various devices. One procedure is to alter the meter with each measure.[58] The same effect, however, may be achieved by simply shifting the stresses or accents from point to point within the measure, but without changing the meter signature. In conducting rhythmic patterns with shifting accents, the conductor should limit the scope of his patterns and utilize a precise rebound to each beat. On accented notes—whether on a downbeat or an upbeat —the stress should be reflected in the tension of the arms and shoulders, while limited, yet precise, movements should occur on the unaccented notes.

Additive rhythm, in which each measure includes one more or one less pulsation than the preceding measure, *e.g.,* 4/4, 3/4, 2/4, or 2/4, 3/4, 4/4, is also frequently employed. Still another rhythmic device is the use of traditional rhythmic patterns in non-symmetrical forms. For example, in 4/4 meter the eighth-notes might be divided as $3+3+2$, or $3+2+3$, rather than $4+4$. (Another way of stating these rhythmic groupings is 1 2 3 1 2 3 1 2, or 1 2 3 1 2 1 2 3.)

---

[57] *Ibid.,* p. 257.

[58] See, for example, various works by Jean Berger: *It Is Good to Be Merry* (Neil A. Kjos), *The Good of Contentment* (Theodore Presser), *Lift Up Your Heads* (Summy-Birchard), and *Seek Ye the Lord* (Augsburg).

In 6/8 meter, a two-measure pattern might be alternately written as 3+3+2+2+2. In conducting rhythms in non-symmetrical forms, the conductor must alter his patterns to conform to the basic rhythm of the music.[59]

While the Neo-Romantic composer will use many of the rhythmic devices of the Neo-Classicist, he will do so in moderation. He places a greater emphasis on the poetical aspects of music and a means of personal expression that is more universally understood. When modern-day rhythmic devices contribute to this end they are used, and when they do not they are avoided.

Dynamics

In contrast to music of the Romantic period, Impressionistic music possesses a relatively low level of dynamic intensity. *Fortissimo* occurs rather infrequently, with the medium and the lower dynamic levels, *i.e., mezzo forte, piano,* and *pianissimo,* being used primarily. *Crescendo* and *decrescendo,* when employed, should be used with considerable care and restraint. In performing music from this period, the conductor should take care to adapt the scope of his beat to the dynamic levels of the music. In conducting a *pianissimo* passage, for example, the movements should be very slight.

Following the Impressionistic period there has gradually developed an increasing use of dynamic extremes. Contrast is often achieved through a rapid change from an extremely low dynamic level to one of great intensity and volume. Modern-day composers are inclined toward using a multiplicity of dynamic effects in their music, including extreme contrast in dynamic levels, rapid *crescendos* and *decrescendos,* dynamic accents, and uniform levels of intensity.[60]

Tempo

With Impressionistic music most tempi tend toward the moderate and the slow, with exceptionally fast tempi usually being avoided. A considerable degree of modern music following this period, however, exhibits a strong rhythmic drive. As movement and speed are an

---

[59] For a further discussion of this technique, see pp. 30-32.

[60] Howerton, *op. cit.,* pp. 179–180.

integral part of our modern-day life, so too are these characteristics reflected in much of our modern-day music. The rhythm of Expressionistic music is generally somewhat irregular and rather complex. As a result of the normal accent of words being sometimes deliberately distorted, the tempo, therefore, often fluctuates with the use of pauses, *ritardandos,* and *accelerandos.*

Tempo, of course, is related to both rhythm and mood, and, in determining the proper tempo, the conductor should consider carefully both of these factors. As clarity of line is essential to the performance of Neo-Classic music, a tempo that is too fast will impede the articulation, while a tempo that is too slow will sometimes lessen the intensity and rhythmic drive. Mood is an important consideration in determining the tempi of Neo-Romantic music. With emotional expression being relatively important, the projection of textual meanings often necessitates a greater flexibility in tempi.

Texture

Composers of the Romantic period were highly interested in harmonic experimentation. This interest, however, was intensified by composers of the Modern period. The Impressionists sought to escape the restrictions of the major-minor system of tonality. In the process, Debussy used a variety of devices including the medieval modes, the whole-tone scale, and the pentatonic scale. Parallel fourths, fifths, and octaves were often used above a pedal point, which resulted in unusual effects from the clash between the sustained and the moving harmonies.

While previous harmonic systems focused upon the relationship of chords and their progression from one to another, the Impressionists utilized individual chords for the sonorous and coloristic effects they created. Thus the tendency for chord resolution was certainly lessened. While triads were sometimes used, seventh, ninth, and eleventh chords were frequently employed either separately or in succession. Composers, furthermore, often utilized these chords on various scale degrees by shifting them up and down without alteration. This "gliding" use of chordal movement, utilizing blocklike chords in parallel motion, was an integral stylistic feature of Impressionism. Escaped chords, *i.e.,* those that are not resolved, but seem to "escape" to another key, were also an important characteristic of Impressionistic music. Impressionist composers often achieved a feeling of rest, or point of harmonic arrival, by simply using a less dissonant chord than those preceding it. Tonal color became equated with melody, harmony, and rhythm during this era.

Debussy often deliberately created a vagueness within his music, coupled with an indefiniteness of phrase structures. Ravel, on the other hand, utilized traditional forms and phrases to a much greater extent. The whole-tone scale was not utilized by Ravel, as it was by Debussy, as he desired a more definite triad outline, clearer phrase structures, and more functional harmony.

Expressionism is generally considered to have begun with Schoenberg, and, as twelve-tone music is associated with him, the two terms have become somewhat synonymous. It should be understood, however, that all Expressionist music is not twelve-tone music, as the Expressionistic movement began before this development. In Schoenberg's earlier works (his oratorio *Gurre-Lieder,* for example), he developed his use of chromaticism to its maximum potential. He then began to seek new means of expression.

Schoenberg's experimentation led to the development of the *twelve-tone method* or *serial technique* about 1923. With this method, all compositions are based upon an arbitrary arrangement or *set* of the twelve chromatic tones. Each tone row or set is handled in such a manner that no particular tone becomes any more important than the others. No tone is allowed to be repeated until every other tone has been used at least one. This is in marked contrast to the conventional major-minor tonal system. The row or set serves as a unifying factor in the music. After the basic set has been introduced, it may be repeated through a variety of means. It may be inverted— that is, turned upside down—it may be performed backwards (retrograde), or inverted and performed backwards (a retrograde of the inversion). The tone row is a type of variation technique in which great variety is achieved with only a minimum of material.[61] The guiding thought is that no idea should be repeated except in a new form. The older style of repetition and sequence, and balanced phrases and cadences was rejected by the Expressionists.

In the nineteenth century, rhythm, harmony, and tone color were often considered as entities unto themselves, while Neo-Classicism considered each of these separate elements as subservient to the whole. The use of counterpoint by the Neo-Classic composers became increasingly important. To differentiate it, however, from the "harmonic" counterpoint of the Romantic era, this new polyphony is often referred to as "linear counterpoint." It is often marked by its transparency of texture and its dissonance and driv-

---

[61] Machlis, *Introduction to Contemporary Music, op. cit.,* pp. 340–342.

ing rhythm. While striking dissonance often occurs as a result of clashes between vocal lines, each line must maintain its forward drive or thrust.

In the music of the Neo-Romanticists, extreme harmonic complexity is usually avoided. Their music is generally characterized by its sensuous lyricism and its richness of harmony. It is often simply and directly stated, although some music possesses considerable rhythmic drive and intensity. Neo-Romantic music is primarily tonal in nature. Dissonance is used, but generally for comparatively brief periods to highlight the emotional and poetical aspects of the text. While a considerable portion of Neo-Romantic music is harmonically conceived, some composers utilize contrapuntal devices as well. While their compositional techniques vary considerably, their one common characteristic is a more personal means of expression.

Expressive Aspects

The Impressionist composer's aim was simply to suggest rather than boldly to state. Music of this period, therefore, should be approached in an objective manner and performed with considerable restraint. The excesses and extremes of the Romantic period should be avoided.

Expressionistic and Neo-Classical music should be approached with an even more objective point of view. Perhaps the most outstanding characteristic of Expressionistic music is its continuous dissonance (and lack of consonance which allows for a lessening of the tension). Dissonance, along with such other devices as angular melodic fragments, irregular rhythm, and abrupt changes in tempi, are used as a means of expressing the conflicts of man's inner self. The composer's concern is the use of these varied devices to portray these inner feelings, rather than the expression of pure emotion in itself.

The Neo-Classicist is concerned largely with craftsmanship and with the statement of his material in an impersonal, objective manner. Emotional expression is minimized. Although it will vary from composer to composer, it is always carefully controlled. The Neo-Classicist endeavored to recapture the classic spirit by striving for symmetry and balance in his music, by utilizing more transparent textures, and by limiting the size of his musical forces.

The Neo-Romanticist, however, seeks a more universalized type of expression. His goal is different from the Neo-Classicist, as he desires his means of communication to be more personal in nature. While he uses many musical devices similar to those of the Neo-

Classical composer, since his purpose is different, he uses them in a different way. The conductor should analyze his music and determine the *raison d'être* for each device if he is to employ it for its intended purpose.

In performing music of the Modern period, particular attention should be given to the tone quality and the manner of articulation. With Impressionistic music, the singers need to use a *legato* style of diction, so as not to disturb the smooth flow of the carefully voiced chords often moving in parallel motion.[62]

The melody of Expressionistic music often moves in wide angular leaps, thus creating some serious intonation problems for the performers. Singers, obviously, need to listen carefully. And, as any rigidity in the jaw will inhibit proper articulation, they need to maintain a rather relaxed jaw to facilitate a cleaner articulation of the various interval jumps.

In Neo-Classic music it is usually desirable to lessen the dramatic qualities of the voice, so that the clarity of the structure may be brought out. Voices with excessive vibrato or tremolo are particularly detrimental to the interpretation of this style of music. In performing music in a Neo-Romantic style, the voice quality should be warm and expressive so as to best convey the subjective aspects of the music.

Certainly one characteristic of twentieth-century music is the wide diversity of musical styles. It is often difficult to place composers neatly in the previously mentioned categories, as some change their styles during their composing years. Other composers might be said to possess an "eclectic" style; *i.e.*, they draw from the techniques and devices of various schools, depending upon the musical thought to be expressed. The conductor, therefore, if he is to interpret properly the works of any particular modern-day composer, should study and analyze the music, as well as the writings of the composer under consideration. What a composer says about his own music has obvious implications for the conductor seeking the proper interpretation. Whenever such writings do not exist, or are unavailable, the conductor may well turn to the vast number of books on twentieth-century composers (as well as those of other periods). What others have written about the lives and music of particular individuals will often provide the inquiring, analytical reader with fresh insights into the interpretation of music.

---

[62] For a discussion of *legato* diction, see p. 66.

The study of style and interpretation is not a subject to be dealt with on a terminal basis—it should be studied throughout one's musical career. The intent of this chapter has been to provide a summary of the most salient points for consideration. To be most meaningful, however, they must be studied in connection with actual music. With this background information, the conductor should carefully study and analyze his scores. Only through reflective thought on the composer's intentions will the proper interpretation be achieved. The choral conductor should also listen critically to the interpretations of various choral organizations—on recordings and in the concert hall. The listener will most likely find that the interpretation of a particular composition will vary somewhat from one conductor to another. "What is stylistically correct and what is incorrect about these performances?" and "What do I like and dislike about the performances?" These questions must be always present on the listener's mind if he is to make the proper evaluation essential to further musical growth. The young conductor must give these questions careful consideration if he is ultimately to achieve the correct interpretation for his own choral groups.

Finally, the effective conductor must also be a scholar. He should devote considerable time to further reading in various sources of the main points discussed in this chapter. He should also develop a broad historical understanding of the various periods of artistic achievement. For these purposes, a selected list of publications recommended for further study is included at the end of this chapter.

Topics for Discussion

1. What are some problems one might encounter when trying to perform Baroque music as it was originally intended?

2. Discuss the benefits and drawbacks of the old system of princely patronage of composers. What ideas have been advanced for the support of composers in our present-day society?

3. What specific techniques might a choral conductor use in teaching an appropriate style for any given period and/or composer? Discuss each historical period and cite particular composers and works.

4. How should the conductor's beat vary in conducting music of various periods?

5. In striving toward an authentic performance, to what extent should authenticity give way to the conductor's personal idiosyncrasies?

6. Discuss the effect of geographical influences upon the style and mode of expression of particular composers.

7. The Romantic era has been referred to as a "period of opposites." What is meant by this expression, and what are the implications for understanding the music of particular composers?

8. What is meant by the term "an eclectic style"? Give some examples.

References

Aldrich, Putman C., "The 'Authentic' Performance of Baroque Music," *Essays on Music in Honor of Archibald T. Davison.* Cambridge, Mass.: Harvard University Press, 1957.

Apel, Willi, *Harvard Dictionary of Music.* Second Edition, revised and enlarged. Cambridge, Mass.: Harvard University Press, 1969.

———, *The Notation of Polyphonic Music, 900–1600.* Cambridge, Mass.: Mediaeval Academy of America, 1942.

Artz, Frederick, *From the Renaissance to Romanticism.* Chicago: University of Chicago Press, 1962.

Bukofzer, Manfred F., *Music in the Baroque Era: From Monteverdi to Bach.* New York: W. W. Norton & Company, Inc., 1947.

———, "On the Performance of Renaissance Music," *Music Teachers National Association, Volume of Proceedings,* 1941. Pittsburg: The Association, 1942, pp. 225–235.

Calvocoressi, M. D., *A Survey of Russian Music.* Baltimore: Penguin Books, Inc., 1944.

Dart, Thurston, *The Interpretation of Music.* Revised Edition. London: Hutchinson University Library, 1960.

Dolmetsch, Arnold, *The Interpretation of the Music of the XVIIth & XVIIIth Centuries.* London: Oxford University Press, 1946.

Donington, Robert, *The Interpretation of Music.* London: Faber and Faber Limited, 1963.

Dorian, Frederick, *The History of Music in Performance*. New York: W. W. Norton & Company, Inc., 1942.

Einstein, Alfred, *The Italian Madrigal* (3 vols.). Princeton, N.J.: Princeton University Press, 1949.

———, *Music in the Romantic Era*. New York: W. W. Norton & Company, Inc., 1947.

Etherington, Charles L., *Protestant Worship Music: Its History and Practice*. New York: Holt, Rinehart & Winston, Inc., 1962.

Fellowes, Edmund H., *The English Madrigal Composers*. Second Edition. London: Oxford University Press, 1948.

Gore, Richard T., "The Performance of Baroque Church Music," *Music Teachers National Association, Volume of Proceedings, 1950*. Pittsburg: The Association, 1953, pp. 155–163.

Grout, Donald Jay, *A History of Western Music*. New York: W. W. Norton & Company, Inc., 1960.

Grove's Dictionary of Music and Musicians. Fifth Edition (9 vols.). New York: The Macmillan Co., 1954.

Hansen, Peter S., *An Introduction to Twentieth Century Music*. Second Edition. Boston: Allyn and Bacon, Inc., 1967.

Harman, R. Alec, and Anthony Milner, *Late Renaissance and Baroque Music*. London: Barrie & Rockliff, 1959.

Howerton, George, *Technique and Style in Choral Singing*. New York: Carl Fischer, Inc., 1957.

Jeppesen, Knud, *The Style of Palestrina and the Dissonance*. Copenhagen: Ejnar Munksgaard, Publisher, 1946.

Lang, Paul Henry, *Music in Western Civilization*. New York: W. W. Norton & Company, Inc., 1941.

Leonard, Richard, *A History of Russian Music*. New York: The Macmillan Co., 1957.

Machlis, Joseph, *The Enjoyment of Music*. Regular Revised Edition. New York: W. W. Norton & Company, Inc., 1963.

———, *Introduction to Contemporary Music*. New York: W. W. Norton & Company, Inc., 1961.

Morley, Thomas, *A Plain and Easy Introduction to Practical Music*. London, 1597. Modern edition by R. Alec Harman, London, 1952.

Palisca, Claude, *Baroque Music.* Englewood Cliffs, N.J.: Prentice-Hall, Inc., 1968.

Pattison, Bruce, *Music and Poetry of the English Renaissance.* London: Methuen & Co., Ltd., 1948.

Quantz, Johann Joachim, *Versuch einer Anweisung die Flöte traversiere zu spielen.* Berlin, 1752. Translation and study by E. R. Reilly. Unpublished Ph.D. dissertation, University of Michigan, 1958.

Reese, Gustave, *Music in the Renaissance.* New York: W. W. Norton & Company, Inc., 1954.

Rothschild, Fritz, *The Lost Tradition in Music: Rhythm and Tempo in J. S. Bach's Time.* New York: Oxford University Press, Inc., 1953.

————, *Musical Performance in the Times of Mozart and Beethoven: The Lost Tradition in Music,* Part II. New York: Oxford University Press, Inc., 1961.

Sachs, Curt, *Rhythm and Tempo: A Study in Music History.* New York: W. W. Norton & Company, Inc., 1953.

Scott, Charles Kennedy, *Madrigal Singing.* London: Oxford University Press, 1931.

Sparks, Edgar, *Cantus Firmus in Mass and Motet, 1420–1520.* Berkeley, Calif.: University of California Press, 1963.

Stevenson, Robert, *Music Before the Classic Era.* London: The Macmillan Co., Ltd., 1955.

Strunk, Oliver, Ed., *Source Readings in Music History.* New York: W. W. Norton & Company, Inc., 1950.

Tartini, Giuseppe, "Treatise on Ornamentation" (translated and edited by Sol Babitz), *Journal of Research in Music Education,* Vol. IV, Number 2 (Fall, 1956), pp. 75–102.

Ulrich, Homer, and Paul A. Pisk, *A History of Music and Musical Style.* New York: Harcourt, Brace & World, Inc., 1963.

4

Rehearsal Techniques

THE SUCCESS OF THE choral concert is determined in the rehearsal room. Effective musical results are dependent upon a conductor's well-defined concept of his musical objectives, and his ability to transmit them to the members of the choral group. Although careful planning assists in the clarification of objectives, the conductor must possess various techniques for implementing his ideas. Through judicious employment of these devices, he will strive toward a consistently improved performance. Efforts in this direction will result in higher musical standards and increased satisfaction for both the performers and the audience.

PRE-REHEARSAL PLANNING

Choral directors are constantly asked to perform, and many, especially school music directors, feel that allocated rehearsal time is inadequate to develop their groups to the proper performance standard. In view of this situation, rehearsals must necessarily be well planned if the director is to make the most effective use of his time. Careful pre-rehearsal planning is also likely to result in more meaningful learning experiences, which in turn provide the climate necessary for subsequent learning experiences. Following are some general suggestions concerning over-all rehearsal planning.

A director should include in the choral rehearsal a variety of music from all eras. If choir members are to develop an understanding of, and appreciation for, various types of music, they should have some experience with choral music of the Renaissance, Baroque, Classic, Romantic, and Modern periods, as well as with folk music.[1] Furthermore, when variety is provided by alternating selections with contrasting styles, moods, and tempi, student interest is more readily maintained.

A conductor should never attempt to learn the music concurrently with his singers, but should study it carefully prior to each rehearsal. To familarize himself with the music, he should read through the choral parts on the piano. Specific difficulties or pitfalls that the singers are likely to encounter, such as intricate rhythmic patterns, difficult intervals in the various parts, unusual harmonic progressions, and particular diction problems, all should be noted. It is helpful for the conductor to mark his score with a colored pencil, indicating the anticipated difficulties.

Consideration should be given, of course, to teaching procedures for clarifying and solving rhythmic and tonal problems, and specific conducting techniques should be analyzed and practiced. It is advisable to sing through any portions of the vocal parts that are likely to cause the singers difficulty, so that they may be demonstrated adequately to the choir. The conductor should also examine the text for words with an unusual pronunciation, and when in doubt, he should consult a dictionary. Any textual subtleties reflected in the score should also be noted as a basis for achieving the proper interpretation.

In addition, the conductor will want to draw upon all his resources and musical background in achieving an effective musical interpretation. The practical application of knowledge gained in music theory and history classes will at this point be of inestimable value. The conductor should apply his knowledge of musical styles in various historical periods, and more specifically his understanding of the unique styles of individual composers.

Prior to the rehearsal, the conductor should determine the order of the selections to be rehearsed and place them on the chalkboard. Singers, after they enter the rehearsal room, can then place their music in order, thus saving time and eliminating or minimizing any unnecessary confusion prior to working on each selection.

Make certain the accompanist is provided any new music in ample time prior to the rehearsal, with instructions as to tempo,

---

[1]For a chronological listing of choral composers, see the Appendix, pp. 222-230.

dynamics, mood, etc. The most carefully laid rehearsal plans can be of little avail, unless the accompanist is adequately prepared.

After each rehearsal, it is desirable to take a few moments to evaluate the group's progress and to notate, either on the music or in a notebook, those points in the score that need further attention, and any approaches that might be effectively used in subsequent rehearsals.

THE FIRST REHEARSAL

The success of a choral group depends to a great extent upon the success of the initial rehearsal. In recruiting members, one of the best advertisements is a group of inspired singers. The word soon "gets around" that choral singing is an exciting adventure, and the question, "Why don't you join too?" may be frequently asked.

Young singers entering the rehearsal room for the first time may possess mixed feelings about choral singing—they may eagerly anticipate an activity that they feel may be exciting and enjoyable, and yet may be somewhat dubious of the outcome or the wisdom of their choice. It is the responsibility of the director to plan the rehearsal so that it will move smoothly toward its objective.

After the group has been seated, the conductor should endeavor to set the group at ease with a few words of welcome. Next, it will be necessary to explain the general rehearsal procedures, and tell the singers what they must do in order to retain their membership. Initial remarks, however, should be kept to a minimum, and the business of the actual rehearsal should be undertaken without unnecessary and needless delay. Also it should be kept in mind that overemphasis upon technique in the beginning can have a deadly effect upon a young choral group. These details are generally best introduced as the requirements of the music dictate—and only a few at a time.

In selecting the music for the first rehearsal, the conductor should consider the musical background of the group. Perhaps the singers have not been exposed to the standard choral literature and are generally unaware and unappreciative of its inherent beauties. In the beginning, it is helpful to concentrate upon a variety of folk-song arrangements of a rhythmical nature. In situations where the singers' backgrounds are extremely limited, it will be found desirable to intersperse a few easy rounds and canons with the rest of the repertoire. By providing the singers with music commensurate with their abilities and backgrounds, the conductor can minimize individual feelings of frustration and a more successful and enjoyable rehearsal will result. In the beginning, the singers should be provided with music they like, as long as it is within the limits of good musical taste. There will be ample time for raising musical standards and improving individual tastes.

The importance of having the first concert as soon as possible cannot be underestimated. Individuals constantly need a goal before them to guide their work if they are to make strides toward a consistently improved performance. This is especially important in the early stages of the development of a newly organized group. Soon the singers will anticipate the rehearsals for the sheer beauty of the music itself and the enjoyment and satisfaction that they receive. At this point the conductor should implement his plans, on a gradual basis, for broadening the singers' musical interests and raising their tastes and musical standards.

INTRODUCING MUSIC

In teaching new music, the best procedures are those which facilitate learning and achieve artistic singing in the shortest period of time. Some choral directors employ what is called the "note approach"—that is, after an attempt is made to read the music, each part is worked out separately with the aid of the piano, and finally all the parts are sung together. Such a procedure is extremely tedious, discipline is often difficult to maintain, and artistic singing is not readily achieved. One of the greatest objections to this procedure is that few of the emotional qualities of the music survive this mechanical approach. The following suggestions are given in an attempt to remedy this dilemma.

If the singers have a fair amount of reading power, they should endeavor to sing the entire number through from beginning to end (with or without the aid of the piano—depending upon the development of their musicianship). In this way, not only will the reading ability of the group improve, but also an over-all concept of the music will be attained.

In presenting difficult compositions, the accompanist may play the music on the piano while each singer follows his part. If a good recording is available, it can be an invaluable aid in presenting new music. Although one would certainly not recommend that choral recordings be slavishly imitated by any group or conductor, they can serve as an extremely useful guide and rehearsal aid. After the choir members have been introduced to the music and have an over-all conception of it, then sections of it may be rehearsed in detail.

Many outstanding choral conductors have found through years of experience that once the rhythmic problems have been overcome, the notes and parts come faster. In studying sections of the music, a very helpful device is to have the singers recite together the text of the composition in correct musical rhythm. Such an approach helps to solve simultaneously problems of rhythm, diction, phrasing, and the proper dynamics.

This procedure does not preclude the necessity for occasionally devoting special attention to a particular voice part. At a specific point in the rehearsal, this may be the only means of achieving the desired musical results. Difficulties do sometimes arise, however, when directors devote too much time to this procedure. Discipline problems may be lessened considerably if the director strives to maintain the group's interest at all times and if he stresses the importance of using all of the rehearsal time to the group's best advantage. In achieving this objective, the following procedures may be used alternately: (*a*) While one part is being rehearsed, each of the other singers should be asked to study his part and listen to it in relation to the other parts. (*b*) All singers might be asked to sing a troublesome part in unison. This procedure also has value in developing an awareness of various relationships between parts. (*c*) Request the choir members to *hum* their own parts softly while the troublesome part is being rehearsed.

Successful directors have found that effective rehearsals must be stimulating and must move quickly. When the director maintains a fast pace and the singers are kept busy, not only is a great deal more accomplished, but also confusion is reduced to a minimum.

IMPROVING MUSIC READING

In most areas of learning, conceptual understandings are likely to be most meaningful when learning is through a discovery process, and not through simply being told the answer. Similarly, in music, sightreading skills will improve most when a singer has to struggle a bit to interpret the score. Once he hears the music through a recording or on the piano, he no longer needs to rely on his musical memory in an attempt to recall the correct rhythm and pitches, for he already *has* the answer. To improve music-reading skills, singers need to be provided with challenges involving a wide variety of rhythmic and tonal experience.

If individuals are to improve, they must recognize and feel a need for improvement. Some persons are strongly motivated toward achieving success in all areas and have a strong desire for self-improvement. Such minds are highly receptive to improving music-reading skills. However, everyone does not possess this degree of motivation and the director can assist these other persons best by helping them to feel the satisfaction of achievement. He should be positive in all his remarks and plan all music-reading experiences so that they are as challenging and interesting as possible. Any devices used should generally grow out of a problem in actually reading music. At least, they should relate to a specific problem of music reading. Abstract drills, unrelated in any way to actual music, can become most dull and serve little purpose.

If the sight-reading abilities of a choir are to be developed, then attention must be given to their development during each rehearsal period. Sight-reading can be improved only by practice, based upon musical understanding. Perhaps just past the midway point of each rehearsal, it is desirable to include at least one selection for sight-reading purposes. Procedures followed at music competition-festivals are suggested. The music should be carefully examined by the choir members while the director points out and discusses various pitfalls inherent in it. Upon first examination, singers should accustom themselves to looking first at the meter and key signatures, and at the beginning chord, and then scanning their respective parts for intricate rhythmic patterns or figures, unfamiliar intervals (particularly wide ones), any chromatic alterations, and expression markings. Next, pitches should be given and the group should attempt to sing the music completely through from beginning to end without a break. General suggestions which the group should keep in mind are: (*a*) keep the eyes moving ahead to grasp patterns or groups of notes; (*b*) respond to the pulse of the music in some way—perhaps by wiggling the toes inside the shoes;[2] (*c*) keep going and do not stop or fret about mistakes; (*d*) look for familiar patterns in the music both before and during the reading process. Following the initial reading, difficult aspects of the music should again be discussed and,

---

[2] For other means of encouraging a response to the pulse of the music, see pp. 135-137.

if time allows, the selection should be repeated in an effort to eliminate previous errors.

In many instances, problems of rhythm and pitch arising from reading sessions will be dealt with simultaneously. In other cases, the learning process may be facilitated when each is dealt with separately. Suggestions for achieving rhythmic responsiveness and tonal awareness follow.

Rhythmic Responsiveness

A singer's perception of rhythmic patterns and the accuracy of his response constitute an important part of music-reading skills. The following approaches are suggested as a means of increasing a choir's responsiveness to rhythm.

1. Reciting the text of the music in correct musical rhythm, as discussed in the preceding section, is an excellent means of facilitating the learning of difficult rhythm patterns. To develop individual rhythmic responsiveness, however, the singers should be asked to peruse the rhythmic patterns silently by themselves before the group endeavors to chant them together.
2. Clapping the troublesome rhythm patterns is a good way to elicit a bodily response to rhythm. Opportunity should be provided for everyone to respond in various ways—individually, in quartets, or in sections, rather than just in the entire group.
3. The director may accumulate a number of rhythmic problems confronted by the singers. To encourage more careful listening coupled with bodily response, he should chant a one- (or two-) measure pattern, with the group responding immediately afterwards. The response is more effective if the group taps the heel or toe prior to the chanting, and maintains this steady response to the pulse throughout the activity. Rhythmic patterns may vary from the simple to the complex and encompass all musical styles. (For an illustration of this idea, see the discussion on rhythmic precision as it relates to attacks and releases, and Figure 40, on pp. 135-137.)
4. Isolate particular rhythm problems in the music and write them on the chalkboard. Analyze them and then respond in some way by chanting or clapping, or by some counting system.
5. Some students have difficulty reading music in meters other than 3/4 and 4/4 because, as a result of their limited experience, they usually expect each beat to be a quarter-note. To correct this misconception, and to broaden their experience, it is helpful to write on the chalkboard a familiar tune in a meter other than the orig-

inal. A tune originally in 4/4 meter might be written, for example, in 4/8, 4/2, or 12/8 meter. The familiar tune serves as a common element and through singing and comparing different ways of notating a tune, students gain insight into the relatedness of rhythms.

6. Write a phrase of a familiar song on the chalkboard and, after the group has sung it through once, alter the rhythm in some way. Use simple rhythmic alterations, but soon include the more difficult until a considerable number of rhythm patterns have been experienced. The familiar song provides a base from which to begin, so that attention may be focused on the rhythm and not the tonal problems.

Tonal Awareness

The ability to perceive differences and relationships in pitch and to reproduce them accurately is essential to achieving any degree of skill in music reading. The following procedures are suggested as a means of developing greater tonal awareness.

1. A keen awareness of the tonal relationships between various intervals is essential to the achievement of good intonation, as well as to skill in sight-reading. One suggested device is the singing in unison of various intervals without aid from the piano. The director may request the group to sing "up a major third" and back to the initial pitch, then "up a perfect fifth" and back, then "down a perfect fourth" and back, etc., until various intervals have been sung. Extended over a period of time, this device may encompass a wide gamut of interval experience, which will contribute substantially to the singers' musicianship. The introduction of this procedure presupposes, of course, some preliminary instruction in the theoretical aspects of intervals, and some initial practice in singing them with the aid of the piano and observing them on the chalkboard as they are sung. The practicality of this device, in terms of improving sight-reading skills, lies in the singers' ability to establish the connection between this aural experience and the visual recognition of the intervals. Therefore, to establish the connection more firmly, the director should, during the rehearsal of certain selections, ask the singers to identify specific intervals, recall their relationships and then sing them with a reasonable degree of accuracy.[3]

---

[3]Some teachers prefer to cement these tonal relationships by relating the intervals to those found in familiar songs. For a listing of intervals and suggested songs, see Robert L. Garretson, *Music in Childhood Education.* New York: Appleton-Century-Crofts, 1966, pp. 189-190.

Another device closely related to the above is to train the group to sing the pitch A = 440 without aid from the piano. In the initial stages, periodical checking of the pitch with the piano will be necessary and will illustrate to the group their relative degree of success. After a while the singers will develop this skill and a degree of confidence will result from the accomplishment. Once the pitch has become firmly established in the singers' minds, a basic starting point is also provided for the singing of various intervals.

2. When intonation difficulties occur within the group, the pitch variation is usually less than a half-tone, since otherwise the group would be singing a wrong note, and most individuals would recognize such a discrepancy. A helpful device is therefore to train the choir to sing *quarter-tones*. First, select a note in the middle range and have the group sing downward a whole-tone and back, then down two half-steps and back, then down two *quarter-tones* and back. Immediately check the pitch with the piano. In the beginning, the choir will find this procedure difficult, but after repeated daily attempts they will soon be able to sing quarter-tones with comparative ease. One might ask: "Just what is the value of such an exercise?" After singers have developed an acute consciousness of pitch, the director often will be able to signal various sections of the choir to make the slight adjustments sometimes necessary for maintaining accurate pitch.

3. Singing the resolutions of dominant seventh chords develops a feeling for tonality and for modulation to new keys and, as a result, has a direct relationship to music-reading skills. A seventh chord creates tension and each pitch possesses a "pull" toward another. Initially, it is desirable for the choir to experience all the resolutions in the different inversions of the chord. Then, they may sing the key circle progression given in Figure 39. The use of notation, however, is not necessary. Each section is asked, upon signal, to move to the closest possible note that will create a feeling of rest. The soprano, alto, and tenor parts will move upward or downward either a half- or whole-step, or they will remain on the same tone. The bass part moves downward a fifth and upward a fourth, except in third inversion chords (V$_2$) when the seventh is in the bass part. Begin on a major triad, then direct one of the upper voice parts doubling the root of the chord to move downward a whole-step, thus creating the dominant seventh chord. Give the choir lots of time to feel the "pull" of their notes before resolving each seventh chord.

4. An excellent device for developing tonal awareness is for the director to teach the choir members to recognize the chord progressions that they sing. A good starting place is to identify the cadences. Too many individuals sing the simple V-I cadence with-

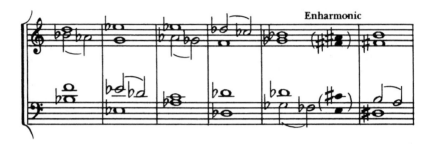

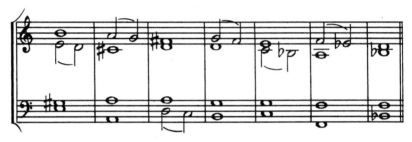

Figure 39.

out knowing what it is. A few minutes of each rehearsal can be well spent in explaining to the group the function and purpose of the cadence, and the part each note plays in the chord. The director may want to take the chord progression out of context and drill each chord until it is perfectly in tune—each time making sure that the singers are able to identify the progression.

As the group improves in their identification of chord sounds, the director will be able to extend the process to more complicated chord progressions and eventually even to modulation. Such a practice, if carried on over a long period of time, will most certainly show results not only in improved reading ability, but also in better intonation and all-around musicianship.

5. Encourage the choir to maintain the pitches in their minds when they are stopped for corrections and/or suggestions. Do not always provide the pitch on the piano, but ask them to remember it and sing upon direction. At first they may flounder and begin to sing in a variety of keys. Soon, however, they will retain and recall the correct pitches. The general alertness necessary to remember the pitches will often have a beneficial effect on the rehearsal.

6. As a further means of developing tonal awareness, and as a check to determine how well the singers know their notes and if they are hearing them in tune, the device of "silent singing" is suggested.

First, give the pitch of a selection the group knows reasonably well. Then ask the choir to sing the music "silently" together at the tempo indicated by the conductor. At the appropriate time, the conductor should prepare the group to sing aloud with the verbal command, "Sing!" spoken on the previous beat. Initially, the group may sing silently for only four to eight measures, but as they become more proficient, the activity may be extended in length. The choir may also be directed to sing aloud at the beginning of a new phrase or, again, as they develop proficiency, at any point within the phrase. Silent singing will be found to be an excellent means to stimulate concentration and alertness and to "rejuvenate" a sluggish choir.

ATTACKS AND RELEASES

Precision of attacks and releases is essential to artistic choral singing and is dependent upon several factors—namely, the general attentiveness of the group, the rhythmic response of the group, and the basic technique of the conductor.

A choral group with high morale, in which each individual possesses a feeling of "belonging" and exhibits a singleness of effort toward the group's objectives, is relatively easy to motivate toward a consistently improved performance. The attentiveness of the choral group depends to a very great extent upon this group morale and upon a high degree of motivation. Difficulties usually arise not in the early stages of rehearsing a selection, but in the later stages, just prior to the perfection of the number. The conductor should therefore be constantly in search of means to stimulate interest and capture the singers' imagination. Individuals who are highly motivated and desirous of improving their group's musical standards will not succumb to the pitfalls of slovenly bodily attitudes and the resultant lack of precision.

Rhythmic security in the music not only aids in the precision and the vitality of the performance, but also reduces to some extent excessive muscular tension and improves the tone quality of the group. Rhythmic security can be increased by encouraging a stronger rhythmic response to the music.

Here is an approach to rhythmic responsiveness which usually creates enthusiasm on the part of the singers. After setting the tempo, instruct the choir members to tap their feet (not too loudly) in response to this basic pulsation. Continue for several measures until the group is responding together precisely. While the group continues the tapping, the director sings a rhythmic or melodic pattern one or two measures long. In the following measure or measures, the group responds and imitates the pattern previously sung by the director (Figure 40). The patterns should be varied from the simple to the

Fig. 40. *A device for developing responsiveness to music of a rhythmic, synco-pated nature.*

complex, and should become progressively more difficult over a period of time. School-age youth especially enjoy syncopated rhythm patterns. Try it—the possibilities are unlimited! In addition to evoking rhythmic response, this procedure is beneficial as an ear-training device.[4]

Singers should develop a strong feeling for the pulsation of the music they are singing, especially if it is in a *staccato* or *marcato* style. They are more likely to feel the pulsation if they make some

---

[4]This device is intended to be used in conjunction with music of a rhythmic syncopated nature, such as the vigorous spiritual *Rock-A My Soul*. It would provide an excellent means of evoking the necessary excitement and rhythmic awareness required for effective singing of this selection. Conversely, using the procedure immediately prior to a Bach chorale would by comparison make the chorale seem rather dull and would serve no purpose.

large bodily movements while singing. Having the group either beat out the basic pulsation of the music on the knee or conduct the traditional conducting patterns can be exceedingly helpful.

The conductor should thoroughly prepare for all attacks and releases if they are to be clear to the performers. Many choral directors take too much for granted in this respect. Most singers soon learn to adjust to the indecisive movements of the conductor, yet as a group they are never quite sure of his intentions. The choral conductor's movements should be clear, precise, rhythmical, and should reflect the mood of the music. Daily practice in front of a mirror can be very helpful. *See if you can follow yourself!*

BALANCE AND BLEND

In achieving correct balance, one must consider the voice quality of the individual singers, the range in which the voices are singing, the number of persons singing the various parts, and the harmonic aspects of the chords and the relative importance of the various vocal lines.

Voices of unusual and distinct tone quality oftentimes protrude from their sections, thus destroying the choral balance and blend. These voices must be subdued and blended with the group if artistic choral singing is to be achieved. The director must be continually on the alert for such occurrences and should strive to develop the singers' awareness of the problem. Often the difficulty results from poor voice production and improper breath control. In such instances, especially in the case of a wide tremolo, individual assistance is often necessary to correct the problem.

The problem of the tremolo, or excessively wide vibrato, usually occurs when a person endeavors to sing with an overly large, dramatic quality and does so without the proper breath support. To eliminate this condition, the director should emphasize adequate breath support, a somewhat lighter tone quality, and practicing with a fairly straight tone. Through constant attention, the situation can be remedied.

When individuals are singing in the extreme high range of the voice, distortion is likely to occur. Voices wtih greater power and brilliance (resonance) in the upper registers must be subdued to the level of the entire group. If the proper balance and blend is to be maintained throughout the vocal range, then choral groups should avoid using all their bodily energy in an effort to sing "as loud as possible." Distortion cannot help but result. The best advice is always to save some energy in reserve by singing up to approximately 75 per cent of the maximum vocal effort, and by concentrating on resonance and improved tone quality. Maximum dynamic levels will, of course, vary from group to group, and the most effective dynamic ranges must necessarily be determined by the director for each specific group.

In music with divided parts, it may be necessary to redistribute some of the voices and assign them to the weaker parts in order to achieve the proper balance. It is suggested that a few selected voices in the chorus be designated as "roving" singers. This would mean, for example, that a few of the second sopranos need not be given a definite voice assignment, but may sing either the soprano or alto part as the musical situation demands.

Moving parts, especially when they occur in the lower voices, should be emphasized and brought out. When some of the parts are sustained, these moving parts indicate a change of harmony and are of special interest to the listener. A much more musical effect often can be created by emphasizing the rhythmical movement of the vocal line, rather than by just singing the part a little louder. The problem of bringing out the melody usually occurs when it is in the lower parts. In such instances it might be well to mark the melody on all the music. Close attention to dynamics is most essential in securing balance between the melodic line and the supporting harmonic parts.

Other factors influencing choral blend, aside from those previously mentioned, pertain specifically to uniform vowel production and tonal and harmonic awareness. In singing, the tone is sustained upon the various vowel sounds. Each vowel produced must be clear and distinct and uniform in production throughout the choir if any degree of blend is to be achieved. The choral director should stress the importance of *singing on the vowel*. As a basis for achieving good blend, it is suggested that the following two concepts be presented to the group and continually emphasized.

1. Following the initial consonant, move to the vowel sound as quickly as possible—and *sing on the vowel*.
2. Listen carefully and endeavor to blend your vowel sounds with the group.

Many directors have found it profitable to utilize all of the primary vowel sounds in an exercise in which careful attention can be given to uniform production within the group. (See Exercise 13, for blending the vowels.)

Exercise 13.

Mah may mee moh   moo,   mah   may   mee   moh   moo,

1. Vocalize within the middle range of the voice only.
2. Move smoothly from one vowel to another.
3. Listen carefully—strive for uniform production within the group.

Some singers appear to be completely unaware of the other voices in the group. Good blend, balance, and intonation will not be achieved unless all the singers are trained to listen to the entire ensemble as well as to themselves.[5] Singers should be advised never to sing so loudly that they can't hear the people and the parts next to them. Humming the music sometimes will allow the individuals to hear the other parts better. This device can be used to improve the blend of all the parts, especially in *legato* singing. On easy and familiar choral selections, it has been found profitable for the singers occasionally to switch parts. This helps to develop an awareness of the other parts and subsequently may improve the blend of the group.

A procedure that has been found to give the most immediate (and sometimes startling) results is to place the entire choral group in quartets (SATB), or in the arrangement known as the "scrambled set-up."[6] Achieving results from these arrangements presupposes that the students know their parts. These seating arrangements separate the students who lean upon each other and lessen the stridency in voices of students accustomed to sitting together. They generally result in a tone quality and blend extremely satisfying to the group. In addition, they reveal the extent to which students have learned their parts.

A tape recorder can be put to very effective use in the choral rehearsal. Recordings of the group serve to re-emphasize the suggestions made by the director. They are also valuable as a means of evaluating progress and determining future lines of endeavor.

---

[5] For a further discussion of the importance of singing without accompaniment, see p. 146.

[6] For diagrams of both these seating arrangements, see p. 191.

PITCH AND INTONATION

Faulty pitch and intonation in choral groups are one of the most troublesome problems confronting choral directors today. Some have learned to live with the problem, so to speak, and have accepted it as being common to untrained voices. The majority, however, continue to strive for perfection, and many have achieved a reasonable consistency of performance in their groups.

Accurate pitch and intonation are basically dependent on (*a*) correctly produced tones, properly supported by the breath, and (*b*) the degree of tonal awareness that each individual singer possesses. In addition to these two basic factors, both previously discussed, there are other varied causes of poor intonation, which the director should be cognizant of if he is to deal effectively with the problem.

The Slurring Attack

Attacking the notes from below and sliding or slurring to the proper pitch is a particularly obnoxious fault common to singers. The problem can be somewhat alleviated if the choir members are instructed to think of approaching the notes from above, rather than from below the pitch. Another helpful device is to think of singing the consonants on the same pitch as the vowels.

Repeated Tones and Scale Passages

Intonation difficulties frequently occur on repeated tones. Since there is sometimes a tendency to sing each repeated tone a bit lower, it is helpful if the singers are instructed to think of each repeated tone as being a bit higher.

Intonation difficulties also often occur on ascending and descending scale passages. Many individuals are likely to sing the ascending scale steps too small and the descending scale steps too large. Both practices, of course, result in flatting. It is therefore suggested that choir members be asked to think purposely of singing the ascending scale steps larger and of singing the descending scale steps smaller.

Diction

Lack of attention to careful enunciation of the words can create intonation difficulties. The best advice that can be given the singers in such instances is: "Vitalize your words," or "Be more precise in your tongue, lip, and jaw movements and work for clarity of diction."

Breath Control

The problem of breath control usually occurs on long, extended phrases. Singers should be advised to refrain from using all their available breath supply, since this would result in an irregular flow of the breath and resultant gradations in volume and slight variations in the pitch. The group should be instructed in the "staggered" method of breathing. On long, extended phrases, each individual should drop out when in need of breath, take a full breath, and unobtrusively reenter. For best results, certain sections or groups should probably be told when to breathe in order that the best possible effect may be achieved.

Classification of Voices

Adolescent voices are unsettled and generally in a state of change. For this reason, and for the protection of the voices against unnecessary strain, it is advisable to retest each singer's voice frequently. Baritones singing tenor parts and altos singing soprano parts can lead to many difficulties.

Bodily Attitudes and Fatigue

Incorrect bodily attitudes, which generally reflect a lack of genuine interest, can have a decided effect upon performance. It behooves the director to be ever alert to this problem and to convince the choir members as best he can that they should maintain correct posture while singing. Correct posture and alert bodily attitudes are essential to properly supported tones, and when singers fully realize this fact they are usually more eager to cooperate. One idea found profitable in action is to insist that the group maintain correct posture only when singing; between numbers they should relax in a position most comfortable to themselves. Good posture can become a habit. Strive for it!

The best time of day for the choral rehearsal is believed to be the middle or late morning hours. Individuals generally do not sing as well immediately following lunch or late in the afternoon when bodily fatigue begins to occur. It is recognized that some school schedules prohibit the utilization of the most desirable hours for rehearsal, and that many directors have little voice in determining the scheduling of classes. It is felt, however, that the director should at least discuss the problem with his school administrator. Administrators are eager to provide the best possible education for their students and, if presented with a reasonable argument for making changes in the schedule, are usually most anxious to cooperate if they can.

When rehearsals become dull and uninteresting, bodily fatigue is bound to occur regardless of the time of day or the length of the rehearsal. Directors should, therefore, carefully plan and endeavor to make all rehearsals exciting events for the choir members.

Tempo

The tempo of the music can have a decided effect upon intonation. The tempo selected for a previous choral group—or the tempo originally chosen by the conductor—may not always be the best one. The conductor should become most sensitive to the problem and should endeavor to determine through experimentation the tempo that is most suitable for his present group and, of course, for the most effective rendition of the music.

Seating Arrangements

In choral groups where a strict tryout is not mandatory for membership there will usually exist a few voices that might be classified as "chronic flatters." If these individuals are allowed to sit together, their tone qualities are seemingly reinforced and can cause havoc within the group as regards intonation. The problem, however, can be somewhat alleviated by judiciously placing each of those offenders between two or more stronger singers. In this way they will more likely produce the tone qualities desired.

Acoustics

Many factors, including the size and shape of the room and the finishing materials utilized, affect the acoustics of the rehearsal room or the auditorium stage. Again, the tempo in which the music is performed should be determined to some extent by the acoustical properties of the performance room. As a general rule, it will be found that in rooms with little reverberation one should avoid singing the music too slowly if accurate pitch is to be maintained, while in rooms that are "exceedingly alive," one should avoid singing the music at too fast a tempo, lest the sounds emitted meet each other coming and going and produce a discordant and distasteful result.

Atmospheric Conditions

Atmospheric conditions also have their effect upon intonation. On dark, dismal days most individuals do not respond physically in the same way they do on bright, clear days. At such times, spirits are sometimes low and the group does not always display an abundance of vitality. It has been said that a person's vitality is to some extent dependent upon the relative degree of humidity present in the atmosphere. During humid times, bodily fatigue occurs sooner, the tone is generally not supported correctly, and many intonation problems result. What can be done to alleviate the situation? The director can only point out to the group the pitfalls that may occur, and through increased group effort hope to avoid some of the difficulties. If this procedure does not produce the desired results, then all concerned would be wise to charge the difficulty to "just one of those days."

Ventilation

Poor ventilation in the rehearsal room creates a stuffy, stale atmosphere that can have a decidedly detrimental effect upon intonation. The director should recheck this condition periodically during the rehearsal. It is often advisable to assign the task to one or more interested persons.

Growing Stale

Most directors have experienced the problem of having choral selections grow stale. There is only one solution to this problem. Set the number aside and return to it at a later date. The problem can be somewhat avoided if the season's repertoire is planned early in the year. This provides ample time to learn a new selection which can then be set aside until rehearsals are renewed just prior to its presentation. This procedure can have a definite beneficial effect upon improving standards of musical performance.

OTHER REHEARSAL CONSIDERATIONS

The effectiveness of a given rehearsal begins from the moment the choir members enter the rehearsal room. The conductor should encourage the singers to secure their music folders and immediately take their seats so that the rehearsal may begin promptly with a minimum of confusion. This process is facilitated if each singer's music is kept in an assigned folder and stored in music cabinets near the entrance door. Following are suggestions that will contribute to more effective and satisfying rehearsals.

Rehearsal Pace

Rehearsals should move quite rapidly—when they lag, disciplinary problems are sometimes encouraged. Confusion between selections can be lessened if the rehearsal order is carefully planned and written on the chalkboard prior to the rehearsal. Choir members should not be given the opportunity to waste time. In most cases, they will appreciate the director's efforts to make the most efficient use of rehearsal time.

Warm-up Exercises and Ear-Training Devices

Many directors prefer to begin their rehearsals with a warm-up exercise or an ear-training device. To avoid monotony, it is desirable to alternate these exercises and devices, and above all to keep them *short*. Get to the music as soon as possible.

Establishing and Maintaining Rapport

It is advisable to begin rehearsals with *familiar* music of a reasonably vigorous nature that is straightforward, uncomplicated, and not too demanding vocally. Selections that are demanding vocally and/or include various subtle nuances and shadings may be better dealt with later in the rehearsal when the singers are more adequately warmed up.

The conductor should study the technical aspects of the music before each rehearsal, and know what he want to accomplish. He should use the music as a reminder—glancing at it only when necessary. Thus he is free to concentrate upon maintaining "eye" contact with the group. Whenever possible, the conductor should inject a bit of humor into the rehearsals. A good laugh can lessen group tension and contribute substantially to the rehearsal's outcome. Through bodily attitudes, the conductor should project his enthusiasm for the music to the group and endeavor to spur the singers toward greater musical accomplishments.

Maintaining Correct Posture

If tones are to be adequately supported, correct posture must be maintained while singing. Unless the singers are continually encouraged, they are likely to fall into poor posture habits. Since the length of many choral selections will average about three minutes, choir members should be expected to maintain 100 per cent effort for this minimum length of time. Between selections they should be instructed to stretch and relax. This same philosophy applies to those individuals who feel they must communicate with each other during the singing of a specific selection. The following rule should apply: *No talking during actual rehearsal! Time between selections will be allotted for questions and communication regarding musical problems of concern to the group.*

Avoiding Fatigue and Vocal Strain

There is a limit to what can be accomplished with a given selection during a single rehearsal. When the singers show signs of fatigue and boredom, set the music aside and return to it at the following rehearsal.

It also is highly desirable for the director to provide a short break at the midway point in the rehearsal period. This time may be effectively utilized for special announcements, such as forthcoming concerts and musical events.

Rehearsing A Cappella

Too often singers become overly dependent upon the piano as a means of tonal and rhythmic support. As a result, they listen primarily to this instrument and not to the other vocal parts. Therefore, it is absolutely essential to rehearse some of the choral selections without accompaniment. Only in this way will the maximum degree of vocal independence, rhythmic security, and effective blend and balance be achieved.

Making Corrections

Errors in rhythm, pitch, and phrasing, etc., should be corrected immediately, before they become habitual. The conductor, however, should not be overcritical in his remarks or belittle the singers, as this may have a discouraging and detrimental effect upon the group. The director should be positive in his remarks—commenting about progress already made, as well as about the portions of the music that still require improvement.

When the conductor resorts to excessive talking, however, the singers' enthusiasm is lessened and valuable rehearsal time is lost. Therefore, he should be succinct in his comments and proceed with the rehearsal as quickly as possible.

The conductor should concentrate on rehearsing the troublesome parts of a choral selection. Much time can be wasted by simply repeating the sections that the singers already know. It is also advisable to rehearse periodically the treble and male sections of the choir separately. This practice is essential if minor discrepancies in rhythm and pitch are to be corrected and if sectional tone quality and blend are to be improved.

Prior to the repetition of selections, the conductor should avoid merely saying "Let's sing it again." If singers are to improve, they must know what they are striving for. Therefore, he should tell them clearly what he wants in every repetition.

Consideration should be given to possible starting points after the choir is stopped for corrections. A general procedure is to identify the point by referring to first the *page,* then the *score,* the *measure,* and finally the *beat* within the measure. After the choir is reasonably familiar with the music, a particular word or phrase may be identified as the starting point. After the singers have gained even further knowledge of the musical score, starting points may be identified as, for example: (*a*) after the double bar, (*b*) at the key change, (*c*) at the tenor entrance (thus forcing the other singers to identify this portion of the music to orient themselves).

Although demonstrating desired musical improvements and occasionally singing certain entrances is justifiable, the director should avoid continually singing with the group. Instead, he should devote his attention to critical listening and assisting the group to a more effective interpretation of the music through his conducting technique.

Stimulating Concentration

It is important that singers give their undivided attention to the conductor and that they concentrate upon achieving artistic singing. Following are suggestions that will contribute toward this objective.

1. *Rehearsing from a Standing Position.*
   Singers become weary and fatigued when rehearsing all the music from a sitting position. In addition, the maximum group effort cannot always be achieved unless the singers stand, assume the correct singing posture, and concentrate upon artistic singing. Therefore, alternate selections should be sung from a standing position.

   As a further means of developing more careful attention, it is advisable for the conductor to time each selection with a stop watch. While the resulting information is essential in planning the length of the final concert program, it has the added advantage of stimulating an extra group effort, particularly if the singers understand the purpose of the timing and the importance of being alert and responsive to the director's conducting movements.
2. *"Erratic" Conducting.*
   When singers seemingly have their eyes glued to the music, and are unresponsive to the subtleties of the conductor's movements, then it is helpful for him to purposely alter the tempo—faster and slower and employing the *fermata* at will. Singers enjoy this activity, and the challenge of "following" the conductor is an excellent means of developing attentiveness and responsiveness in a choir.
3. *"Silent Singing."*
   Mentally thinking together the pitch, rhythm, and tempo of a selection under a conductor's direction, before being asked to sing aloud at a designated point, is an excellent means of stimulating concentration and alertness. (For a more detailed discussion of this procedure, see pp. 134-135.)

Encouraging Individual Responsibility

The conductor should encourage the choir members to analyze their difficulties and to request assistance with particularly troublesome parts or sections of the music. Although the conductor necessarily must use discretion and be the final judge as to which problems should be undertaken first, he should encourage individual responsibility in regard to the various problems encountered in the music. Encouraging individual effort produces greater group solidarity, improved musicianship, and eventually a more effective interpretation of the music.

Ending the Rehearsal

The conductor should schedule a selection relatively familiar to the group during the final portion of the rehearsal—one that the singers particularly enjoy, so they will leave the rehearsal room with a feeling of genuine aesthetic accomplishment. The director should be prompt in ending the rehearsal, since most individuals have a demanding time schedule. Nevertheless, the dismissal time must be considered the director's prerogative—the singers should not be mere "clock watchers," but should wait to be dismissed.

INTERPRETATION

In achieving artistic interpretation of choral selections, a conductor must take into consideration a number of factors. The following suggestions will assist the conductor in achieving his goals.

Style of the Music

Prior to the initial rehearsal of a choral selection, the conductor should give ample thought to the style of the music. These thoughts will provide a guide to the achievement of a more artistic interpretation. Essential points for consideration are the characteristics of music in various historical periods, and the specific treatment that should be given in regard to meter and stress, tempo, dynamics, texture, and expression. The unique characteristics of the music of each individual composer should also be understood.

Consideration should also be given to the stylistic features or characteristics of particular types of compositions, such as the chorale, the motet, the madrigal, the cantata, the oratorio, the mass, liturgical music, the folk song, the ballad or love song, and music in a popular idiom.

Another facet of style is the technical manner in which it is executed, that is, *legato, staccato,* and *marcato.* The mood of the text as well as the musical markings will generally reveal these basic styles. Each musical selection requires a specific treatment in terms of diction, as well as in the projection of the mood or spirit of the song to the audience. The singers, therefore, must become aware of the differences in style if artistic interpretation is to be achieved.

Dynamic Range and Contrast

The dynamic range of a particular choral group depends upon the age level, physical maturity, and vocal development of the singers in the group. The relatively immature voices of a junior high school chorus, for example, are obviously unable to achieve the same full *fortissimo* effects as an adult choral group. Directors should avoid being overambitious and striving for effects that may prove harmful and injurious to younger students' voices. Contrast of dynamics is, of course, one of the objectives of the director. One should remember, however, that dynamics are relative, and that to achieve this goal the dynamic extremes of one group need not necessarily equal those of another choral group. Through experimentation, a conductor should determine the maximum dynamic level that voices of his particular group may sing without distortion of sound and undue vocal strain—and then compensate at the other extreme of the dynamic range by reducing the level of the *pianissimo* effects. Although immature vocal groups will be unable to achieve the same *pianissimo* effects as an adult group, some adjustment toward the goal of achieving dynamic contrasts must necessarily occur at this end of the continuum. Only in this way will the voices be protected from undue vocal strain.

A director must devote considerable attention to the achievement of effective dynamic contrasts. *Crescendo* and *decrescendo* markings should be adhered to. In the absence of such markings a slight *crescendo* on ascending vocal lines and a slight *decrescendo* on descending vocal lines will generally enhance the effectiveness of the interpretation. When in doubt about the general dynamic level, a thorough study of the text will reveal certain subtle implications— each suggesting, sometimes from phrase to phrase, a change in dynamic effects; to achieve effective interpretation the director must assist the singers in developing an awareness of the importance of dynamic contrasts. Through the use of teacher demonstrations, the tape recorder, choral recordings, and other means, the ineffective portions of a selection must be brought to the singers' attention and the importance of dynamic contrasts should be continually stressed.

Tempo

Although choral conductors will often differ in their opinions concerning the "correct" tempo of a selection, most will agree that they must determine the most effective tempo for their own groups. Factors determining the proper tempo are the basic style of the music, the mood of the text, the given musical markings, the physical maturity of the group, and the acoustical properties of the rehearsal room and the auditorium. One may best advise the conductor to experiment in an effort to determine the most effective tempo for his particular group.

Nuances

Nuances may be defined as delicate changes in musical expression, either in tone, color, tempo, or volume. The various nuances and shadings necessary for the most effective performance of the music quite naturally develop as the singers gain increased understanding of the text. The singers should recite and study the words of the music individually and as a group. Only through this approach will certain subtle, hidden meanings—essential to the best interpretation of the music—be revealed.

One type of nuance, perhaps obvious only to the director, is the slight degree of phrasewise tension and relaxation essential to the most effective interpretation of choral music. The tension or emotional surge is usually characterized by a slight quickening of one phrase, while the relaxation aspect of the cycle is reflected through a slight slowing down of the tempo. The tension is not only balanced but also complemented by the relaxation. Improvement of a problem moves through three stages: an awareness of the problem, an evaluation or appraisal of present progress, and a renewed effort toward improvement. Therefore, to implement these effects in the music, the conductor must demonstrate his desired objective by singing various vocal lines, and by playing back tape-recorded portions of the music, in order that the group may evaluate their performance.

Projecting the Mood

Projection of the mood or spirit of a song is essential to an effective choral performance. Capturing the proper mood of a selection may occur only through diligent study of the text. The director should discuss the implications of the text with the singers, the proper mood should be established for each selection, and an effort should be made to improve the projection with each subsequent rehearsal.

In achieving this goal, it has been found helpful to give special attention to the consonants. For example, in certain words such as *thunder, glory,* etc., the prevailing thought is quite dynamic. Therefore, the initial consonants should be stressed—almost "exploded." Often the advice, "Sing these as *Capital Consonants,*" assists in creating in the singers' minds the desired mental picture. Conversely, other initial consonants in such words as *dreams, softly, lullaby,* etc., demand the opposite treatment and must be handled more subtly and sung in a smooth *legato* style.

Finishing the Musical Phrase

Perhaps one of the most obvious differences between a professional and an amateur choral group is the seeming inability of the latter to complete their musical phrases. Often, because of lack of proper breath control, choral groups anticipate the release of the phrase ending. A choral director may eliminate this difficulty, to some extent, by employing what is called "staggered breathing," thus enabling the singers to sustain the phrase until it is released by the conductor. Singers often are inclined to anticipate the release of the phrase. It is often helpful if, during rehearsals, the director employs a slightly modified type of interpretation by holding certain phrases a bit longer than others. In this way, choir members are trained to watch the conductor more carefully, especially at the beginning and the end of phrases.

One of the greatest faults in choral singing is that groups do not finish their words. Such singing is slovenly and detrimental to an effective projection of the mood or spirit of the music. Singers should be trained to include the final consonants on all words, and should

Fig. 41. Excerpt from "April Is in My Mistress' Face" (by Thomas Morley).

be especially careful to include the final consonant upon the release of the phrase by the conductor. For example, a problem often arises when one or more sections of the choir release the phrase at the end of the second beat, while another section begins a phrase on the third beat of the music. This is essentially a conducting problem, and the difficulty can be avoided if the singers are instructed that the attack for one section will serve as the release for the other section (Figure 41).

Eliminating Excessive Slurring

Exaggerated slurring or scooping is the scourge of effective choral singing. According to studies by the music psychologist Carl Seashore, some degree of "gliding attack" is characteristic of the human voice and is even desirable.[7] However, definite steps should be taken to avoid excessive slurring. Most objectionable slurring occurs because the jaw is tight and rigid and the mouth is kept too tightly closed. Slurring can be eliminated, to a considerable extent, if the singers are requested to drop their jaws prior to the initial attack or prior to wide pitch changes. When choir members learn to anticipate wide pitch or interval changes, and properly adjust the vocal mechanism, choral singing can be performed much more effectively.

Facial Expressions and Bodily Attitudes

Many choral concerts are rendered less effective as a result of the stoic, expressionless faces of the singers. Especially since the advent of television, choral directors are becoming more cognizant of the importance of facial expressions and bodily attitudes to the ultimate success of the concert program. A correct bodily attitude may be defined as that entire bodily posture or stance which reflects the mood of the music. Appropriate facial expressions are equally important to the effective performance of a selection, and considerable attention must be devoted to each individual singer if the desired results are to be achieved.

Memorizing the Music

If the mood of the music is to be effectively projected to the audience, then music performed for programs and concerts must be thoroughly memorized. When music is memorized the singers are able to watch the director more closely and concentrate on the interpretive apects. The director is able to establish better rapport with the group and to transmit, through his conducting technique, his bodily attitudes, and his facial expressions, the desired musical interpretation.

Some choral groups are seemingly able to memorize music more quickly than others. Memorization can be facilitated through increased musical understanding and through the principle of association. Students with a greater understanding of the musical score— that is, knowledge of form, harmonic structure, styles of music, etc.— will memorize their parts more quickly. Memorization of the text may be facilitated by identifying particular key words in the text and

[7]C. E. Seashore, *Psychology of Music.* New York: McGraw-Hill, Inc., 1938, p. 271.

associating them with many facets of personal experience. When one connection fails, often one can rely upon others to assist in the "recall" process.[8] Memorization is dependent upon a well-defined concept of the whole composition, and the relationship of the various parts to the whole. In short, a systematic, well-planned program of instruction, designed toward the goal of improving the musicianship and understanding of the singers, will reap many benefits—only one of which is improved memorization.

Topics for Discussion

1. What are some of the personal characteristics of successful choral directors you have known?

2. In your experience as a participant in various choral groups, have you ever sensed or felt that the director was unprepared for the rehearsal? What were your feelings? What was the reaction of the group?

3. Discuss the effects upon a chorus of a mechanistic approach to the teaching of new music.

4. Identify, if possible, the causes of poor pitch and intonation in some of the choral groups in which you have participated.

5. Recall the techniques utilized by the conductor for achieving effective interpretation in groups in which you have participated. Which techniques were most effective? Which were relatively ineffective?

6. Select a specific choral publication and try to analyze the difficulties that a particular group might encounter in rehearsals.

7. Why should accompanied selections be rehearsed, at least part of the time, without accompaniment?

---

[8]An approach to the identification of key words is as follows: Write the complete text of the choral selection on the chalkboard, and ask the group to follow it when singing, rather than the text in the octavo publication. Prior to the next repetition, erase certain nonessential words, such as *and, or, to,* etc. Then gradually on each subsequent repetition erase other words, until only a small group of key words remains. Then suggest to the group that they give vent to their imaginations and associate these key words with as many related ideas as possible. Finally, erase all the words from the chalkboard and test the singers' recall ability.

8. Discuss the factors that prevent the attainment of effective balance and blend in a choral group. How would you remedy them?

9. Analyze the difficulties, if any, that hamper your memorization of music.

10. Should music be memorized for all performances? For what reasons would you justify memorizing the music? For what reasons would you justify using the music at programs and concerts?

References

Cain, Noble, *Choral Music and Its Practice.* New York: M. Witmark & Sons, 1942. (Chapters 9, 11 and 12.)

Christy, Van A., *Glee Club and Chorus.* New York: G. Schirmer, Inc., 1940. (Chapters 4 and 5.)

Davison, Archibald T., *Choral Conducting.* Cambridge: Harvard University Press, 1945. (Chapters 4 and 5.)

Ehret, Walter, *The Choral Conductor's Handbook.* New York: Edward B. Marks Music Corp., 1959. (Chapters 1–7.)

Finn, William J., *The Art of the Choral Conductor.* Boston: C. C. Birchard & Co., 1939. (Chapters 5–12.)

Garretson, Robert L., *Helpful Hints for the Choir Director.* Champaign, Ill.: Collegiate Cap & Gown Co., 1956. (Chapter 2.)

Hoggard, Lara G., *Improving Music Reading in the Choral Rehearsal.* Delaware Water Gap, Pa.: Shawnee Press, Inc., 1947.

Jones, Archie N., Ed., *Music Education in Action: Basic Principles and Practical Methods.* Boston: Allyn and Bacon, Inc., 1960, pp. 172–184 and 186–199.

Krone, Max T., *The Chorus and Its Conductor.* Chicago: Neil A. Kjos Music Co., 1945. (Chapters 3, 6, and 7.)

Murray, Lyn, *Choral Technique Handbook.* Great Neck, N.Y.: The Staff Music Publishing Co., 1956.

Sunderman, Lloyd F., *Some Techniques for Choral Success.* Rockville Center, L.I., N.Y.: Belwin, Inc., 1952. (Chapters 6 and 7.)

Van Bodegraven, Paul, and Harry R. Wilson, *The School Music Con-ductor*. Chicago: Hall & McCreary Co., 1942. (Chapters 2, 4, 5, and 6.)

Wilson, Harry R., *A Guide for Choral Conductors*. New York: Silver Burdett Co., 1950. (Chapter 2.)

———, *Artistic Choral Singing*. New York: G. Schirmer, Inc., 1959. (Chapters 3, 4, 9, and 11.)

5

Programs and Concerts

PRACTICALLY ALL CHORAL CONDUCTORS have at one time or another encountered difficult problems in the preparation and presentation of choral programs. Problems of special concern are: locating a variety of worthwhile choral materials, planning and staging programs of an artistic nature, and planning and implementing effective publicity. The individual conductor solves these problems as best he can, and, in so doing, is constantly obtaining new ideas. Following are suggestions that may be helpful.

SELECTING THE MUSIC

The basic consideration in planning a choral program is selection of the music, since the success of the program depends to a great extent upon the quality and appropriateness of the music performed. Following are criteria that will serve as a guide and help the director select good, usable choral materials.

1. Is the text worth-while? Does it contain a message of sufficient value?

2. Is the music artistically conceived, and does it reflect the mood of the text?

3. Does the selection fit the needs and interests of the particular age group for which it is being selected?

4. Does the music fit the physical limitations of the singers? Is the *tessitura* of the parts too extreme? Are there extreme, awkward jumps in the voice parts which might prove difficult to execute?

5. Are the voice parts handled in such a manner as to make each part sufficiently interesting?

6. If the selection is an arrangement, is it done in an authentic musical style? Is the authenticity of the music sacrificed for clever musical effects? (This criterion applies to arrangements of the masters, as well as to folk-song arrangements.)

7. Does the music justify the rehearsal time necessary to prepare it?

8. Are all the various types and styles of choral music being represented in your selections, so that the singers may have the broadest educational experience possible?

CONSIDERING THE AUDIENCE

The choral conductor should consider the audience in his selection of music for particular programs. Music has a variety of moods and must be appropriate to the occasion. Aside from individual musical tastes, the nature of the event quite often determines the receptivity of the group to various types of music. Performances provided for certain festive banquets, for example, quite often preclude the exclusive use of sacred music. If the occasion warrants the use of popular and novelty tunes, they should be used. This need not imply a lowering of musical standards, for to include in the program a variety of styles and types of music is often the most effective way of evoking enthusiastic audience reaction.

It is important to the success of the program that rapport be established as soon as possible between the audience and the performers. Prior to the beginning of the choral concert, the audience is usually unsettled, as evidenced by considerable shuffling around, coughing, and general confusion. The conductor, therefore, should begin the program with music of a reasonably straightforward and vigorous nature in order to gain the complete attention of the audience. Placing selections of a quiet and subdued nature at the beginning of the program should be avoided, for here their effect would be lost. Such numbers would be more effective if placed later in the program when the audience is in a more receptive mood.

The conductor also should consider the audience in planning the length of the program. Fatigue-causing factors decrease not only the efficiency of the singers, but also the receptivity of the audience. Choral programs generally should not exceed an hour and a quarter, including intermission. It is desirable to end the program with the audience wanting to hear more, since such attitudes will promote more enthusiastic support of the choral organization.

ACHIEVING UNITY AND VARIETY

For an effective choral program, it is important that both unity and variety be maintained. Musical *variety* may be achieved by selecting numbers that contrast in style, mood, length, mode, and key. Variety in the program also may be obtained by:

1. featuring vocal and/or instrumental soloists, either within or in addition to the choral selections;

2. featuring either or both the treble and male sections of the choir in selected SSA and/or TTBB literature;

3. presenting several of the school's music groups, both vocal and instrumental, in a combined program.

Unity, as well as variety, is often achieved in the choral program by selecting publications that fall into three or more groups, and that have some definite literary or stylistic relationship to each other; for example, sacred songs, folk songs, and contemporary music. A prevalent practice is to begin the program with a group of sacred selections, representing various historical periods, and end the program with music of a lighter mood—either folk songs or contemporary music, depending upon the nature of the music. Program I illustrates this idea.

Program I

I

SACRED MUSIC

Jubilate Deo . . . . Orlandus Lassus

Day by Day We Magnify Thee . . . . . . George F. Handel

Contentment . . . . W. A. Mozart

Nunc Dimittis . . . . B. S. Kalinnikov

The Last Words of David . . . . Randall Thompson

II

CONTEMPORARY MUSIC

It Is Good to Be Merry . . . . Jean Berger

The Lobster Quadrille . . . . Irving Fine

Old Abram Brown . . . . Benjamin Britten

Sure on This Shining Night . . . . Samuel Barber

Whether Men Do Laugh or Weep . . . Ralph Vaughan Williams

III

FOLK SONGS

My Pretty Little Pink . . . . American Folk Song
arr. Joyce Barthelson

Dance to Your Daddie . . . . Scottish Nursery Song
arr. Edmund Rubbra

I Know My Love . . . . Irish Folk Song
arr. Parker-Shaw

May Day Carol . . . . English Folk Song
arr. Deems Taylor

Didn't My Lord Deliver Daniel? . . . . Spiritual
arr. Ralph Hunter

The program sequence from serious to lighter moods and from early periods to contemporary compositions is, of course, heavily enmeshed in tradition and has many merits. However, some directors feel that the group of sacred songs is likely to be better received if it is placed later in the program. Furthermore, they believe that audience rapport may be more firmly established if the program is begun with music of a lighter mood. Program II is presented as an alternative approach. The use of a choral prelude and a choral postlude may contribute further to the over-all effectiveness of the program.

Program II[1]

CHORAL PRELUDE

O Sing Your Songs . . . . Noble Cain

FOLK SONGS

Chiapanecas . . . . Mexican Dance Tune
arr. Harry R. Wilson

Shenandoah* . . . . Early American Barge Song
arr. Tom Scott

Soon-Ah Will Be Done† . . . . Spiritual
arr. William L. Dawson

Charlottown . . . . American Folk Song
arr. Charles F. Bryan

SACRED MUSIC

O Filii et Filiae . . . . Volckmar Leisring

Ave Verum Corpus . . . . W. A. Mozart

Salvation Is Created . . . . Paul Tschesnokov

Glory to God in the Highest . . . . Randall Thompson

CONTEMPORARY MUSIC

Younger Generation . . . . Aaron Copland

Old Abram Brown . . . . Benjamin Britten

Monotone . . . . Normand Lockwood

Stomp Your Foot (from *The Tender Land*) . . . Aaron Copland

CHORAL POSTLUDE

Onward, Ye Peoples . . . . Jean Sibelius

As any given audience will usually contain persons with varied
musical tastes, the conductor may wish to evoke maximum audience
response and enthusiasm by including on the program a variety of
musical styles and ensembles. In Program III, for example, Part I
includes sacred choral literature from various periods. In Part II,

---

[1] In this and subsequent programs, symbols indicate that selections are
to be sung by: (*) girls' glee club, (†) boys' glee club, and (‡) choir and
audience. Undesignated selections are to be sung by the mixed chorus.

while the singers are given a brief rest, the accompanist may be featured in two or three piano selections. Including an extended choral work of some type in Part III serves to highlight the first portion of the program, as well as providing a valuable musical experience for the participants. Following an intermission, it is often desirable to include music of a less serious nature. A group of folk songs from various countries, therefore, is appropriate at this point (Part IV). Further variety may be achieved by featuring one or more smaller vocal ensembles. Part V includes music particularly suitable for a men's octet, while in Part VI is included music most appropriate for a small mixed ensemble of 12/16 voices. As the culminating part of the program, the entire chorus may be featured in music of a light character. Selections from light opera and Broadway musicals are particularly appealing to most audiences and generally are enthusiastically received. Program III illustrates these ideas.

Program III

I

Cantantibus Organis . . . . Luca Marenzio

Cantate Domino Canticum Novum . . . . . Heinrich Schütz

Plorate Filii Israel . . . . Giacomo Carissimi

Ave Maria . . . . Sergei Rachmaninoff

Alleluia . . . . Alan Hovhaness

I I

Reflets dans l'eau . . . . Claude Debussy

Alborada del gracioso . . . . Maurice Ravel
Mary Jones, Pianist

I I I

Polovetzian Dance and Chorus
(from *Prince Igor*) . . . . Alexander Borodin

INTERMISSION

I V

Marching to Pretoria . . . . South African Veld Song
arr. Joseph Marais & Ruth Abbott

Ho-La-Hi . . . . German Folk Song
arr. Roger Fiske

Ching-A-Ring Chaw . . . . Minstrel Song
arr. Aaron Copland & Irving Fine

When Love Is Kind . . . . English Folk Song
arr. Salli Terri

Ezekiel Saw the Wheel . . . . Spiritual
arr. Harry Simeone

V

Josh'a Fit de Battle . . . . Spiritual
arr. Harvey Enders

All Through the Night . . . . Old Welch Song
arr. Roy Ringwald

Men's Octet

V I

Guantanamera . . . . Traditional Cuban Guajira
arr. Lou Hayward

Tenderly . . . . Walter Gross
arr. Harry Simeone

Mame . . . . Jerry Herman
arr. Martin Albert

The Modernaires

V I I

Neighbor's Chorus (from *La Jolie Parfumeuse*) Jacques Offenbach

Man of La Mancha (Choral Selections) . . . . . Mitch Leigh

Utilizing a Theme

Another means of achieving unity is to build the choral program
around some central theme. In choosing a theme, the conductor
should consider the various alternative subtopics around which the
music may be grouped. Provided the text of the music under consideration is related to the central theme or topic, a careful analysis of it
will often reveal many possibilities for natural groupings. Christmas,
Easter, and other important holidays or seasons provide a most natural opportunity for this type of thematic treatment. For the imaginative choral director the possibilities are unlimited. Consider the following suggestions.

Christmas programs

A most effective Christmas choral program may be achieved by selecting numbers that fall into one of the following three categories or groups: "The Advent," "The Nativity," and "The Rejoicing." By utilizing this theme, directors will find their problems somewhat minimized, since most of the choral publications of Christmas music may be placed into one of these three important periods of the Christmas season. Program IV illustrates this idea.

Program IV

CHORAL PRELUDE

Fanfare for Christmas Day . . . . Martin Shaw

THE ADVENT

While Shepherds Watch'd . . . . Old Yorkshire Carol
arr. Gustav Klemm

As Joseph Was A-Walking . . . . Don Malin

Lost in the Night . . . . Finnish Folk Melody
arr. F. M. Christiansen

The Three Kings . . . . Healey Willan

THE NATIVITY

Jesus, Jesus, Rest Your Head . . . . . . Appalachian Carol
arr. Niles-Warrell

Gentle Mary and Her Child . . . . . . Finnish Folk Melody
arr. Lundquist

Slumber Song of the Infant Jesus . . . François Auguste Gevaert

Silent Night* . . . . Franz Gruber

THE REJOICING

Hodie Christus Natus Est . . . . Jan Pieters Sweelinck

Go Tell It on the Mountain . . . . Spiritual
arr. John W. Work

Glory to God in the Highest . . . . G. B. Pergolesi

CHORAL POSTLUDE

Joy to the World‡ . . . . George F. Handel

Other categories that may be utilized in a similar manner for a Christmas program are: "The Star of Bethlehem," "The Nativity of the Christ Child," and "Joy to the World."

"Christmas Around the World" is a flexible theme for a school assembly program. The program may be built around carols from all countries. The use of a narrator may further enhance the effectiveness of the program.

While some directors prefer to use all-sacred music at Christmas, others may wish to include some secular, as well as sacred, music on their programs. When this is done the selections must be given careful consideration and judiciously placed on the program according to some particular plan. To help achieve this purpose, the theme "Music at Christmastide" is suggested. Appropriate categories for developing this theme are "Christmas Hymns and Carols," "Christmas Symbols and Greetings," and "Songs of Youth and Childhood." The program may be made even more effective through the use of an organ prelude, a brief choral prelude or "fanfare" prior to the processional, and the inclusion of selected masterworks for combined choirs immediately after the processional and just before the recessional. Further variety may be achieved by featuring different choral groups on all or part of each of the three major sections of the program. Program V illustrates this idea.

Program V

𝕸𝖚𝖘𝖎𝖈 𝖆𝖙 𝕮𝖍𝖗𝖎𝖘𝖙𝖒𝖆𝖘𝖙𝖎𝖉𝖊

ORGAN PRELUDE

Pastorale . . . . Arcangelo Corelli

Carol Rhapsody . . . . Richard Purvis
Organist: Mary Jones

CHORAL PRELUDE

Fanfare for Christmas Day . . . . Martin Shaw

PROCESSIONAL AND GLORIA

Adeste Fideles . . . . Old Latin Hymn

Gloria in Excelsis Deo . . . . Joseph Haydn
Combined Choirs

CHRISTMAS HYMNS AND CAROLS

Christmas Hymn . . . . 17th Century German

God Rest Ye Merry, Gentlemen . . . . . Old English Carol

Still, Still, Still . . . . Austrian Carol

Carol of the Drum . . . . Czech Carol
Concert Choir

CHRISTMAS SYMBOLS AND GREETINGS

Now Is the Caroling Season . . . . Dorothy Priesing

O Tannenbaum . . . . Traditional German

Silver Bells . . . . Jay Livingston

Mistletoe . . . . Fred Waring and Jerry Toti
Mixed Chorus

SONGS OF YOUTH AND CHILDHOOD

Sleigh Ride . . . . Leroy Anderson

Winter Wonderland . . . . Felix Bernard

Chestnuts Roasting on an Open Fire . . . . Torme and Wells

Toyland . . . . Victor Herbert
The Modernaires

CHORAL POSTLUDE AND RECESSIONAL

Hallelujah Chorus (from *Messiah*) . . . . George F. Handel
Combined Choirs

Joy to the World‡ . . . . George F. Handel
Audience and Combined Choirs

Other categories or titles for grouping choral selections are: "Music of the Masters," "Now We Go A-Caroling!," "The Many Moods of Christmas," "Christmas Favorites," "Yuletide Carols," "Loud Their Praises Sing!," and "Carols from Faraway Lands."

Inter-faith programs
In schools and colleges, where the student body or the membership of a choral group is representative of several faiths, a particularly appropriate program may include music from various religions. Program VI illustrates this idea.

Program VI

I

O Magnum Mysterium	Tomas Luis da Vittoria
Verbum Caro	Gaspar von Weerbeke
Angelus ad Pastores	Hans Leo Hassler
Weihnachts Motette	Luca Marenzio

I I

Mi Y'Mallel (Hanukkah Song)	Julius Chajes
Shuvu Adonay (Psalm 126)	Joseph Topel
Harken to My Pray'r (based on a Hebrew motif) .	Julius Chajes
El Yivneh Hagalil ("The Lord Will Build Galilee") .	Julius Chajes

I I I

Break Forth, O Beauteous Heavenly Light	J. S. Bach
Joseph Tender, Joseph Mine	Seth Calvisius
Lo, How a Rose E'er Blooming	Michael Praetorius
Hallelujah Chorus (from *Messiah*)	G. F. Handel

Easter program

An effective grouping of music for a sacred Easter program may be achieved by selecting music that falls in one of the following three categories: "The Holy Week," "The Crucifixion," and "The Resurrection."

General sacred programs

Groupings which may be used for general sacred choral music programs are: "The Spirit of Glorification," "The Spirit of Trust," and "The Spirit of Peace."

Secular programs

Appropriate groupings for a secular program are: "Songs of Work," "Songs of Love," and "Songs of Play," or "Songs of Nature," "Songs of Love," and "Songs of Travel." "I Hear America Singing" may be used as an appropriate title for a spring concert in which both sacred and secular music is included (Program VII).

Program VII

I HEAR AMERICA SINGING

CHORAL PRELUDE

A patriotic selection

OF HER FAITH

Sacred music of various faiths

OF HER PEOPLE

Secular or sacred music about particular societal organizations or famous individuals

PRAISE TO THE LAND OF THE FREE

Appropriate patriotic music

CHORAL POSTLUDE

America the Beautiful‡

Memorial Day program
An effective Memorial Day program may be achieved by grouping the music into the categories, "The Ideals," "The Men," and "The Land." Program VIII illustrates the use of this theme.

Program VIII

LEST WE FORGET

CHORAL PRELUDE

The Star-Spangled Banner‡ . . . . John S. Smith

THE IDEALS

Born to Be Free . . . . Ralph E. Williams
What Makes a Good American? . . . . . . Singer-Gearhart
Give Me Your Tired, Your Poor . . . . Irving Berlin

T H E   M E N

Anchors Aweigh . . . . Miles & Zimmerman

The Caissons Go Rolling Along . . . . E. L. Gruber

The Marines' Hymn . . . . L. Z. Phillips

The U.S. Air Force Song . . . . Robert Crawford

Reading: *O Captain! My Captain!* . . . . . . Walt Whitman

T H E   L A N D

This Is My Country . . . . Al Jacobs

Homeland . . . . Noble Cain

God Bless America . . . . Irving Berlin

America the Beautiful . . . . Samuel A. Ward

P O S T L U D E

Taps‡ . . . . U.S. Army Bugle Call

PUBLICIZING THE CONCERT

Adequate publicity is essential to the over-all success of concerts and programs. Singers perform best before an interested and enthusiastic audience; therefore, the director should continually search for means to increase the size and quality of the audience and to develop community support for the choral music program. Following are some suggested publicity techniques.

Newspaper Articles

Newspaper articles should be well written, giving all the vital information, such as date, time, place, soloists, and other special features of the program. This information, along with a copy of the program, should be forwarded to local newspapers well in advance of the program date. Most newspaper editors welcome such information and are usually willing to allot a limited amount of space in their publications as a public or community service. The younger set may be best reached by placing articles and announcements in the school newspaper. To provide a desirable learning experience for secondary school students, the director should designate individuals in the choral organization to handle this latter aspect of public relations.

Radio Announcements

In communities displaying a high degree of interest in school, church, and community affairs, certain local radio stations have cooperated by broadcasting spot announcements of programs, sometimes during local news broadcasts, a few days before the event is to occur. Some radio stations provide this assistance as a public service, without charge. In certain instances, stations have been known to interview choir members on radio broadcasts concerning aspects of a coming musical event or program.

Complimentary Tickets

Perhaps one of the most effective means of publicity is the distribution of a specified number of complimentary tickets to concerts for which there normally would be no admission charge. Tickets may be mailed to selected persons or a certain number may be provided each choir member for distribution. Individuals do not, as a rule, destroy so quickly items to which they attach some value; tickets may lie around a person's home in various conspicuous places, or be shuffled daily from one coat pocket to another. In this way, the tickets are a constant reminder of the coming event.

Mailing of Programs

In many instances, a certain clientele may be lured by mimeographed copies of the actual program. In contrast to the more formal appearance of a printed announcement, the actual program creates greater interest for the reader. Recognition of a familiar or favorite choral selection sometimes provides the necessary extra motivation for one to leave the confines of a comfortable home on a cold winter night.

Posters

Attractive, eye-catching posters also can be an effective means of attracting attention and stimulating interest in choral programs. Posters may be printed by local printing shops for a nominal fee, or in the school printing shop, where facilities exist. In most organizations there are a number of persons with artistic ability who are willing to prepare some attractive posters. These same individuals will usually assume the task of distribution. Posters should be placed where traffic is heavy—in locations where they will be seen by the largest number of persons—in schools, churches, stores, and various other locations in the community. Adequate study given to determining the best locations will reap later dividends.

Handbills and Public Carrier Advertisements

Although these media of communication are used infrequently because of their prohibitive cost, the distribution of handbills throughout a specified section of the community and the use of advertisements posted in or outside buses or other types of public transportation, are additional means of publicity. Their use would probably be justified only for certain types of programs which are financially self-supporting and presented on several consecutive evenings.

A less expensive means that may be profitably utilized is the distribution of automobile bumper stickers that advertise a specific event.

"Word-of-Mouth"

For many performances, a large segment of the audience will always consist of parents, relatives, and friends. This group is motivated to attend programs and concerts largely because of their individual interests in particular members of the performing organization. The "personal touch" is exceedingly important in all areas of human relations. Effective results may be achieved, therefore, if each participant in the organization is requested to extend a cordial, verbal invitation to at least 25 persons outside his immediate family. Each singer may be provided with a printed reminder, perhaps in the form of an invitation, to make certain he remembers to pass the word.

THE FINAL REHEARSAL

When programs are to be presented in a school or church auditorium, it is of paramount importance that the final rehearsal be held there so that the choir members may become accustomed to the acoustics and to the routine of the performance. (Indeed, the final rehearsal for any concert should always be held at the place where the concert is to be given.) The group should even practice marching on and off the risers so that this may be accomplished with a minimum of confusion.

Not everyone in an audience is capable of judging the musical accomplishments of a choral group, but most will surely be impressed one way or another by the singers' general appearance. The importance of uniform dress is discussed in Chapter Six. In addition, the director should emphasize the importance of bodily attitudes and facial expressions that reflect the mood of the music. Concentration upon the emotional qualities of the music not only will result in an improved performance and greater audience appreciation, but also will serve to reduce excessive nervousness in the singers.

The choir should be advised always to keep their eyes on the conductor and not on the audience, never to turn their heads to look at the person next to them, never to call attention to any mistakes, and to maintain absolute silence between selections and when off-stage. In short, the group should endeavor to be as "professional" as possible.

It is suggested that the director turn part of the rehearsal over to a student conductor or a qualified assistant and listen from the back of the auditorium for choral balance, blend, precision, intonation, and general effect. Most persons generally wish to do their best, and last-minute suggestions are sometimes taken more seriously than advice given during previous rehearsals.

When the music has been memorized, the singers are able to pay closer attention to the conductor and to his interpretative wishes. Most individuals will have memorized the music by the time it is perfected and ready for performance. There may be occasions, however, when it is necessary to use the music. In such instances the singers should be reminded to hold their music so that they can easily see the director—they should keep their noses out of the music and watch him as closely as possible, especially at the beginnings and ends of phrases.

Final instructions concerning the dress for the performance and the meeting time and place prior to the concert, should be reiterated at the last rehearsal. To avoid any misunderstanding, it is advisable to place these final instructions on both the bulletin board and the chalkboard. When the performance involves a number of different school, church, or community groups, it has been found profitable to mimeograph the instructions and distribute a copy to each individual involved.

The placement of the piano in relationship to the chorus must be considered if it is to enhance the effectiveness of the music, and if the correct balance and maximum security of the singers is to be achieved. Generally, the best location for a grand piano is immediately in front of the chorus, rather than at either side. If it is in this position, generally all singers can hear equally well. If only an upright piano is available, then the risers may be divided in the middle and the piano placed between the two sections in such a position that the director can be easily seen. This arrangement has the obvious disadvantage of dividing the singers, but it is outweighed by the increased tonal and rhythmic security they receive.

When a band or orchestral accompaniment is used, the chorus is usually placed on risers, or on the stage, immediately behind the band or orchestra (Plan 1). From the visual standpoint this arrangement is highly desirable. In addition, it usually enables all the per-

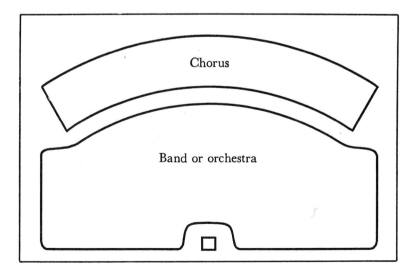

Plan 1.

formers to see the conductor more easily. The major problem that usually occurs with this arrangement lies in achieving a proper balance between the two groups. Unless an especially large choral group is performing, it is necessary to lessen considerably the volume of the instrumental group. This is sometimes best accomplished by assigning only one player to a part.

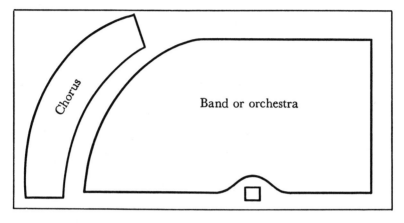

Plan 2.

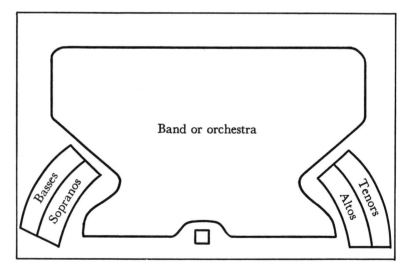

Plan 3.

When a satisfactory balance still cannot be achieved, the problem can be lessened to some extent by placing the chorus on one side of the stage, as illustrated in Plan 2. This arrangement allows for a somewhat better projection of the voices.

Still another possibility is to divide the chorus and place them on both sides of the instrumental group and to the front of the stage (Plan 3). This arrangement allows for the highest degree of voice projection, but has the obvious disadvantage of lessening, to some extent, the tonal and rhythmic security of the singers.

Musical productions presented on a stage with adequate facilities can be made much more effective by utilizing appropriate lighting. Through the use of various colors such as amber, red, blue, green, pink, etc., during the various choral selections, the emotional effects of the music can be heightened considerably. Colored gelatin for covering spot and stage lights may be obtained in a wide assortment of colors and hues (approximately 95). The imaginative director will be able to identify the predominant color mood or moods of each selection by careful analysis of the music. A cue sheet or marked copy of the program should be prepared for the electrician, and all lighting effects should be carefully set during the final rehearsal.

The director should stress the importance of an adequate warm-up before the performance. Choir members should be in the rehearsal room at least 45 minutes prior to the concert. It is important that the temperature of the rehearsal room be approximately that of the auditorium stage. Extreme differences in temperature can have a detrimental effect upon the singers' voices.

A little time devoted to vocalization, reviewing general procedures, and renewing in the singers' minds the tempi and general moods of the choral selections can prove a profitable aid in achieving an improved performance. It is especially important to review the order of the selections. It has been found helpful to start each number and sing at least the first phrase or so. This procedure helps the group accustom themselves to the routine of the program. Singers are often likely to be somewhat nervous and "on edge" immediately prior to the concert. The director, therefore, should endeavor to exert a calming influence on the group by talking and chatting informally with them in the warm-up room, prior to entering the auditorium stage.

Careful planning and attention to all the preceding details will contribute substantially to the over-all effectiveness of the choral concert.

Topics for Discussion

1. Maintain a file of programs of various types. Discuss the aspects of particular programs you like or dislike, in terms of musical value, unity and variety, and general format.

2. Discuss the importance of achieving audience rapport. By what means may this be achieved?

3. As a class project, prepare individual programs utilizing a unique thematic idea. Discuss the strengths and weaknesses of these programs in terms of the purposes for which they were designed.

4. Discuss the lighting effects that you feel would enhance the effectiveness of a particular choral program.

5. Discuss the effects of a good program of public relations upon concert attendance and school-community relationships.

6. Recall from your past experience as a singer, situations in which the director's careful attention to details during the final rehearsal contributed substantially to the effectiveness of the choral concert.

References

Cain, Noble, *Choral Music and Its Practice*. New York: M. Witmark & Sons, 1942. (Chapter 13.)

Christy, Van A., *Glee Club and Chorus*. New York: G. Schirmer, Inc., 1940. (Chapter 8.)

Davis, Ennis, *More Than a Pitchpipe*. Boston: C. C. Birchard & Co., 1941. (Chapter 8.)

Graham, Floyd F., *Public Relations in Music Education*. New York: Exposition Press, 1954. (Chapter 7.)

Krone, Max T., *The Chorus and Its Conductor*. Chicago: Neil A. Kjos Music Co., 1945. (Chapters 9 and 10.)

Wilson, Harry R., *A Guide for Choral Conductors*. New York: Silver Burdett Co., 1950. (Chapter 4.)

6

Planning and Organization

A PRACTICAL KNOWLEDGE OF planning and management procedures is as important to the choral director as the techniques of teaching. It is in this area that the ultimate success of the music program many times depends. The choral conductor is first an organizer, secondly a teacher, and finally a conductor. A conductor without an understanding of organizational procedures may be seriously impaired in his efforts to develop outstanding musical groups. Certain administrators often judge the effectiveness of the music director by his ability to plan and organize, rather than by his musicianship. They generally assume that the music teacher has had an adequate training in music; they cannot, however, always assume that the person is an effective organizer.

RECRUITING MEMBERS

The organization and development of new choral groups in various social institutions, or the improvement of established programs, may in some instances pose a considerable problem to the inexperienced director. A successful choral group demands at least a specific minimum membership, without which it is difficult to achieve any measurable degree of success; naturally the long-range development of a program depends to some extent upon this initial success. Following are suggestions that should prove profitable in the development of the choral music program.

Endeavor to show all individuals that singing can be an enjoyable and rewarding experience—not an uninteresting mechanical ritual! In schools this may be approached, in the beginning, through well-planned assembly sings.[1] In churches, informal sings may be promoted as an integral part of the program provided or sponsored for various age groups; that is, boy and girl scouts, youth groups, young married couples' groups, men's organizations, and women's societies.

At the outset of this program, one should utilize many familiar songs, sung in unison. Unison songs, sung with good tone quality and clear diction, can be a satisfying musical experience. This activity, plus the singing of many rounds and canons, provides the background for and serves as a means of stimulating interest in the later group harmonization of favorite songs. Although the emphasis always should be upon the recreational and not the technical aspects of the music, it is possible for the leader to stress the importance of good tone quality and clear diction as it relates to expressive singing. Remarks such as "When you open your mouths wide, you sound so much better," and "Enunciating your words makes this song more enjoyable to sing" contribute toward this end. Several highly successful choral programs were begun in this manner. From the musical seeds sown in these informal sings and assemblies grew a strong desire on the part of many individuals to explore further the vast wealth of choral literature.

With particular reference to school situations the following suggestions are offered. Inviting outstanding choral groups from neighboring schools and from the community at large to present assembly programs may serve to stimulate interest in singing and provide further impetus to the choral music program. One of the local barbershop quartets might prove of special interest to the male students. If individuals are to improve they must know what they are striving for. Hearing other choral groups provides a means through which students may evaluate their own attitudes and progress.

In certain schools, the problem of recruiting students for choral groups centers not in enrolling girls, but in obtaining an adequate

---

[1] For a variety of songs for recreational singing, see the listing at the end of this chapter.

number of boys in order to sing four-part music. The reasons for this problem are many, including schedule conflicts with other school activities and athletics. The problem usually resolves itself to ferreting out the remaining number of boys and/or making the choral program so attractive that an adequate number of singers are drawn from the other conflicting activities. The organization of a male quartet or octet, that may be called upon to sing in the school assembly or elsewhere in the community, can have a most desirable effect upon boys who consider choral singing to be a non-masculine activity. To combat this attitude, many successful directors have devoted special attention toward establishing rapport with, and subsequently recruiting in the organizations, the "leaders" of the school athletic teams. Once this group has been won over, the problem of recruiting additional boys is, for obvious reasons, lessened considerably.

Enlisting the cooperation of other teachers in the school to be on the lookout for students who display an interest in music, and who from all indications will be able to meet the established membership qualifications, has in many cases proved most profitable. Some are, to a greater or lesser extent, desirous of participating in choral groups, but are either unaware of their capabilities or lack courage enough to express their desires to the choral director.

It is advisable to heed the old adage, "Nothing succeeds like success." The director should assume an attitude of believing in the success of his choral groups. In other words, he should avoid pessimistic attitudes and should always be optimistic; he should think in positive terms and avoid negative thoughts. Such a positive attitude is contagious and can have a decidedly beneficial effect on one's singers.

STIMULATING INTEREST

Individuals are normally motivated in a variety of ways toward music participation. There are relatively few persons whose initial interest is entirely *intrinsic;* that is, whose desire to study music emerges primarily from a love of the music itself. Nevertheless, such interest not only is admirable, but also might well be considered one of the ultimate goals of music education. The skilled director who displays a great enthusiasm for music will normally make great strides in developing in individuals a love for music and the desire to explore and experience the vast wealth of music literature. It is not suggested, however, that the choir director depend entirely upon this intrinsic interest in the development of the choral music program. In a normal situation one will find that everyone is interested in music to a greater or lesser extent. The problem usually occurs with the half-interested person who either is "exploring" the activity or is merely anxious to remain in the company of his friends. The experienced director, however, takes a realistic attitude and utilizes many means to help accomplish his goal or purpose. Sometimes these techniques or methods are described as *extrinsic* means of motivation; that is, the director motivates such a person by taking advantage of interests that lie outside the music itself.

Following are suggestions that might be placed in either of the previously mentioned categories and, if utilized, will not only stimulate interest in music participation, but will also result in other values that contribute toward the development of the choral music program.

Exchange Concerts

Exchange concerts with neighboring communities are valuable in that they provide the singers a "yardstick" for the evaluation of the progress of their own music groups, as well as serving as an introduction to varied types of music literature. In addition, valuable and lasting friendships are sometimes made with individuals from other schools or communities.

Guest Conductors

Utilizing guest conductors for rehearsals and/or concerts can be a valuable musical experience for chorus members. As a result of this experience, singers necessarily become more alert to the conducting movements of the director and develop an awareness of varying types of musical interpretation. Such an arrangement can usually be made on an exchange basis with directors from neighboring institutions. Whenever financial arrangements can be made, however, it would seem highly desirable to invite a nationally known choral director to work with the choir or chorus for a day or two. These rehearsals may be culminated with a public concert. A practice that is quite prevalent, and certainly more economical, is for a number of neighboring schools or churches to join together and direct their efforts toward one large music festival. In the schools, lines of communication usually are set up by the principals; therefore, it is quite natural for those in the same athletic conference to join together for this event.

Attending Concerts

Group solidarity and a feeling of belonging—so important to the ultimate success of an organization—is often facilitated when members of a choral organization attend as a group various musical events presented in the community or in nearby towns or cities. In addition, a broader understanding and appreciation of music is often developed by the group.

Choral Recordings

Recordings of professional, collegiate, church, and community choral groups often are utilized for the introduction of new musical selections to the group, and as a means of studying various types of interpretation. A variety of listening experiences is helpful in broadening the singers' musical horizons, and in improving their musical tastes.

Tape Recordings as a Rehearsal Aid

The use of a tape recorder during rehearsals can be a most effective means of facilitating the singers' musical development. As an aid in improving the interpretation of a musical selection it is in many ways unsurpassable. Often the well-chosen words of the director, expressing a specific desired effect, are comparatively ineffective, whereas the playback of a tape recording usually has a profound effect on the listeners.

Production and Sale of Recordings

Provided the musical development of the organization warrants it, it may be found profitable to produce and sell recordings of the group. Such a project not only serves to stimulate the singers' interest, but also focuses the community's interest on the choral music program—certainly a most desirable objective.

Group Photographs

The experienced director is well aware of the enthusiasm created
when organization pictures are taken. They have for a long time
been utilized as a means of developing an *esprit de corps* in groups.
Persons of all ages enjoy pictures; however, school-age youth are
especially interested in photographs that include themselves and
their peers.

The Rehearsal Room Bulletin Board

The bulletin board may be used advantageously in many ways. It
may be utilized for posting general announcements, magazine or
newspaper articles of general interest, organization photographs, and
various other types of pictures and cartoons dealing with music
topics. All of these are effective means for stimulating interest in
music.

Radio and Television Broadcasts

The choral group that is fortunate enough to participate in radio or
television broadcasts will usually be highly motivated to prepare
for the program.[2] As a result, most directors would agree that such
opportunities are a profitable educational experience for the persons
involved. Many local stations, it will be found, are desirous of
scheduling programs of general public interest. Because the nature
or content of choral music programs is especially appropriate for
programming during the Christmas and Lenten seasons, many community music groups may be heard at these times. Unfortunately, in
some localities, opportunities such as these are not frequently available for all choral groups. In such instances, however, many directors endeavor to utilize these educational media in other ways—by
announcing at rehearsals various noteworthy programs, or posting
notices of them on the bulletin board. In this way the choir members
may benefit considerably from the programs themselves, as well as
from discussions of them later.

---

[2] Choral conductors should acquaint themselves with the hand signals
utilized in television studios. See the Appendix, p. 322.

Publication of Yearbooks or Newsletters

Many school music groups have found it extremely profitable, in terms of developing individual interest, to publish a yearly booklet in which photographs, comments on noteworthy performances, and various anecdotes of the organization's members are included. Other groups have published periodically a newsletter with equal success. In most groups there will be found persons who have a keen interest in writing, and who will benefit especially from this experience.

Awards

The presentation of letters, pins, or keys to outstanding students, or to students who have participated for a specified length of time, has long been found to be an effective means of stimulating interest in school music groups. Some directors have found the establishment of a point system to be quite effective in implementing such a plan. That is, to receive an award a student must be accredited with a specified number of points. For example, points may be given for attendance at regular and special rehearsals, participation in concerts and music festivals, or participation as a soloist or a member of an ensemble at competition-festivals or at various functions in the community. It is usually advisable for a committee, selected by the students, to work with the director in setting up the system of awards.

Social Events

Dances, mixers, and parties provide a splendid opportunity for the development of *esprit de corps* and the feeling of belonging which can contribute so much to the eventual success of an organization. In addition to serving as a means of strengthening personal relationships within the group, they can be utilized as money-making activities.

Newspaper Publicity

Adequate newspaper coverage of concerts can be of considerable assistance in the development of the choral music program. Newspaper editors are eager to receive information concerning news events that they believe will be of special community interest. Many newspapers have a prescribed format to be followed in preparing news items. Learning and following these procedures will often facilitate communication and the release of the news item. Also, early submission of an item that has no particular release time enables a paper to use it whenever it will fit their makeup. The importance of maintaining friendly relationships with the local newspaper staff, and submitting articles that are carefully written, cannot be overemphasized.

Competition-Festivals

Music competition-festivals may contribute substantially to the development of the music program. Adjudicators' remarks may prove helpful to singers and director alike. Opportunity is also provided for hearing other school music groups and for making many lasting acquaintances with individuals from other communities. Perhaps the major criticism levied against contests—not the only one, however— is that too much emphasis is placed upon the competitive aspects, and that singers often become emotionally disturbed and upset over the preparation, performance, and the final ratings. In certain instances this criticism may be true; however, it should not be interpreted as a final condemnation of contests. Prior to participation in such events, the director must prepare his groups emotionally for any eventual outcome. He will encourage concentrated effort during rehearsals and performances. Nevertheless, he will strive to develop in his singers a realistic life attitude. In our present-day society, too much emphasis is placed upon winning "first prize" in various fields of endeavor, or being named the star of the show or hero of the game. Individuals failing to reach their goals often assume a defeatist attitude. The director can render a genuine service to his singers by helping them to develop a proper perspective.

TESTING AND CLASSIFYING VOICES

Among choral directors, it is accepted procedure to audition individuals before admitting them to membership in an organization. In some cases, the audition is utilized as a means of limiting membership and obtaining the best voices for the choir or chorus. Directors using the procedure primarily for this purpose justify it as a necessary means of providing the selected singers with the best possible musical experience. It is most desirable to develop and maintain highly selective choral groups, provided that the remaining individuals are not prevented from participating in some group as a result. Opportunity for participation in a wide variety of choral groups and ensembles should be provided, in order that the musical and social needs of *all* interested persons are met. Auditions also provide a means of determining the singer's vocal range and voice quality, so that he may be assigned the voice part to which he is best suited, and by which he can make the best contribution to the group. Since most adolescent voices are quite unstable and are still in the process of change, it is advisable to retest voices periodically in order to avoid unnecessary strain from singing in the improper vocal range.

In classifying voices, two criteria must be taken into consideration—*range* and *quality*. The following procedure is suggested as a means of determining these factors.

Exercise 14.

Exercise 15.

1. Determine the approximate middle range of the student's voice and start there.
2. Utilizing Exercise 14, vocalize upward, noting the point at which excessive strain occurs and/or when the quality of the voice changes to any noticeable degree.
3. Utilizing Exercise 15, vocalize from the middle range downward, noting the point at which the quality of the voice changes. The low range is as important as the higher limits of the voice. Little benefit can come to a voice that is forced downward in an attempt to sing too low a part.

The voice ranges in Figure 42 are only approximate classifications, and the ranges of many singers do not always fall easily into

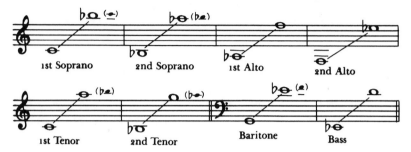

Fig. 42. A general classification of voice ranges of untrained singers.

these categories. The vocal range of some individuals may be considerably smaller than, and some may conceivably cover the ranges of two or more of, the classifications presented. In any case, one must listen carefully to the quality of the voice and determine the range in which it sounds most natural; that is, where the person sings with the best voice quality and with the least amount of strain or effort. This is most readily accomplished by utilizing some easy song material. The well-known English folk song "Drink to Me Only with Thine Eyes" is excellent for this purpose, and may be found in many song books compiled for community singing.

As a further guide in determining the proper voice classification of singers, the following voice qualities are considered characteristic:

1st Soprano—light, flutelike, lyric quality.
2nd Soprano—similar in range to the first soprano, but has a fuller, more dramatic type of voice quality.
1st Alto—similar in quality to the second soprano, but has a more fully developed lower range.
2nd Alto—a heavier, deeper voice quality, especially in the lower range, which is more fully developed than the first alto voice.
1st Tenor—light, lyric quality, especially in the upper range limits.
2nd Tenor—similar in range to the first tenor, but has a fuller, more dramatic, voice quality.
Baritone—often similar in quality to the second tenor, yet has a more fully developed middle and lower range. (Initial voice characteristics may be deceiving—it is in this category that many true tenor voices may be identified and developed. Periodical retesting is recommended.)
Bass—a heavier, darker, deeper quality, especially in the middle and lower ranges of the voice.

In addition to determining voice quality and range, many directors like to test the singer's ability to read music and to carry a harmony part independently. The above-mentioned song is also excellent for this purpose. A suggested procedure is as follows:[3]

1. For all treble voices, request the person to sing the alto part. For male voices, request the individual to sing either the bass or tenor part, depending upon the singer's vocal range and previous musical experience.
2. Provide the starting note and/or a short introduction. Accompany the singer, playing all the voice parts *except* the one he is requested to sing. (Omitting this part enables the director to determine more readily the extent to which a person can carry a part without help from others in his section. This information is invaluable in assigning seating in an organization. "Followers" may be judiciously placed between "leaders," and from the reading standpoint the total effectiveness of the choral group will be enhanced.)
3. With some singers, because of their lack of experience, it may be necessary to provide occasionally some assistance with their parts. This procedure is justifiable, because the director really is desirous of determining just how quickly the individuals "catch on." In some instances, repeating the song a time or two (with less assistance each time) will enable the director to determine the singer's musical memory and his ability to adjust and profit from assistance provided during rehearsals.

Following is a suggested list of other songs that might also be utilized for voice auditions. These selections may be located in most song books compiled for community singing.

1. *All Through the Night* (old Welch air)
2. *Tell Me Why* (College song)
3. *My Homeland* (from *Finlandia*)
4. *Believe Me if All Those Endearing Young Charms* (old English air)
5. *Annie Laurie*
6. *Fairest Lord Jesus* (German folk song)
7. *Juanita* (Spanish air)
8. *Jacob's Ladder* (spiritual)

Many choral directors have found it advantageous to maintain a permanent record of each choir member. Readily available information, included on personnel cards, can be helpful to the director in

---

[3] It is assumed that the individual has been oriented to the song through singing the melody during the previous part of the audition.

PERSONAL DATA

Name: _____

Address: _____

_____ Phone: _____

Previous musical experience: _____
_____

Part(s) previously sung: S1, S2, A1, A2, T1, T2, B1, B2

Height:_____ Weight: _____ Chest Measurement: _____

. . . .

Range: _____   Voice timbre: S. A. T. B.
                            Comments: _____
                            _____

Quality: 1 2 3 4 5   Part assigned: S1, S2, A1, A2
Intonation: 1 2 3 4 5   T1, T2, B1, B2
S. Reading: 1 2 3 4 5   Robe no. assigned: _____

*Fig. 43.   A sample personal data card. The vocal range in which the indi-
vidual sings with comparative ease may be indicated in red; the undeveloped
part of the vocal range may be indicated in blue.*

administering the total choral music program. Figure 43 shows a
sample card, which may be altered or adapted to suit individual
tastes.

SEATING ARRANGEMENTS

Choral directors generally have found, through experimentation, that
certain seating arrangements are preferable to others. The type of
arrangement selected usually depends upon several factors, including
the number of voices assigned or available for each part, the comparative voice qualities of various members, and the relative musical
experience of the singers. Following are several suggested seating
arrangements for mixed voices, and the advantages of each are mentioned.

The advantages of the arrangement of Plan 4 are as follows:

1. One of the problems confronting choral directors seems to be
   the development of tenor voices. When placed in the front of
   the choir the tenors are more easily heard and may therefore

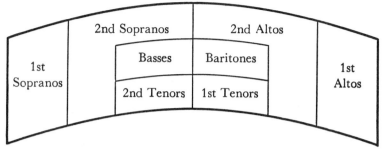

Plan 4.

sing in a more natural voice, thus improving the blend of the group.

2. At times the tenor part may need to be reinforced. If some of the second altos need to be utilized for this purpose, they will be close enough to effect a reasonably good blend.

3. The soprano and the bass sections are relatively close together. The proximity of these two sections, which are the outside two parts of the harmonic structure, can effect a stability to the chord and thus help to improve intonation.

4. The placement of a limited number of girls behind the boys can assist in the development of a better blend among the various sections. Choral blend is dependent to a great extent upon the ability of the singers to hear adequately the other parts. This seating arrangement in which the treble voices literally surround the male section increases the latter's awareness of the treble parts and provides increased tonal support, which is especially desirable for unstable adolescent male voices.

Another suggested arrangement may be utilized effectively when the membership of boys is adequate from the standpoint of both quantity and quality.

Plan 5.

The advantages of the arrangement of Plan 5 are as follows:

1. With the taller students in each section standing toward the outside, a more uniform appearance is achieved—producing a total
   effect noticeably different from the first arrangement. The difference in height between boys and girls is not pointed up by having
   them placed in the same row.
2. Both choirs are reasonably close together and may function as separate units if necessary. (In terms of providing variety to a choral
   program, the inclusion of numbers arranged exclusively for male
   or female voices is highly desirable.)
3. In the event the first tenor part needs to be reinforced with altos,
   the proximity of the second alto section would provide the maximum support and enable the singers to achieve a reasonably good
   blend.
4. The proximity of the soprano and bass sections effects a certain
   stability to the harmonic structure and assists in improving intonation.

The preceding arrangements have one advantage in common;
i.e., by grouping together the voices on the same part, a degree of
security is provided the singers, particularly those in young choirs.
However, with the security of singing next to others on the same part,
also goes the danger of some singers becoming overly dependent upon
certain leaders within their section. If these leaders happen to be
absent on a particular day, then the effectiveness of the entire section
is often hampered. It behooves the choral conductor, therefore, to
seek ways to strengthen the aural sense of all the singers in his
groups. The director's objective should be the development of individual security through vocal independence, not dependence. Seating arrangements may make their contribution to this end. After the
choir members have had a certain minimal musical training, it is desirable for the director to experiment with different seating arrangements, in which each singer will be better able to hear himself and to
evaluate his efforts properly.

One arrangement, used for a number of years, is the placement
of choir members by quartets; that is, SATB, or any combination
thereof.[4] The quartet seating arrangement usually results in the
achievement of better balance and blend. While the voice parts are
arranged in rows from the front to rear of the choir, each singer is
nevertheless able to hear himself better as well as the other voice

---

[4] Some directors utilize the arrangement of TSAB, while others prefer
BSAT.

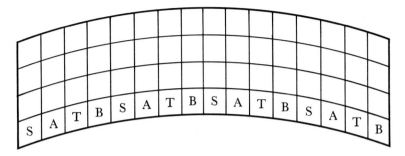

Plan 6.

parts. Some directors assign singers to quartets (or octets) on a continuing basis and utilize these groupings periodically for small ensemble practice. In school situations some directors, at intervals of about every six weeks, will request each quartet to sing a portion of selected music for evaluative purposes.

Another arrangement involves placing each singer as far as possible from another singing the same part, thus enabling him to hear his own voice better, and to evaluate his efforts toward improved tone quality, diction, balance and blend, and intonation. This arrangement, used by Robert Shaw, has been designated the "scrambled set-up" by Louis Diercks. Plan 7 is for a choir of nine first sopranos, seven second sopranos, eight first altos, seven second altos, five first tenors, seven second tenors, eight baritones, and seven basses.[5]

One of the most striking results that occurs through the use of this arrangement is that of improved balance and blend. The weaker singers are not in a position to affect the others in the section adversely, all singers can hear themselves better, and, with the sound

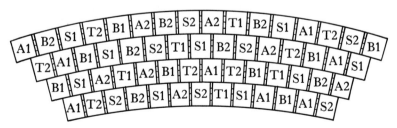

Plan 7.

[5] Louis H. Diercks, "The Individual in the Choral Situation," *The NATS Bulletin,* Vol. 17, No. 4, May 15, 1961, p. 7. Used by permission.

of any particular part coming from all areas of the choir, there seems to result a better fusion of sound.[6]

As the voices in the front row are nearest to and the first to reach the audience, it is desirable, with this set-up as well as with the quartet arrangement, to place the more selected singers in this position to serve as a "mask" to the choir.[7] Also, when a sufficient number of choir risers are available, it is desirable to space the singers slightly farther apart than usual. This also contributes to the objectives of this arrangement.

Some directors prefer to use either the quartet arrangement or the "scrambled set-up" exclusively, even when introducing new music. Others prefer to use a more conventional set-up until they feel the singers possess at least a minimal understanding of, and ability to sing, their parts. For this latter group, the following plan is suggested. While the singers are learning the music in their respective sections, the voice parts are at least divided or arranged so as to achieve a somewhat better blend, or fusion of sound, than in some of the traditional arrangements.

Basses	1st Tenors	Baritones	2nd Tenors
2nd Altos	1st Sopranos	1st Altos	2nd Sopranos

Plan 8.

Directors of junior high school choirs often use SAB music arrangements because of a lack of well-developed tenor voices. Plan 9 is suggested for this voice combination. Because of the insecurity of the male voices of this age group, it is desirable to place them toward the front of the choir where they will be partially surrounded by the

---

[6] Both the quartet arrangement and the "scrambled set-up" are desirable for use primarily with music of a homophonic texture. When performing polyphonic music, the choir should utilize a traditional formation, as the beauty of polyphony results from the interplay of the voice parts stemming from various sections of the choir.

[7] Diercks, *op. cit.*, p. 7.

female voices. This will insure their being heard more easily and will result in a better balance and blend. As the group progresses, and as the individual voices mature, it will become feasible to introduce some easy four-part (SATB) music. At this particular stage of devel-

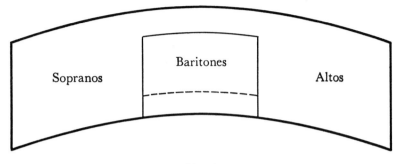

Plan 9.

opment, the tenor voices are likely to be especially insecure, and perhaps fewer in number. Therefore, seating this group of voices in front of the baritones will also contribute to the balance and blend of the group.

For directors of treble voice choirs, the following seating arrangements are suggested.

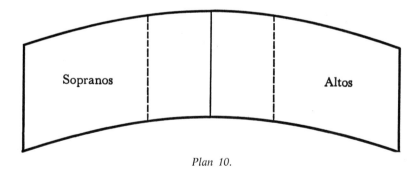

Plan 10.

Plan 10 is for grade school choirs comprised of selected fifth- and sixth-grade students. This plan allows for flexibility in rehearsing and programing a variety of music suitable for this age group. The repertoire will usually include a combination of two- and three-part music, some of which is learned in the general music class. When singing two-part music, the group placed in the center will sing their respective soprano or alto parts. When singing three-part music, they will sing the second soprano part. The group of students for this shifting, flexible role should be carefully selected through auditions held prior to the first rehearsal.

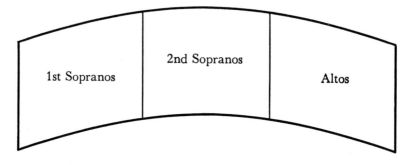

Plan 11.

Plan 11 is suggested for use with girls' glee clubs in junior and senior high school, and for women's choruses on the college or adult level. Although a sufficient amount of three-part music is available for use with girls' glee clubs, the more proficient organizations may ultimately desire to include some SSAA music in their repertoire, because of the more complete harmonic effects. In such instances, the alto parts will necessarily have to divide as indicated in Plan 12.

Since both SSA and SSAA arrangements may be utilized in a given program, both Plan 11 and Plan 12 will be found practical

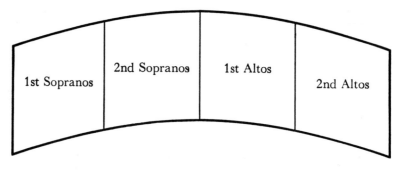

Plan 12.

because of the adjacency of the second soprano and the alto parts. To achieve an adequate balance, it may be necessary, for example, to assign a few second sopranos, designated as "roving singers," to the first alto part. Or, in other instances, a few first altos may be used to bolster the second soprano part. These two seating arrangements allow for a flexible assignment of adjacent parts to meet the requirements of the music being performed.

Following are two plans suitable for use with male glee clubs. The first arrangement generally will be found to be the most suitable, especially when an adequate number of boys is available to balance the parts. When, however, there occurs a definite lack of tenor

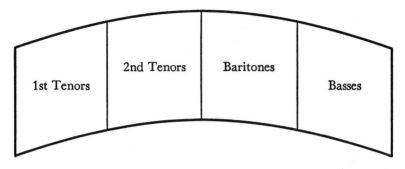

Plan 13.

voices, Plan 14 may provide an alternative solution. When the tenor voices are placed toward the front, they are more likely to be heard, and a more effective balance may be achieved.

In seating the students, it is advisable to place the stronger voices and some of the better readers toward the back of the group. In such a position they will be better able to assist the rest of the

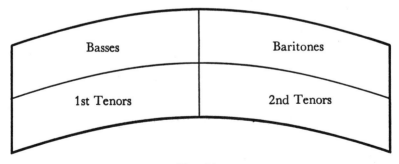

Plan 14.

singers. It is also advisable to scatter some of the better readers throughout the choir, in order to stabilize the group.

In an effort to achieve the best choral blend, it is advisable to place singers with strident voices between singers with a more natural vocal production. Individuals are inclined to simulate or assume the voice qualities of the persons nearest them. When several singers of a similar voice quality are seated together, this particular quality is sometimes strengthened and the resultant tone becomes stronger and out of proportion to the number of singers with that particular quality. The same principle may also adversely affect intonation. When several chronic flatters (caused by faulty voice production) are seated together, intonation problems are sometimes magnified. By distributing these singers within the group, intonation problems usually are lessened considerably.

Another factor to take into consideration is the height of the choir members. It is recommended that the taller individuals be placed toward the outside and the back of the group. Especially when the singers are on choral risers, this arrangement will enable them to see better the conducting movements of the director and will result in greater security of the entire group.

Directors will find it highly profitable to experiment with a variety of seating arrangements. Given plans may be found more effective with certain groups than with others, and periodical changes in arrangements will sometimes contribute to the betterment of the choral organization.

ASPECTS OF SCHEDULING

Scheduling classes appears to be one of the most troublesome of the administrative problems confronting high school choral directors today. In general, the problem is simply one of not enough time being allowed in the school schedule for the adequate rehearsal of choral groups. This lack of sufficient rehearsal time restricts the progress of the choral groups and, because of scheduling difficulties, talented pupils are sometimes "lost" to the music program. In some ways the problem is linked with a school's financial difficulties (the budget problem). Because of lack of funds for additional teachers, the music instructor is sometimes assigned additional classes to teach. Such is possible when the number of class meetings per week is either reduced or kept to a minimum. In any event, the result is the same—the teacher's effectiveness is lessened because his efforts are spread too thin.

The causes of poor scheduling will vary, of course, since very few school situations are identical in every respect. Some directors are concerned primarily because of the conflicts with athletics and other extracurricular activities. Of this group some are concerned about the problem of personnel, and others about the lack of adequate rehearsal facilities—the school gym sometimes being the only place to rehearse. Many directors express concern because they have little voice in determining class schedules. They believe the administration could benefit a great deal by discussing the problems with the teachers involved.

Of course, if the wishes of every teacher were adhered to the school schedule could conceivably run far into the night. Setting up the school schedule in order to meet best the needs of the students is, indeed, a difficult task for the school principal. It is understandable that pressure from various teachers, and parents too, could at times be quite annoying.

School music programs have made great strides in recent years. Since administrators have recognized the values of music, it has in an increasing number of cases progressed from a largely extracurricular subject, offered before or after school hours only, to a regular part of the school schedule. In larger school systems where it is necessary to offer duplicate classes in most subjects, fewer conflicts result between music and the other subjects. In smaller school systems, duplicate scheduling of classes is not always economically feasible, and music classes may therefore be offered only in the hours immediately before and after school. In such instances, a conflict usually results between the music classes and the school athletic program and other extracurricular activities.

In some cases, administrators have endeavored to meet the problem by shortening the periods in the school schedule, thus providing an opportunity for additional classes such as music and art to be offered during the regular school day. Also, in an effort to meet the problem, some schools have put into operation what might be termed the "sliding" or "staggered" schedule. In this plan the music class meets at a different period during each day of the week. Assuming that the student has at least one daily study period in a six-period schedule, he normally would not miss the same regularly scheduled class more than once every six days. Such a plan allows the music teacher to schedule the choral group for five rehearsals a week—the desirable number of rehearsals if one is to develop a topnotch choral group. If, however, the music class were scheduled only twice a week, the student would then miss a regularly scheduled class only once in every three-week period. When the sliding schedule is utilized for only two periods a week, for example on Tuesday and Thursday, it may be combined with rehearsals before or after school, or during an activity period, on Monday, Wednesday, and Friday. Thus, a total of five weekly rehearsals may be scheduled. From the standpoint of minimizing the amount of other classwork which the students would miss, this latter plan is perhaps more feasible and certainly more acceptable to other teachers than the former. For such a plan to operate successfully, it is necessary for the entire teaching staff, as well as the administration, to be in sympathy with the aims of the school music program. At best, however, the sliding schedule has drawbacks and should be utilized only as a stopgap measure until a time when the choral rehearsal may be scheduled at a definite and regular period during the school day.

Before a solution to scheduling problems can be achieved, it may be necessary for the music teacher to "sell" the administration on the values of music instruction and the importance of an adequate number of weekly rehearsals to the growth and development of the school music program. Effective solutions to scheduling problems usually can be achieved and will exist where an honest effort has been made, and where the administration is thoroughly cognizant of the values of music in meeting the individual needs of the students. Where the administration realizes the value of music, one will usually see not only a minimum of scheduling problems, but also a thoroughly trained and excellent music department staff.

Because the scheduling of classes is one of the most troublesome administrative problems confronting choral directors, it deserves concentrated study by both music teachers and administrators. Although an ideal solution to the problem is not always possible, a great deal can be accomplished by teachers and administrators sitting down together at the conference table. Increased insight into the other points of view will usually result in greater understanding and effect a more smoothly functioning school program.

SCHEDULING OF CLASSES

In developing a balanced choral music program, the director may frequently ask himself the question: "How many and what types of choral groups should I have?" Certainly the answer to this question depends upon the situation as it exists in a specific school. The size of the school and the existing need are both determining factors. The most successful school choral programs usually include a selected mixed choir or chorus with other junior groups utilized as "feeders" to the advanced group. This does not mean to suggest the exclusion of particular students from the advanced groups. Rather, it implies the necessity for choral experience commensurate with the level of each singer's musical development. The choral program should be based upon meeting the needs of all students and everyone with the desire should have the opportunity to participate in some choral group.

Students enter the junior high school with a variety of previous experiences and backgrounds. Although most of them have benefited from the general music program in the elementary school, certain pupils may have been fortunate enough to participate in grade school choruses comprised of selected fifth- and sixth-grade students. Figure 44 illustrates the type and variety of choral groups that the secondary school may endeavor to maintain. It also illustrates two alternative approaches in the basic pattern of organization. Both programs are predicated upon the philosophy of meeting the needs of all students; that is, providing an opportunity for all students who desire to participate in choral singing.

The general music class is usually required by most junior high schools. In some instances this class is required only of seventh-grade pupils, while being optional or elective for eighth-grade students. In general music classes students are provided the opportunity for exploring special music areas of particular interest. Although some schools enroll seventh-grade students in selective choral groups, it is felt desirable to delay this particular experience until the eighth grade. At this point the music program usually becomes somewhat more selective, and students are encouraged to participate in some activity of special interest, whether it be choral or instrumental music, fine or industrial arts, home economics, or some other area. In the late spring, before the close of school, seventh-grade students may be offered the opportunity of auditioning for the more selective eighth- and ninth-grade choral groups.

Junior High School Choral Groups

As indicated in Figure 44, the organization of special groups may follow one of several patterns. Some schools organize a boys' and girls' glee club for eighth- and ninth-grade students. Where school enrollments are particularly large, separate boys' and girls' glee clubs are often maintained for *both* eighth- and ninth-grade students. This plan of organization is predicated on the belief that during early

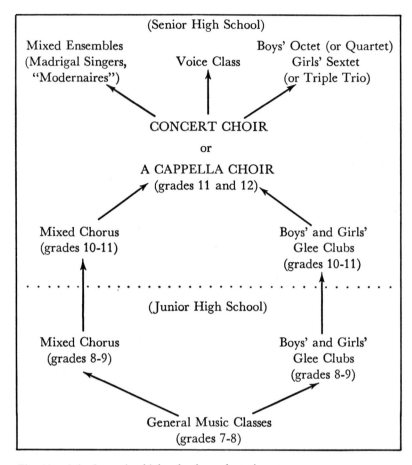

Fig. 44. *A junior-senior high school vocal music program.*

adolescence boys and girls enjoy participating in activities with their own sex. Another reason advanced is that the music composed or arranged for boys' and girls' glee clubs is more closely in line with their particular interests and musical tastes. Advocates of this position advance the argument that these types of musical experience differ considerably from the standard choral literature for mixed voices, and should be an integral part of the junior high school students' background.

Administrators and music educators in other schools feel that boys and girls should have experiences that bring them together under socially desirable conditions; thus they advocate the *mixed chorus* as the most ideal plan of organization. Still other schools, recognizing the values of both glee clubs and mixed groups, compromise between these two alternatives and thus capitalize upon the strong points of both plans of organization. In such instances, the girls' glee club will rehearse during school hours on Monday and Wednesday, and the boys' glee club on Tuesday and Thursday. Then on Friday the two groups are scheduled to meet together.[8] Thus, during their separate rehearsals the students have the opportunity to become better acquainted with the literature for either treble or male voices and also to rehearse separately their parts for the SATB (or SAB) music, which they will rehearse jointly on Friday of each week. For junior high schools this plan is advocated as the one that best meets the needs of the majority of students.

Senior High School Choral Groups

In the senior high school, the "combined" plan may also be followed for the "junior" groups, but owing to scheduling difficulties students generally participate in either a mixed chorus or a boys' or girls' glee club. (In certain schools, where the enrollment is exceptionally large, both types of organizations may be maintained.) It is desirable to schedule these groups for a minimum of three periods a week. In four-year high schools (grades 9–12) the membership in the mixed chorus (sometimes referred to as the junior choir) and the glee clubs is generally comprised of ninth- and tenth-grade students. In three-year high schools (grades 10–12), the membership in these organizations will consist primarily of tenth-grade students, plus a limited number of eleventh-grade students who were not accepted for membership in the advanced choir. Because of the greater variety and amount of literature available for mixed voices, and since in many cases it may be found more practical to schedule one organization than two, the mixed chorus is felt to be the most flexible arrangement. In addition, since all "senior" or advanced choral groups depend upon a "feeder" organization for their ultimate success, student experiences in singing music for mixed voices, prior to membership in the advanced choir, may contribute substantially to the degree of proficiency that the latter organization is able to achieve.

---

[8] Under this plan of organization, each student has the opportunity of participating in choral music activities for three periods a week; that is, either M.W.F. or T.Th.F. On alternate days he may be scheduled to participate in physical education, art, home economics, industrial arts, or some other class, depending upon the particular school situation.

The Concert Choir or the *A Cappella* Choir are two names commonly given the selective choral group in the high school. By maintaining a selective choral group, higher musical standards may be achieved and the participating singers will benefit from a higher quality of musical experiences. As the school's musical groups provide a "bridge of understanding" between the school and the community, it is highly desirable to develop and maintain a choral group that achieves and maintains high musical standards. The membership will usually consist of eleventh- and twelfth-grade students (juniors and seniors). A selective choral group, to achieve the maximum degree of musical proficiency, should rehearse at least five days a week, Monday through Friday. The most effective rehearsal time is during the morning, since students often become overly fatigued during the afternoon hours.

Small Vocal Ensembles

For particularly talented and interested students, experience in various small ensembles also should be provided. Participation in either an octet or a quartet will provide an outlet for boys who desire male companionship and the opportunity to explore the literature composed and arranged especially for male voices. Participation in a sextet or a triple trio will provide a similar opportunity for the especially talented girls in the school.

The mixed ensemble, however, will provide perhaps an even more unique musical experience. Many schools organize a group of "madrigal singers," with a membership usually of about 12 to 16 voices. These groups generally devote themselves to a thorough study of madrigal singing and related types of choral literature. Other schools will organize an ensemble, ranging from 16 to 32 voices, devoted to the study and performance of contemporary choral arrangements necessitating, for the most effective performance, a relatively small group of experienced singers. Although this latter group is given various names, the title "The Modernaires" is perhaps the most descriptive of the choral music performed. Often the school enrollment and the degree of student interest necessitates the maintenance of both types of small mixed choral ensembles. If only enough students are available for one mixed ensemble, however, then the group should study, rehearse, and perform a wide variety of choral literature, rather than devote itself to only one specific type or style of choral music.

Small vocal ensembles should rehearse at least twice weekly. In some cases the singers will find a "free" period during the day in which rehearsals can be scheduled. When this is not possible, rehearsals will necessarily have to be scheduled before or after school hours or during the noon period. The smaller ensembles, such as trios, quartets, sextets, and octets, may be encouraged to schedule, during the evening hours, an additional weekly rehearsal at one of the members' homes. Although the most desirable arrangement would have the director meet with the singers during every rehearsal, his busy schedule may not permit him to do so. Thus these evening rehearsals, if deemed necessary and desirable according to the local situation, may be conducted by one of the more talented student leaders. Such opportunity provides valuable experience for students who may eventually enter teacher training programs.

The Voice Class

The high school voice class is an adjunct of the choral program. It is usually taught by the choral director and may serve as a valuable training ground for student soloists in the advanced choir. Membership in the voice class should be highly selective and limited to those students who possess at least a reasonable degree of innate vocal and musical ability, and who display a keen interest in developing vocal proficiency. The particular value of the class approach to vocal training lies in the opportunity for singers to observe each other and discuss, as a group, common vocal difficulties. Although private vocal study is highly desirable, it may be financially prohibitive to many students; in addition, the opportunity for valuable group experience does not present itself. Therefore, by meeting the needs of a particularly interested and musically talented group, the high school voice class makes its unique contribution to the balanced vocal music curriculum.

THE MUSIC BUDGET

The cost of educating our children and running our schools has risen almost continually since World War II, and with increasing school enrollments the problem is likely to become more and more acute.

School administrators, therefore, must necessarily become more watchful of the amount of the budget allotted to each department. Departments not demonstrating a definite need for the funds allotted them are likely to suffer a decrease. Many music educators are especially concerned with the problem because, as their program develops and more students participate in it, additional funds are needed to purchase music and equipment necessary to provide the best musical education for the students. It will be found, however, that many administrators will become more interested in music classes as enrollments increase, because the more students enrolled, the lower the per capita cost.

Among administrators there seems to be a growing interest in a performance type of budget, where the emphasis is upon values received rather than upon only facts and figures. It might, therefore, prove most profitable for the music educator to discuss with his administrator the benefits of music study in terms of its aesthetic, expressive, cultural, personal-social, avocational, and vocational values. Although it will be found that most administrators are familiar with these benefits, it is nevertheless desirable for them to understand the music educator's particular point of view.

It is suggested that music educators demonstrate an interest in matters of budget. They should familiarize themselves with the proper procedures for requisitioning materials and keeping accounts and records. They should set up a system of filing and maintaining music materials, and should demonstrate knowledge of how to repair music. If administrators feel the music educator is spending money wisely, and if they feel that materials are well cared for, they are more inclined to grant a request for an increase in the music department budget.

After careful planning and estimating of future choral department needs, the director should discuss the budget problem with his administrator, emphasizing the fact that the quality of instruction depends to a great extent upon adequate teaching materials and equipment. A long-term approach to departmental needs is highly recommended. The budget for the approaching school year might be divided into three categories: "Desirable and Helpful," "Highly Desirable," and "Essential and Necessary" for the operation of the program during the ensuing school year. Administrators are generally most appreciative of such a businesslike approach to the budget problem. (See Budget 1.)

Another approach to the budget problem is simply to list the items under two rather than three categories. Under "Operating

Expenses," list the items necessary for the efficient functioning of the department for the ensuing year. Under "Non-recurring Expenses," list the items that are important to the further development of the program. As the funds for special purchases are not likely to be available in any one year for the acquisition of all special needs, the items in this category should be listed in the order of importance. This will be of considerable assistance to the administrator in making his final budget allotments. Any items that the school is unable to acquire in a particular year may be included on the following year's

Budget 1.

CHORAL MUSIC DEPARTMENT

Proposed Budget for the Academic Year ⸺.

A. *Essential and Necessary Items**   *Amount*

    1. Octavo music (SATB, SSA, TTBB) . $⸺
    2. Music folders . . . . ⸺
    3. Music storage boxes . . . . . . ⸺
    4. Choir robe maintenance and repairs . ⸺
    5. Equipment maintenance . . . . . ⸺
    6. Choral recordings and magnetic tapes . ⸺

        Total . . . . $⸺

B. *Highly Desirable Items†*

    1. Additional storage cabinets . . . . $⸺
    2. Photographs (for publicity purposes) . ⸺
    3. Additional rehearsal-room risers . . ⸺
    4. Additional chairs (for rehearsal room) ⸺
    5. Additional standing risers
       (for concerts) . . . . ⸺
    6. New bulletin board . . . . . . ⸺

        Total . . . . $⸺

C. *Desirable and Helpful Items*‡

1. Film rentals . . . . $_____
2. New tape-recording equipment . . . _____
3. Stereophonic record player . . . . _____
4. Transportation expenses
   (festivals and contests) . . . . _____
5. Additional piano (for student practice) _____
6. Visiting conductors' fees . . . . . _____

   Total . . . . $_____

   Grand Total . . . . $_____

   * Essential and necessary for operation of the department or activity during the ensuing school year.
   † Highly desirable for the future growth of the program.
   ‡ Desirable and helpful in terms of providing the best educational experiences for the students.

budget request and perhaps ranked proportionately higher in their order of importance. Sample Budget 2 illustrates this idea.

Budget 2.

CHORAL MUSIC DEPARTMENT

Proposed Budget for the Academic Year _____.

A. *Operating Expenses*   *Amount*
   1. Octavo music . . . . $_____
   2. Music folders . . . . _____
   3. Music storage boxes . . . . . . _____
   4. Choir robe maintenance . . . . . _____
   5. Equipment maintenance . . . . . _____
   6. Choral recordings and magnetic tapes . _____
   7. Photographs . . . . _____
   8. Film rentals . . . . _____
   9. Transportation expenses . . . . . _____

   Total . . . . $_____

B. *Non-recurring Expenses*

1. Additional chairs (for rehearsal room) $\$$_____
2. Additional risers . . . . _____
3. Additional piano . . . . _____
4. Additional storage cabinets . . . . _____
5. Choir robe replacements . . . . . _____
6. New tape-recording equipment . . . _____
7. Stereophonic record player . . . . _____

       Total . . . . $\$$_____

       Grand Total . . . . $\$$_____

Regardless of the type of form used, it has been found helpful to attach to the proposed budget a concise description of each item and the reasons for its need. This information will minimize questions of a general nature and thereby will facilitate the budget conference held between the choral director and the school administrator. Whenever conferences are held with administrators, a businesslike approach to the budget problem will be appreciated by the administrators and will be to the director's advantage. Choral directors should study carefully their groups' needs and be prepared to explain the importance of each item. They should be thoroughly familiar with the exact specifications of each requested item and be able to explain its desirability over other products of a similar nature but lower in cost.

CARE OF CHORAL MUSIC

Indexing and Storing

A practical method of indexing and storing choral music has many advantages. It protects the music from unnecessary wear and tear, selections are more easily located, and a much neater appearance usually is created in the rehearsal or storage room. In general, choral directors find one of the following two methods most suitable for their particular situations. Some directors prefer to place each choral selection into a separate 9 × 12-inch manila filing envelope, and to file the music alphabetically by title in a metal filing cabinet. So that selections may be easily located, the title is placed in the upper left-hand corner of the envelope, along with other pertinent information such as the composer, arranger, voice arrangement, and the number of available copies. For easy reference, these data may also be kept on 3 × 5-inch cards and maintained in a metal file box.

Fig. 45. Music file boxes provide a convenient means of music storage. Any selection may be easily located through the use of a file card system.

Other music directors prefer to file their music in 7½ × 11-inch reinforced cardboard boxes and to place them on conveniently situated shelves. (Boxes are available in 1-, 2-, and 3-inch widths.) Each box is labeled and/or numbered so that selections may be easily located. Again, all pertinent information, as previously described, should be placed on 3 × 5-inch cards, along with the number of the box in which the music is stored. All cards are filed alphabetically by title in a file box in order that pertinent data or particular selections may be easily located. If so desired, a separate index by composers is oftentimes helpful in quickly locating certain sought selections. Although file boxes are slightly more expensive than manila envelopes, the latter system will be found to be less expensive to maintain. As the music library grows, it will be found slightly less expensive to build additional shelves for storing music than to purchase additional filing cabinets.

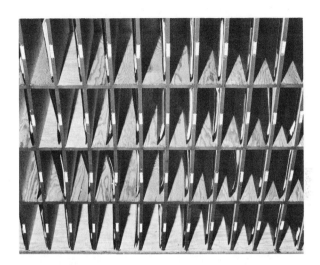

Fig. 46. Music cabinets conveniently situated enable each singer to obtain his music folder immediately upon entering the rehearsal room.

Distribution

Choral directors distribute the music in various ways. Most find it a practical time-saver to insert the music in a folder of some type. Some use a plain 9 × 12-inch manila filing folder; others use a folder with cloth reinforced edges (8½ × 11-inch) with flaps that hold the music in place and prevent it from falling out. This type of folder, although a bit more expensive than manila folders, is well worth the invest-ment; it is described in several music distributors' catalogs. Some directors utilize the services of student librarians to distribute the choral folders. Others put the music in a convenient place near the door so that each student may pick up a folder as he enters the room (cabinets may be constructed or purchased ready-made for this pur-pose). Choir members are instructed to leave the music in the same place when they leave the room. This procedure saves the director a great deal of time and energy and is a practice far superior to collect-ing music haphazardly left about the rehearsal room.

Fig. 47. Repairing music after it has been used will protect one's investment.

Repair

After choral selections have been removed from the folders and before they are filed, they should be examined carefully and repaired whenever necessary. A special tape, available in various widths and manufactured by the Minnesota Mining and Manufacturing Company, is particularly suitable for edging the backs of torn octavo publications. A special dispenser is available for applying this tape. The same company also manufactures a transparent, non-drying tape designed for use on torn music pages. All these items may be located in various music distributors' catalogs.

Many of the afore-mentioned duties can be assigned to responsible individuals. In this way, not only can excellent training be provided younger persons, but also the director can be freed from many time-consuming chores and can thereby devote more time to coordinating the total choral music program.

SELECTING CHOIR ROBES

Just what are some of the reasons for wearing choir robes? In the first place, uniform appearance in any organization places emphasis upon the group rather than the individual. It helps to develop pride and a feeling of belonging—a feeling so essential to the success of any organization. Choir robes provide a comparatively cool garment, which may be donned with little effort and in a minimum amount of time. This advantage is especially important when program schedules allow only a limited amount of time for warming-up and dressing. In this section we shall provide the directors of school and church choirs with information to facilitate the selection of choir robes.

Color

To obtain individuality, many school directors select robes and accessories in school colors. Two-tone color effects and pleasing color harmony may be achieved through use of various accessories that can be worn with the choir robe.

Many church choir directors purchase robes that blend with the interior decorations of the church. Some time ago, the Protestant church would not select choir robes in any color except black. However, the trend has recently been to use color in their choir apparel —color that is pleasing and that will blend with the interior of the church.

According to manufacturers, the most popular colors are shades of blue; shades of green are second, followed by black, with maroons in fourth place. White is used on special festive occasions such as Christmas and Easter, and also during the summer months. White not only is cooler, but also gives the congregation a feeling of coolness. In addition to the above-mentioned colors, a wide range of delicate pastels is now available and is becoming increasingly popular. You may choose from such colors as desert gold, spruce green, Neptune, Malibu, and Monarch, to name a few.

Style

Styles are available to fit many individual tastes. There are robes designed specifically for children's, intermediate, and adult choirs.

After the director determines his needs, he should consult various manufacturers' catalogs before any final decision is made. Upon request, manufacturers will provide detailed pictures, swatches of material, and other pertinent information.

Also available are special robes for the director. The director's robe is altered by changing the sleeve construction; this is done by gathering the fullness of the sleeve at the wrist into a cuff. Robes designed in this manner allow the director greater hand visibility and more freedom in his conducting movements.

Fabric

In certain areas or sections of the country in which there is heavy industry, unless the material is specially treated various chemical gases in the air will affect the robes, causing the color to fade. If one lives in such an area, great care should be taken to determine if the fabric has been treated to prevent fading; question the manufacturer before making a purchase. The quality of the fabric will determine the price of any given style. The better fabrics wear longer, retain their shape, have better draping qualities, do not fade, and are less subject to wrinkling.

Yoke

The foundation of any robe is the yoke, and the importance of its construction should not be overlooked. The yoke should be constructed of a substantial material so that it will hold its shape and prevent the body of the robe from drooping. It should be made of a strong, yet lightweight material—lightweight for comfort, but possessing strength so that the body will retain its shape. The yoke shouldn't shrink, and should lie flat when dry-cleaned.

Fluting

The fluting gathers the fullness of the robe over the shoulders and across the back, allowing the robe to hang in attractive folds. It is most desirable to purchase robes that have ample fullness so that large or small persons can wear them.

Size

Choir robes should be purchased in a range of sizes that will fit the average group. If money is available, a few extra robes should be bought, because it may not be possible to purchase the same material in future years to replace damaged robes or to increase the quantity. The mill that manufactures the fabric may discontinue it, and in dyeing new fabrics, it may not be possible to match the shade exactly. There should be at least two or more inches of hem at the bottom so that the robe may be lengthened if necessary.

Closures

Various companies recommend different kinds of closures. Here are some of the advantages and disadvantages of each: (*a*) Zipper— faster and looks neater; care must be taken that clothes are not snagged. (*b*) Hook and eye—hooks may pull out, causing some gapping. (*c*) Snap placket—snaps may pull out if they are merely tacked on; however, if care is taken they are quite satisfactory.

Care and Repair

When robes are purchased it is wise to sew in a numeral near the label; robes can then be assigned by number, and choir members are more readily assured of locating their own robes. The director may then maintain a list of all the choir members, and the robe number that is assigned to each member.

All robes should be treated as one would treat fine clothes. To be protected against moths, they should be stored when not in actual use; they should be kept in a closet, away from light, since light will fade some robes as it will other fabrics. All robes should be dry-cleaned at least once a year, preferably by the same firm. If proper care is taken, choir robes should last at least ten years or more. Money spent for the proper maintenance and upkeep of robes is a wise way in which to protect one's investment.

Topics for Discussion

1. Endeavor to recall, if possible, your personal reactions to hearing an outstanding choral group from a neighboring community. In

what way did this experience serve as a means of motivating your own music study?

2. What musical experiences or events in high school made the greatest impression upon you? In your opinion, why did these experiences make such a lasting impression?

3. Why are certain seating arrangements more effective with some choral groups than with others?

4. From a psychological basis, why is it more desirable to schedule music classes every day, rather than, for example, only twice a week?

5. Outline an instructional program in choral music designed to meet the musical and social needs of a specific school or church. What choral groups and ensembles would you organize, and what membership requirements would you specify?

6. In what way is the budget problem related to the scheduling problem?

7. Discuss the types of attire available for various choral groups. Discuss the appropriateness of attire in relation to various types of musical programs and in relation to particular occasions.

8. Utilizing the criteria of purpose, price or cost, and durability, discuss the strengths and weaknesses of essential musical equipment, such as pianos, risers, tape recorders, record players, directors' stands, music folders, music storage cabinets, choir robes (and storage cabinets), and other suitable attire.

9. What supplies and equipment do you consider basic to the effective operation of a balanced choral program?

References

Andrews, Frances M., and Clara E. Cockerille, *Your School Music Program*. Englewood Cliffs, N.J.: Prentice-Hall, Inc., 1958, pp. 190–216 and Chapter 16.

Cain, Noble, *Choral Music and Its Practice*. New York: M. Witmark & Sons, 1942. (Chapters 6, 7, and 8.)

Christy, Van A., *Glee Club and Chorus*. New York: G. Schirmer, Inc., 1940. (Chapters 2 and 3.)

Dykema, Peter W., and Karl W. Gehrkens, *The Teaching and Administration of High School Music.* Chicago: Summy-Birchard Publishing Co., 1941. (Chapters 29 and 30.)

Graham, Floyd F., *Public Relations in Music Education.* New York: Exposition Press, 1954. (Chapter 3.)

Klotman, Robert H., *Scheduling Music Classes.* Washington, D.C.: Music Educators National Conference, 1968.

Krone, Max T., *The Chorus and Its Conductor.* Chicago: Neil A. Kjos Music Co., 1945. (Chapters 1 and 2.)

Leeder, Joseph A., and William S. Haynie, *Music Education in the High School.* Englewood Cliffs, N.J.: Prentice-Hall, Inc., 1958, Chapter 3 and pp. 214–222.

MENC Committee on Music Rooms and Equipment, Elwyn Carter, Chairman, *Music Buildings, Rooms, and Equipment.* Revised and Enlarged Edition. Washington, D.C.: Music Educators National Conference, 1955.

Snyder, Keith D., *School Music Administration and Supervision.* Second Edition. Boston: Allyn and Bacon, Inc., 1965. (Chapters 7, 8, and 9.)

Sunderman, Lloyd F., *Choral Organization and Administration.* Rockville Centre, L.I., N.Y.: Belwin, Inc., 1954.

————, *Organization of the Church Choir.* Rockville Centre, L.I., N.Y.: Belwin, Inc., 1957. (Chapters 2 and 6.)

Van Bodegraven, Paul, and Harry R. Wilson, *The School Music Conductor.* Minneapolis: Schmitt, Hall & McCreary Co., 1942. (Chapters 10 and 12.)

Wilson, Harry R., *Artistic Choral Singing.* New York: G. Schirmer, Inc., 1959. (Chapter 10.)

———— and Jack L. Lyall, *Building a Church Choir.* Minneapolis: Schmitt, Hall & McCreary Co., 1957. (Chapter 5.)

Songs for Recreational Singing[9]

Introductory songs

Chumbara (*Sing Again,* No. 103)
Hello! (*Lead a Song,* p. 37)

---

[9] In organizing a "community sing," it is suggested that at least one song be selected from each of the categories listed.

How D'ye Do (*Songs for Every Purpose,* p. 217)
Laugh Provoker, A (*Songs for Every Purpose,* p. 226)
More We Get Together, The (Tune—Did You Ever See a Lassie?)
Sweetly Sings the Donkey (*Sing Along,* No. 129)
Viva L'Amour (*Singing Time,* No. 79)

Action songs

Alouette (*Sing Along,* No. 35)
Chiapanecas (*Sing Along,* No. 39)
Daisy Bell (*Sing Along,* No. 9)
Hokey Pokey (*Sing Again,* No. 96)
Little Tom Tinker (*Sing Along,* No. 130)
MacDonald's Farm (*Songs for Every Purpose,* p. 217)
Oh! Susanna (*Songs for Every Purpose,* p. 224)
Paw-Paw Patch (*Sing Again,* No. 100)
She'll Be Comin' Round the Mountain (*Sing Along,* No. 134)
Sweetly Sings the Donkey (*Sing Along,* No. 129)

Rounds and canons

Alleluia (*Rounds and Canons,* No. 24)
Alphabet, The (*Rounds and Canons,* No. 41)
At Summer Morn (*The Ditty Bag,* p. 123)
Are You Sleeping? (*Songs for Every Purpose,* p. 215)
Bell Doth Toll, The (*Songs for Every Purpose,* p. 23)
Christmas Bells (*Sing Again,* No. 94)
De Bezem (The Broom) (*Songs for Every Purpose,* p. 105)
Dona Nobis Pacem (*Sing Along,* No. 78)
Down in the Valley (*Sing Along,* No. 84)
Early to Bed (*Silver Book,* p. 135)
French Cathedrals (*Sing Together,* p. 101)
Haste Thee Nymph (*Sing Together,* p. 101)
Ifca's Castle (Carl Fischer Octavo, No. 4708)
Kookaburra (*The Ditty Bag,* p. 143)
Like as a Father (Cherubini) (*Sing Again,* No. 69)
Little Tom Tinker (*Sing Along,* No. 130)
Lovely Evening (*Sing Along,* No. 128)
Make New Friends (*The Ditty Bag,* p. 33)
Merrily, Merrily (*Songs for Every Purpose,* p. 11)
Merry Lark, The (*Sing Together,* p. 110)
Morning Comes Stealing (*Sing Along,* No. 45)
Morning Is Come (*Sing Together,* p. 111)
Music Alone Shall Live (Old German) (*Sing Again,* No. 68)
Non Nobis, Domine (William Byrd) (*Sing Again,* No. 70)

Old Hungarian Round (*Sing Together,* p. 111)
Old King Cole (*Sing Together,* p. 96)
Ol' Texas (*Sing Again,* No. 58)
Orchestra, The (*Sing Again,* No. 101)
Reuben and Rachael (*Songs for Every Purpose,* p. 200)
Rise Up, O Flame (Praetorius) (*Sing Together,* p. 11)
Row, Row, Row Your Boat (*Sing Along,* No. 141)
Scotland's Burning (*Songs for Every Purpose,* p. 30)
Sing Together (*Sing Together,* p. 99)
Where Is John? (*The Ditty Bag,* p. 65)
White Coral Bells (*The Ditty Bag,* p. 31)
Willie, Willie Will (Brahms) (*The Ditty Bag,* p. 141)
Wise Old Owl (*Singing Time,* No. 142)

Combined songs[10]

Are You Sleeping—Three Blind Mice (*Songs for Every Purpose,* pp. 215, 152)
Old Folks at Home—Humoresque (*Singing Time,* pp. 64, 75)
Keep the Home Fires Burning—The Long, Long Trail (*Twice 55,* No. 177, 178)
Solomon Levi—The Spanish Cavalier (*Songs for Every Purpose,* pp. 210, 211)
Tipperary—Pack up Your Troubles (Chappell Music Pub., N.Y.)
Yankee Doodle—Dixie (*Songs for Every Purpose,* pp. 229, 238)

Songs for harmonizing

All Through the Night (*Songs for Every Purpose,* p. 35)
Annie Laurie (*Sing Along,* No. 53)
Battle Hymn of the Republic (*Songs for Every Purpose,* p. 240)
Carry Me Back to Old Virginny (*Singing Time,* No. 27)
Clementine (*Sing Along,* No. 132)
Down by the Old Mill Stream (Forster Music Publishers, New York)
Down in the Valley (*Sing Along,* No. 84)
Good-bye, My Lover, Good-bye (*Songs for Every Purpose,* p. 191)
Home on the Range (*Sing Along,* No. 30)
In the Evening by the Moonlight (*Singing Time,* No. 62)
I've Been Workin' on the Railroad (*Sing Along,* No. 133)
Jacob's Ladder (*Sing Along,* No. 89)
Little Annie Rooney (*Sing Along,* No. 10)
Lullaby (*The Ditty Bag,* p. 125)

---

[10] For a variety of other combined songs, see Frederick Beckman, *Partner Songs.* Boston: Ginn & Company, 1958.

My Bonnie (*Songs for Every Purpose,* p. 215)
Old Folks at Home (*Sing Along,* No. 20)
On Top of Old Smoky (*Mitch Miller Community Song Book,* p. 5)
Standin' in the Need of Prayer (*Singing Time,* No. 120)
Tell Me Why (*Sing Along,* No. 16)

Closing songs

All Through the Night (*Songs for Every Purpose,* p. 35)
America (*Sing Along,* No. 138)
Auld Lang Syne (*Songs for Every Purpose,* p. 29)
Fare Thee Well (*Sing Together,* p. 12)
God Be with You (*Songs for Every Purpose,* No. 52)
God Bless America (Irving Berlin, Inc., 799 7th Ave., N.Y.)
Good Night (*Sing Together,* p. 49)
Good Night, Beloved (*Sing Together,* p. 58)
Good Night, Ladies (*Songs for Every Purpose,* p. 200)
Good Night to You All (*Rounds and Canons,* No. 60)
Jacob's Ladder (*Sing Along,* No. 89)
Now the Day Is Over (*Sing Along,* No. 66)
So Long, It's Been Good to Know Ya! (Folkways Music Publishers, N.Y.)
Softly Now the Light of Day (*Silver Book of Songs,* No. 170)
Taps (*Twice 55 Plus Songs,* No. 89)

Community Song Books

Abingdon Song Kit (by James F. Leisy). New York: Abingdon Press, 1957.

Choral Adventures (ed. Ruth Heller). Minneapolis: Schmitt, Hall & McCreary, 1951.

Christmas Caroler's Book in Song and Story (arr. Torstein O. Kramme). Minneapolis: Schmitt, Hall & McCreary, 1935.

Ditty Bag, The (by Janet E. Tobitt). Pleasantville, N.Y.: Janet E. Tobitt, 1946.

Golden Book of Favorite Songs, The. Minneapolis: Schmitt, Hall & McCreary, 1923.

Good Fellowship Songs. Delaware, Ohio: Cooperative Recreation Service.

Gray Book of Favorite Songs, The. Minneapolis: Schmitt, Hall & McCreary, 1924.

Mitch Miller Community Song Book (compiled and edited by Guy Freedman). New York: Remick Music Corp., 1962.

Noels (a collection of Christmas Carols by Marx and Anne Oberndorfer). Chicago: H. T. Fitzsimons, 1932.

Rounds and Canons (ed. Harry R. Wilson). Minneapolis: Schmitt, Hall & McCreary, 1943.

Silver Book of Songs. Minneapolis: Schmitt, Hall & McCreary, 1935.

Sing Again (arr. Harry R. Wilson). New York: J. J. Robbins, 1952.

Sing Along (arr. Harry R. Wilson). New York: J. J. Robbins, 1948.

Sing Around the Clock (arr. Howard Ross). New York: Chas. H. Hansen, 1955.

Sing Together. New York: Girl Scouts of the U.S.A., 1957.

Singing Time (arr. Ruth Heller and Walter Goodell). Minneapolis: Schmitt, Hall & McCreary, 1952.

Songs for Every Purpose and Occasion. Minneapolis: Schmitt, Hall & McCreary, 1938 (includes 357 songs).

Songs of the Four Seasons (by Harry R. Wilson). New York: Consolidated Music Publishers, 1960.

Songs of the Gay Nineties (ed. Hugo Frey). New York: J. J. Robbins, 1942.

Songs of Many Nations. Delaware, Ohio: Cooperative Recreation Service, 1962.

Spirituals (arr. William Stickles). New York: Chas. H. Hansen, 1946.

Time to Sing: Folio of Community Songs for Every Occasion (arr. G. M. Compagno). New York: Edw. B. Marks, 1938.

Twice 55 Community Songs (The Brown Book). Chicago: Summy-Birchard, 1957.

Twice 55 Community Songs (The Green Book). Chicago: Summy-Birchard, 1957.

Fred Waring Song Book (comp. and ed. Hawley Ades). Delaware Water Gap, Pa.: Shawnee Press, Inc., 1962.

Appendix

Source Information

CHORAL COMPOSERS

This chronological list does not presume to be complete, but it does include most of the major contributors to choral literature from approximately 1400 to the present. Although some composers may be known as well or perhaps even better for compositions other than choral music, all have made contributions significant enough to justify inclusion here. This list was developed primarily from the choral compositions listed in the Appendix. For representative compositions of these composers, see those lists beginning on pages 231, 286, and 289.

Pre-Renaissance (c. 1200–1400)

Perotin		
(Perotinus Magnus)	b. France	c. 1183–c. 1238
Adam de la Halle	b. Arras, France	c. 1240–1287
Guillaume de Machaut	b. France	c. 1304–1377

Renaissance Period (c. 1400–1600)

John Dunstable	b. Dunstable, Bedfordshire, England	c. 1370–1453
Gilles Binchois	b. Mons, in Hainaut, Belgium	c. 1400–1460
Guillaume Dufay	b. Hainaut, Belgium	c. 1400–1474
Johannes Okeghem	b. East Flanders, Belgium	c. 1430–1495
Pierre de La Rue	b. Tournai, Belgium	c. 1430–1518
Heinrich Isaac	b. Brabant, Belgium	c. 1450–1517
Josquin Després	b. Hainaut, Belgium	c. 1450–1521
Jacob Obrecht	b. Berg-op-Zoom, Netherlands	c. 1452–1505
Loyset Compère	b. ?	c. 1455–1518
Jean Mouton	b. Haut-Wignes, France	c. 1470–1522
Antoine Brumel	b. Flanders	c. 1475–1520
Martin Luther	b. Eislenben, Germany	1483–1546
Clément Janequin	b. Châtellerault, France	c. 1485-1560
Ludwig Senfl	b. Zurich, Germany	c. 1490–c. 1543
Costanzo Festa	b. Rome, Italy	c. 1490–1545
Nicolas Gombert	b. Flanders	c. 1490–1556
Thomas Créquillon	b. Ghent, Flanders, Belgium	?–1557
Claudin de Sermisy	b. France	c. 1490–1562

Passereau	Early 16th-Century French composer	?–?
Adrian Willaert	b. Bruges, Belgium	c. 1490–1562
Robert Carver	b. Scotland	c. 1491–c. 1546
Cristobal Morales	b. Seville, Spain	c. 1500–1553
Christopher Tye	b. England	c. 1500–c. 1572
Jacob Arcadelt	b. Liège, Belgium	c. 1505–1560
Claude Goudimel	b. Besançon, France	c. 1505–1572
Thomas Tallis	b. Leicestershire (?), England	c. 1505–1585
Jacobus Clemens	b. Ypres, Belgium	c. 1510–1556
Antonio Scandello	b. Brescia, Italy	1517–1580
Noe Faignient	b. Flanders, Belgium	?–1595
Hubert Waelvant	b. Tongerloo, Brabant	c. 1517–1595
Andrea Gabrieli	b. Venice, Italy	c. 1520–1586
Philippe de Monte	b. Mons, Belgium	1521–1603
Fernando Franco	b. La Serena, Mexico	c. 1525–1585
Giovanni Pierluigi da Palestrina	b. Palestrina, Italy	c. 1525–1594
Claude Le Jeune	b. Valenciennes, France	1528–1600
Richard Farrant	b. England	c. 1530–1581
Guillaume Costeley	b. Pont-Audemer, Normandy, France	1531–1606
Orlando di Lasso	b. Mons, Belgium	c. 1532–1594
Giaches de Wert	b. Weert, Netherlands	c. 1535–1596
William Byrd	b. Lincolnshire (?), England	c. 1543–1623
Marco Antonio Ingegneri	b. Verona, Italy	1545–1592
Giovanni Maria Nanino	b. Tivoli, Italy	1545–1607
Tomás Luis de Victoria	b. Avila, Spain	c. 1549–1611
Jacobus Gallus (Jacob Handl)	b. Reifnitz, Austria (now Yugoslavia)	1550–1591
Orazio Vecchi	b. Modena, Italy	c. 1550–1605
Giovanni Macque	b. Valenciennes, France	c. 1550–1614
Luca Marenzio	b. Coccaglio, Italy	1553–1599
Johannes Eccard	b. Mühlhausen, Germany	1553–1611
Bartholomeus Gesius	b. Müncheberg, Germany	c. 1555–1613
Sethus Calvisius	b. Gorsleben, Thuringia, Germany	1556–1615
Giovanni Gastoldi	b. Caravaggio, Italy	c. 1556–1622
Thomas Morley	b. England	1557–1602
Jacques Mauduit	b. Paris, France	1557–1627
Giovanni Croce	b. Chioggia, Italy	c. 1560–1609
Don Carlo Gesualdo	b. Naples, Italy	c. 1560–1613
Felice Anerio	b. Rome, Italy	c. 1560–1614
Melchior Vulpius	b. Wasungen, Germany	c. 1560–1615
Hieronymus Praetorius	b. Hamburg, Germany	1560–1629
Peter Philips	b. England	c. 1561–1628

Jacobo Peri	b. Florence, Italy	c. 1561–1633
Jan Pieterszoon Sweelinck	b. Deventer (or Amsterdam), Netherlands	1562–1621
John Dowland	b. Ireland, possibly in County Dublin	c. 1562–1626
John Bull	b. Somersetshire, England	c. 1562–1628
Francis Pilkington	b. England	c. 1562–1638
Ludocico da Viadana	b. Viadana, Italy	1564–1645
Gregor Aichinger	b. Regensburg, Germany	1564–1628
Michael Cavendish	b. England	c. 1565–1628
Adriano Banchieri	b. Bologna, Italy	1568–1634
Paul Peurl	b. Austria	c. 1570–1624
Thomas Tomkins	b. St. David's, England	c. 1572–1656
John Wilbye	b. Diss, Norfolk, England	1574–1638
Thomas Weelkes	b. England	c. 1575–1623
Melchior Franck	b. Zittau, Germany	c. 1579–1639
Michael East	b. London, England	c. 1580–c. 1648
Thomas Ford	b. England	c. 1580–1648
Orlando Gibbons	b. Oxford, England	1583–1625
Adrian Batten	b. London, England	c. 1585–1637

Baroque Period (c. 1600–1750)

Giulio Caccini	b. Rome, Italy	c. 1546–1618
Giovanni Gabrieli	b. Venice, Italy	c. 1557–1612
Hans Leo Hassler	b. Nuremberg, Germany	1564–1612
Claudio Monteverdi	b. Cremona, Italy	1567–1643
Michael Praetorius	b. Kreuzberg, Thuringia, Germany	c. 1571–1621
Gregorio Allegri	b. Rome, Italy	1582–1652
Melchior Teschner	b. Fraustadt, Silesia, Austria	1584–1635
Heinrich Schütz	b. Kostritz, Saxony, Germany	1585–1672
Johann Hermann Schein	b. Grünhain, Saxony, Germany	1586–1630
Samuel Scheidt	b. Halle, Saxony, Germany	1587–1654
Johann Cruger	b. Grossbreece, Prussia, Germany	1598–1662
Pier Francesco Cavalli	b. Crema, Italy	1602–1676
Orazio Benevoli	b. Rome, Italy	c. 1605–1672
Giacomo Carissimi	b. Marino, Italy	c. 1605–1674
Franz Tunder	b. Burg auf Fehmarn, Germany	c. 1614–1667
Matthew Locke	b. Exeter, England	c. 1630–1677
George Jeffries	b. England	?–1685
Jean-Baptiste Lully	b. Florence, Italy	1632–1687

Marc-Antoine Charpentier	b. Paris, France	c. 1634–1704
Dietrich Buxtehude	b. Helsingør, Denmark	c. 1637–1707
Johann Christoph Bach	b. Erfurt, Germany	c. 1642–1703
Pelham Humfrey	b. England	1647–1674
Michael Wise	b. Salisbury, England	c. 1648–1687
Johann Michael Bach	b. Arnstadt, Germany	c. 1648–1694
John Blow	b. Newark-on-Trent, Nottinghamshire, England	1649–1708
Johann Pachelbel	b. Nuremberg, Germany	1653–1707
Philipp Heinrich Erlebach	b. Esens, Germany	1657–1714
Giuseppe Pitoni[1]	b. Rieti, Italy	1657–1743
Henry Purcell	b. London, England	1659–1695
Alessandro Scarlatti	b. Palermo, Italy	1660–1725
Giacomo Antonio Perti	b. Crevalcore, Italy	1661–1756
Antonio Lotti	b. Venice, Italy	1667–1740
François Couperin	b. Paris, France	c. 1668–1733
Antonio Vivaldi	b. Venice, Italy	c. 1669–1741
Antonio Caldara	b. Venice, Italy	1670–1736
D. Pompeo Canniciari	b. Rome, Italy	c. 1670–1744
William Croft	b. Nether Ettington, Warwickshire	c. 1678–1727
Jean-Philippe Rameau	b. Dijon, France	1683–1764
Bohuslav Cernohorsky	b. Nimburg, Bohemia, Czechoslovakia	1684–1742
Francesco Durante	b. Frattamaggiore, Italy	c. 1684–1755
Johann Sebastian Bach	b. Eisenach, Thuringia, Germany	1685–1750
George Friedrich Handel	b. Halle, Saxony, Germany	1685–1759
Benedetto Marcello	b. Venice, Italy	c. 1686–1739
Niccola Antonio Porpora	b. Naples, Italy	1686–1768
Johan Helmich Roman	b. Stockholm, Sweden	c. 1694–1758
Georg Gottfried Wagner	b. Mühlberg, Saxony	c. 1698–1756
Johann Ernst Eberlin	b. Jettingen, Bavaria, Germany	1702–1762
Karl Heinrich Graun	b. Wahrenbrück, Germany	c. 1704–1759
Giovanni Battista Pergolesi	b. Jesi, Italy	1710–1736
Thomas Arne	b. London, England	1710–1778

---

[1] Although Pitoni lived during the Baroque period, he was of the Roman school, which rejected the styles and forms of Baroque music and directed their efforts toward composing liturgical music in the style of Palestrina.

Classic Period (1750–1820)

Wilhelm Friedemann Bach	b. Weimar, Germany	1710–1784
Gottfried August Homilius	b. Rosenthal, Germany	1714–1785
Christoph Willibald Gluck	b. Erasbach, Germany	1714–1787
Karl Philipp Emanuel Bach	b. Weimar, Germany	c. 1714–1788
Johann Heinrich Rolle	b. Quedlinburg, Germany	1716–1785
Johann Christoph Altnikol	b. Bevna (Silesia)	1719–1759
Johann Adam Hiller	b. Wendisch-Ossig, Germany	1728–1804
Johann C. F. Bach	b. Leipzig, Germany	1732–1795
Franz Joseph Haydn	b. Rohrau-on-the-Leitha, Austria	1732–1809
Michael Haydn	b. Rohrau, Austria	1737–1806
Carl Michael Bellman	b. Stockholm, Sweden	1740–1795
Quirino Gasparini	b. Bergamasco, Italy	?–1778
William Billings	b. Boston, Massachusetts	1746–1800
Andrew Law	b. Milford, Connecticut	1749–1821
Dimitri S. Bortniansky	b. Glukhov, Ukraine	1751–1825
Jacob French	Early American composer	1754–18??
Wolfgang Amadeus Mozart	b. Salzburg, Austria	1756–1791
Luigi Cherubini	b. Florence, Italy	1760–1842
Joseph Eybler	b. Schwechat (near Vienna), Austria	1764–1846
Thomas Attwood	b. London, England	1765–1838
John Wall Callcott	b. London, England	1766–1821
Ludwig van Beethoven	b. Bonn, Rhineland	1770–1827

Romantic Period (1800–1900)

Ignaz von Seyfried	b. Vienna, Austria	1776–1841
Johann Kaspar Aiblinger	b. Wasserburg, Bavaria, Germany	1779–1867
Konradin Kreutzer	b. Messkirch, Baden, Germany	1780–1849
Konrad Kocher	b. Ditzinger, Germany	1786–1872
Gioacchino Rossini	b. Pesaro, Italy	1792–1868
Franz Schubert	b. Lichtenthal, Austria	1797–1828
Alexis F. Lvov	b. Reval, Russia	1798–1870
Hector Berlioz	b. Côte-Saint-André, France	1803–1869
Felix Mendelssohn	b. Hamburg, Germany	1809–1847

Robert Schumann	b. Zwickau, Saxony, Germany	1810–1856
Samuel Sebastian Wesley	b. London, England	1810–1876
Franz Liszt	b. Raiding, Hungary	1811–1886
Richard Wagner	b. Leipzig, Germany	1813–1883
Giuseppe Verdi	b. Le Roncole, Italy	1813–1901
Robert Franz	b. Halle, Saxony, Germany	1815–1892
Charles François Gounod	b. Paris, France	1818–1893
Jacques Offenbach	b. Cologne, France	1819–1880
Franz Abt	b. Eilenburg, Germany	1819–1885
Louis Lewandowski	b. Wreschen (near Posen), Poland	1821–1904
César Franck	b. Liège, Belgium	1822–1890
Anton Bruckner	b. Ansfelden, Austria	1824–1896
Johann Strauss (Jr.)	b. Vienna, Austria	1825–1899
Stephen Collins Foster	b. Lawrenceville (Pittsburgh), Pennsylvania	1826–1864
François Auguste Gevaert	b. Huysse, Belgium	1828–1908
Johann von Herbeck	b. Vienna, Austria	1831–1877
August Soderman	b. Stockholm, Sweden	1832–1876
Alexander Borodin	b. St. Petersburg, Russia	1833–1887
Johannes Brahms	b. Hamburg, Germany	1833–1897
César Antonovitch Cui	b. Vilna, Russia	1835–1918
Camille Saint-Saëns	b. Paris, France	1835–1921
Mily A. Balakirev	b. Nizhny-Novgorod, Russia	1837–1910
Alfred Robert Gaul	b. Norwich, England	1837–1913
Theodore Dubois	b. Rosnay, Marne, France	1837–1924
Georges Bizet	b. Paris, France	1838–1875
Modest P. Moussorgsky	b. Karevo, Russia	1839–1881
Peter Ilich Tchaikovsky	b. Kamsko-Votkinsk, Russia	1840–1893
John Stainer	b. London, England	1840–1901
Antonin Dvořák	b. Mühlhausen, Bohemia, Czechoslovakia	1841–1904
Arthur Sullivan	b. London, England	1842–1900
Edvard Grieg	b. Bergen, Norway	1843–1907
Herman Schroeder	b. Quedlinburg, Germany	1843–1909
Nikolai A. Rimsky-Korsakov	b. Tikhvin, Russia	1844–1908
Gabriel Urbain Fauré	b. Pamiers, France	1845–1924
Alexander Arkhangelsky	b. Penza, Russia	1846–1924
Gustav Schreck	b. Zeulenroda, Germany	1849–1918
Vincent D'Indy	b. Paris, France	1851–1931
Hugo Jungst	b. Dresden, Germany	1853–1923
Alexander A. Kopylov	b. St. Petersburg, Russia	1854–1911
Engelbert Humperdinck	b. Siegburg, Germany	1854–1921
Stevan S. Mokranjac	b. Negotin, Serbia	1855–1914
Sergei I. Taneyev	b. Vladimir, Russia	1856–1915

Alexander Kastalsky	b. Moscow, Russia	1856–1926
Edward Elgar	b. Broadheath, England	1857–1934
Reginald De Koven	b. Middletown, Connecticut	1859–1920
Mikhail M. Ippolitov-Ivanov	b. Gatchina, Russia	1859–1935
Horatio Parker	b. Auburndale, Massachusetts	1863–1919
Pietro Mascagni	b. Leghorn, Italy	1863–1945
Richard Strauss	b. Munich, Germany	1864–1949
Alexander T. Gretchaninov	b. Moscow, Russia	1864–1956
Jean Sibelius	b. Tavastehus, Finland	1865–1957
Vassili S. Kalinnikov	b. Voin, Russia	1866–1901
Enrique Granados	b. Lérida, Catalonia, Spain	1867–1916
Granville Bantock	b. London, England	1868–1946
Henry Hadley	b. Somerville, Massachusetts	1871–1937
F. Melius Christiansen	b. Eidsvold, Norway	1871–1955
Max Reger	b. Brand, Bavaria	1873–1916
Sergei V. Rachmaninoff	b. Oneg, Novgorod, Russia	1873–1943
Hugh S. Roberton	b. Glasgow, Scotland	1874–1952
Samuel Coleridge-Taylor	b. London, England	1875–1912
Nikolai D. Leontovich	b. Monastirsh, Russia	1877–1921
Paul G. Tschesnokov	b. Government of Vladimir, Russia	1877–1921
Jean-Baptiste Faure	b. Mouline, Allier, France	1880–1914

Modern Period (1890 to present)

Claude Debussy	b. St. Germain-En-Lave, France	1862–1918
Frederick Delius	b. Bradford, England	1862–1934
Erik Satie	b. Honfleur, France	1866–1925
Ralph Vaughan Williams	b. Down Ampney, Gloucestershire, England	1872–1958
Gustav von Holst	b. Cheltenham, England	1874–1934
Arnold Schoenberg	b. Vienna, Austria	1874–1951
Charles Edward Ives	b. Danbury, Connecticut	1874–1954
Maurice Ravel	b. Ciboure, Basses-Pyrénées, France	1875–1937
Martin Shaw	b. London, England	1875–1958
Ernest Bloch	b. Geneva, Switzerland	1880–1959
Healey Willan	b. Balham, Surrey, England	1880–
Béla Bartók	b. Nagy Szent Miklós, Transylvania	1881–1945
Zoltán Kodály	b. Kecskemet, Hungary	1882–1967
Igor Stravinsky	b. Oranienbaum, Russia	1882–
Marcel Dupré	b. Rouen, France	1886–

Konstantin N. Shvedov	b. Moscow, Russia	1886–
Norris Lindsay Norden	b. Philadelphia, Pennsylvania	1887–1956
Heitor Villa-Lobos	b. Rio de Janeiro, Brazil	1887–1959
Ernst Toch	b. Vienna, Austria	1887–1964
Božidar Širola	b. Žakanj, Yugoslavia	1889–1956
Joseph W. Clokey	b. New Albany, Indiana	1890–
Heinrich Lemacher	b. Solingen, Germany	1891–
Arthur Honegger	b. Le Havre, France	1892–1955
Felix Labunski	b. Ksawerynowo, Poland	1892–
Darius Milhaud	b. Aix-en-Provence, France	1892–
Carl F. Mueller	b. Sheboygan, Wisconsin	1892–
John Jacob Niles	b. Louisville, Kentucky	1892–
Peter Warlock	b. London, England	1894–1930
(Philip Heseltine)		
Paul Hindemith	b. Hanau, Germany	1895–1963
Leo Sowerby	b. Grand Rapids, Michigan	1895–1968
Albert Hay Malotte	b. Philadelphia, Pennsylvania	1895–
Carl Orff	b. Munich, Germany	1895–
Richard Kountz	b. Pittsburgh, Pennsylvania	1896–1950
Howard Hanson	b. Wahoo, Nebraska	1896–
Virgil Thomson	b. Kansas City, Missouri	1896–
Henry Cowell	b. Menlo Park, California	1897–1965
Alexander Tansman	b. Lodz, Poland	1897–
Roy Harris	b. Lincoln County, Oklahoma	1898–
Hugh Ross	b. Langport, England	1898–
Francis Poulenc	b. Paris, France	1899–1963
Carlos Chávez	b. Mexico City, Mexico	1899–
Randall Thompson	b. New York, New York	1899–
George Antheil	b. Trenton, New Jersey	1900–1959
Aaron Copland	b. Brooklyn, New York	1900–
Otto Luening	b. Milwaukee, Wisconsin	1900–
Harry Robert Wilson	b. Salina, Kansas	1901–1968
Jean Berger	b. Hamm, Germany	1901–
Olaf C. Christiansen	b. Minneapolis, Minnesota	1901–
Edmund Rubbra	b. Northampton, England	1901–
Maurice Duruflé	b. Louviers, France	1902–
William Walton	b. Oldham, England	1902–
Paul Creston	b. New York, New York	1906–
Normand Lockwood	b. New York, New York	1906–
Dmitri Shostakovitch	b. St. Petersburg, Russia	1906–
Miklos Rozsa	b. Budapest, Hungary	1907–
Halsey Stevens	b. Scott, New York	c. 1908–
Samuel Barber	b. West Chester, Pennsylvania	1910–
Julius Chajes	b. Lwow, Poland	1910–
William Howard Schuman	b. New York, New York	1910–

Alan Hovhaness	b. Somerville, Massachusetts	1911–
Gian Carlo Menotti	b. Cadegliano, Italy	1911–
Franz Reizenstein	b. Nuremberg, Germany	1911–
Benjamin Britten	b. Lowestoft, Suffolk, England	1913–
Norman Dello Joio	b. New York, New York	1913–
Jan Meyerowitz	b. Breslau, Germany	1913–
Gardner Read	b. Evanston, Illinois	1913–
Irving Fine	b. Boston, Massachusetts	1914–1962
Cecil Effinger	b. Colorado Springs, Colorado	1914–
Vincent Persichetti	b. Philadelphia, Pennsylvania	1915–
Houston Bright	b. Midland, Texas	1916–
Scott Huston	b. Tacoma, Washington	1916–
Vaclav Nelhybel	b. Czechoslovakia	1919–
Paul Fetler	b. Philadelphia, Pennsylvania	1920–
William Bergsma	b. Oakland, California	1921–
Lukas Foss	b. Berlin, Germany	1922–
Anton Heiller	b. Vienna, Austria	1923–
Daniel Pinkham	b. Lynn, Massachusetts	1923–

CHORAL OCTAVO PUBLICATIONS

The octavo publications in this appendix have been included because they are particularly suitable for non-professional choral groups. SAB publications are included for junior high school cho-ruses; also listed are SSA and TTBB publications that are particu-larly appropriate for high school as well as college glee clubs. SATB publications have been included for use with high school, college or university, church, and community choirs and choruses. In addition, there are listed selections that are appropriate for chorus and band and/or orchestra.

Because of the comparatively large number of publications included for use with mixed voices (SATB), all the music below is listed under various categories in order that directors may easily locate certain sought selections. These categories are: "Christmas," "Easter and Lent," "Folk Songs and Spirituals," "Special Occasions," and "General: Sacred and Secular." For the other voice classifica-tions (SAB, SSA, TTBB), publications are included under three categories: "Sacred," "Secular," and "Folk Songs and Spirituals."

Following the title, composer, and/or arranger, the publisher and catalog number are given. This information is provided to facilitate the ordering of music. Since the director will wish to know if the selection is to be performed a cappella or with accompaniment, this information is also provided. All publications have been graded according to difficulty, using the following terms: Easy, Moderately easy, Medium, Moderately difficult, and Difficult. Also indicated are those publications having incidental solos. Prices have not been included since they are subject to change without notice. It is suggested that current prices be requested from local dealers immediately prior to placing an order; in this way, both billing and budgeting problems may be minimized. In selecting music, it is suggested that directors obtain for examination purposes single copies of particular octavo selections from the publisher or their local dealer, whichever is most convenient. The lists below provide a helpful starting point, but only through careful analysis of each selection in relation to the needs of a specific choral group will the most effective programing be achieved.

PUBLICATIONS FOR MIXED VOICES (SATB)

Christmas (Sacred and Secular)

And the Trees Do Moan (Carol of the Mountain Whites)—arr. Gaul
    Oliver Ditson Co. No. 332. Optional accompaniment. Moderately easy.

Angelus Ad Pastores Ait—Gabrieli
    C. F. Peters No. 5930. Two choirs—12 parts. Optional accompaniment. Difficult.

As Dew in Aprille (from *A Ceremony of Carols*)—Britten, arr. Harrison. Boosey & Hawkes No. 1829. Accompanied. Medium.

Behold a Star from Jacob Shining—Mendelssohn, arr. Davison
    E. C. Schirmer No. 1683. Organ accompaniment. Medium.

Birds and the Christ Child, The (Czechoslovakian carol)—arr. Krone
    Carl Fischer No. CM 4612. *A cappella*. Easy.

Born Today (Hodie Christus Natus Est)—Sweelinck
    B. F. Wood No. 291. Accompanied. Moderately difficult.

Break Forth, O Beauteous Heavenly Light—Bach
    Oliver Ditson No. 13744. Accompanied. Easy.

Carol of the Bells (Ukrainian carol; secular)—Leontovich, arr. Wilhousky. Carl Fischer No. CM 4604. *A cappella*. Easy.

Carol of the Birds (traditional French Christmas carol)—arr. Cain

Schmitt, Hall & McCreary No. 1507. Optional accompaniment. Moderately easy.

Carol of the Drum (Czech carol)—arr. Davis
B. F. Wood No. 568. Accompanied. Moderately easy.

Carol of the Italian Pipers (traditional carol)—arr. Zgodava
Shawnee Press No. A-967. Optional accompaniment. Moderately easy.

Carol of the Pifferari (Old Neopolitan Christmas air)—arr. Christy
Belwin No. 2190. *A cappella.* Easy.

Carol of the Russian Children (White Russian carol)—arr. Gaul
G. Schirmer No. 6770. Optional accompaniment. Moderately easy.

Clear and Calm Was the Holy Night—Nikolsky, arr. Gnotov
Witmark No. 5-W2860. *A cappella.* Medium.

Fanfare for Christmas Day—Shaw
G. Schirmer No. 8745. Optional organ accompaniment. Moderately easy.

Fum, Fum, Fum (Catalonian carol)—arr. Parker & Shaw
G. Schirmer No. 10182. *A cappella.* Medium.

Gentle Mary and Her Child (Finnish folk melody)—arr. Lundquist
Elkan-Vogel No. 1152. *A cappella.* Easy.

Glory to God in the Highest—Pergolesi
Wood No. 289. Organ accompaniment. Moderately difficult.

Gloucestershire Wassail (traditional old English yule song)—arr. Scott. Shawnee. Accompanied. Bass or alto solo. Medium.

Go Tell It on the Mountain (Christmas spiritual)—arr. Work
Galaxy No. 1532. *A cappella.* Sop. & ten. solos. Medium.

God Rest You Merry, Gentlemen (old English Christmas carol)—arr. Stevens. Pro Art No. 1420. Accompanied. Easy.

Good Christian Men, Rejoice (traditional German)—arr. Parker & Shaw G. Schirmer No. 10183. *A cappella.* Moderately easy.

He Is Born (Il est né)—arr. Roger Wagner
Lawson-Gould No. 663. *A cappella.* Easy.

Holly and the Ivy, The (traditional English)—arr. Parker & Shaw
G. Schirmer No. 10187. *A cappella.* Moderately easy.

How Unto Bethlehem (traditional Italian)—arr. Parker & Shaw
G. Schirmer No. 10194. *A cappella.* Moderately easy.

I Saw Three Ships (traditional English)—arr. Parker & Shaw
  G. Schirmer No. 10188. *A cappella.* Moderately easy.

I Wonder as I Wander (Appalachian carol)—arr. Niles & Horton
  G. Schirmer No. 8708. Optional accompaniment. Sop. or ten. solo. Medium.

Jesus, Jesus, Rest Your Head (Appalachian carol)—arr. Niles-Warrell
  G. Schirmer No. 8302. *A cappella.* Moderately easy.

Jesus' Christmas Lullaby (Bohemian folk song)—arr. Ehret
  Elkan-Vogel No. 1140. Accompanied. Moderately easy.

Joseph Dear, Oh Joseph Mild—Calvisius
  Associated No. A-396. *A cappella.* Medium.

Let Heaven Rejoice and Sing (German carol)—arr. Ehret
  Sam Fox No. CC7. Accompanied. Easy.

Lo, How a Rose E'er Blooming—Praetorius
  G. Schirmer No. 2484. *A cappella.* Easy.

Lost in the Night (Finnish folk melody)—arr. F. M. Christiansen
  Augsburg No. 119. *A cappella.* Sop. solo. Moderately difficult.

Mary Had a Baby—William L. Dawson
  Tuskegee No. 118. *A cappella.* Sop. solo. Medium.

Masters in this Hall (traditional French)—arr. Parker & Shaw
  G. Schirmer No. 10192. *A cappella.* Medium.

O Filii et Filiae—Leisring, arr. Row
  Row No. 283. *A cappella.* Medium.

O Magnum Mysterium (O Wondrous Nativity)—Vittoria
  G. Schirmer No. 7626. *A cappella.* Medium.

O Sanctissima (Sicilian folk melody)—arr. Parker & Shaw
  G. Schirmer No. 10194. *A cappella.* Medium.

Old Polish Christmas Carol—arr. Liszniewski
  Huntzinger No. 4049. *A cappella.* Easy.

Our Day of Joy Is Here Again (Swedish folk melody)—arr. Lundquist
  Elkan-Vogel No. 1151. *A cappella.* Easy.

Rocking (traditional Czech carol)—arr. Cashmore
  Oxford No. X 33. *A cappella.* Medium.

Saviour Is Born, The (Austrian carol)—arr. Warner
  Summy-Birchard No. 1578. Accompanied. Easy.

Shepherds All, and Shepherdesses (Allon, gay, gay)—Costeley
  Oxford No. OCS 1667. *A cappella.* Medium.

Shepherds' Chorus (from *Amahl and the Night Visitors*) —Menotti.
G. Schirmer No. 10801. Accompanied. Sop. and bass solos.
Medium.

Silent Night—arr. Sargent
Oxford No. OCS 876. *A cappella.* Moderately easy.

Sleep in Peace, O Heavenly Child—Michael Haydn
G. Schirmer No. 11043. Accompanied. Moderately easy.

Slumber Song of the Infant Jesus, The—Gevaert
E. C. Schirmer No. 1163. *A cappella.* Easy.

So Blest a Sight (English traditional) —arr. Parker & Shaw
G. Schirmer No. 10196. *A cappella.* Moderately easy.

Songs of Praise the Angels Sang (Swedish folk melody) —arr.
Lundquist. Elkan-Vogel No. 1145. *A cappella.* Easy.

Still, Still, Still—Luboff
Walton No. 3003. Accompanied. Easy.

There Shall a Star from Jacob—Mendelssohn
Carl Fischer No. CM 6228. Accompanied. Medium.

Three Far-Eastern Carols—Sargent
Oxford No. X73. *A cappella.* Moderately easy.

Three Kings, The—Willan
Carl Fischer No. OCS 718. *A cappella.* Medium.

Three Old English Carols—arr. Holst
Schmidt No. APS 15171. Accompanied. Moderately easy.

Two Folk Carols (Star in the South and Zither Carol) —arr. Sargent
Oxford No. X50. *A cappella.* Moderately easy.

We Wish You a Merry Christmas (English folk song; secular) —arr.
the Krones. Kjos 4006. Accompanied. Easy.

What Child Is This? (old English) —arr. Parker & Shaw
G. Schirmer No. 10199. *A cappella.* Moderately difficult.

When Christ Was Born of Mary Free—Fissinger
World Library of Sacred Music No. AC-1523-8. Percussion
accompaniment. Easy.

While by My Sheep (17th century Christian hymn) —arr. Jungst
G. Schirmer No. 2532. *A cappella.* Easy.

While Shepherds Watch'd (old Yorkshire carol) —arr. Klemn
Galaxy. Optional accompaniment. Moderately easy.

Ye Watchers and Ye Holy Ones (17th century German melody) —
arr. Davison. E. C. Schirmer No. 1780. Accompanied. Moderately easy.

Easter and Lent

Alleluia—Thompson
E. C. Schirmer No. 1786. *A cappella.* Moderately difficult.

Alleluia, Alleluia—Buxtehude
Theodore Presser No. 312-40668. Accompanied. Medium.

All Glory, Laud and Honor (Palm Sunday) —Teschner, arr. Cain
Flammer No. 81127. Accompanied. Easy.

Ave Verum Corpus—Byrd
Associated No. NYPMA 7. *A cappella.* Moderately easy.

Christ Is Arisen—Hassler
Edward B. Marks No. 26. *A cappella.* Moderately easy.

Christ Is Arisen—Schubert
E. C. Schirmer No. 2686. *A cappella.* Moderately easy.

Crucifixus (from *Mass in B minor*) —Bach
E. C. Schirmer No. 1174. Accompanied. Medium.

Ecce, Quomodo Moritur—Jacobus Gallus (Jacob Handl)
G. Schirmer No. 8424. *A cappella.* Moderately easy.

Four Chorales from the *Saint Matthew Passion*—Bach, ed. Ehret
Lawson-Gould No. 686. *A cappella.* Moderately easy.

God So Loved the World—Stainer
G. Schirmer No. 3798. *A cappella.* Easy.

Go to Dark Gethsemane—Noble
Gray No. CMR 501. *A cappella.* Medium.

He Never Said a Mumbalin' Word (spiritual) —arr. Wilson
Paull-Pioneer. *A cappella.* Moderately easy.

Hosanna (Palm Sunday) —F. M. Christiansen
Augsburg No. 57. *A cappella.* Difficult.

Lamb of God (Chorale 1540) —arr. F. M. Christiansen
Augsburg No. 133. *A cappella.* Easy.

Lamb of God—Hassler
Lawson-Gould No. 800. *A cappella.* Moderately easy.

Light Divine (scene and prayer from *Cavalleria Rusticana*) —Mascagni
G. Schirmer No. 5959. Accompanied. Moderately difficult.

Magdalena—Brahms
G. Schirmer No. 9953. *A cappella.* Medium.

My Saviour Dear, What Woe of Soul—Bach, arr. Lundquist
Willis No. 5503. *A cappella.* Medium.

O Lamb of God—Kalinnikov, arr. Ehret
Pro Art No. 1513. *A cappella.* Moderately easy.

Palms, The (Palm Sunday)—Faure, arr. Howorth
Belwin No. 790. Accompanied. Medium.

Ride On! Ride On! (Palm Sunday)—Thompson
Gray No. CMR 1154. *A cappella.* Medium.

Sunrise Alleluia—Bright
Shawnee Press No. A-852. Accompanied. Moderately easy.

Surely, He Bore Our Sorrows (Lent)—Victoria
E. C. Schirmer No. 2217. *A cappella.* Medium.

Surely He Hath Borne Our Grief (from *Messiah*)—Handel
G. Schirmer No. 6598. Accompanied. Medium.

Surrexit Pastor Bonus (The Shepherd Has Arisen)—Lasso
G. Schirmer No. 7685. *A cappella.* Medium.

This Is the Day which the Lord Hath Made—Bortniansky
Bourne No. BL3041. *A cappella.* Medium.

Three Lenten Poems of Richard Crashaw—Pinkham
E. C. Schirmer No. 2693. Accompanied. Medium.

Tree of Sorrow—Chávez
Mercury No. MP-113. *A cappella.* Difficult.

Were You There? (Negro spiritual)—arr. Burleigh
Ricordi No. NY423. Optional accompaniment. Medium.

Folk Songs and Spirituals

Ain'a That Good News? (spiritual)—arr. Dawson
Tuskegee No. 103. *A cappella.* Moderately easy.

An Eriskay Love Lilt (Irish folk song)—arr. Roberton
G. Schirmer No. 8107. *A cappella.* Moderately easy.

A Red, Red Rose (Scotch folk tune)—arr. Parker & Shaw
Lawson-Gould No. 645. *A cappella.* Ten. solo. Medium.

Ash Grove, The (Welsh air)—arr. Jacob
Oxford No. F9. *A cappella.* Easy.

Black Is the Color of My True Love's Hair (Appalachian folk song)
—arr. Churchill. Shawnee. Accompanied. Moderately easy.

Charlottown (Southern folk song) — arr. Bryan
J. Fischer No. 8136. *A cappella.* Medium.

Chilly Waters (Negro spiritual) — arr. Roberton
Curwen No. 61420. *A cappella.* Easy.

Ching-A-Ring Chaw (minstrel song) — arr. Copland-Fine
Boosey & Hawkes No. 5024. Accompanied. Medium.

Cicirinella (Italian folk song) — arr. Krone
Witmark No. 5-W2952. Accompanied. Easy.

Climbin' up the Mountain (spiritual) — arr. Smith
Kjos No. 1001. *A cappella.* Easy.

Czechoslovakian Dance Song — arr. Krone
Witmark No. 5-W2608. Optional accompaniment. Moderately
easy.

Dance to Your Daddie (Scottish nursery song) — arr. Rubbra
Mills No. 322. *A cappella.* Moderately easy.

Dark-Eyed Sailor, The (English folk song) — arr. Vaughan Williams
Galaxy No. 128. *A cappella.* Medium.

Didn't My Lord Deliver Daniel? (spiritual) — arr. Hunter
Lawson-Gould No. 957. Accompanied. Moderately easy.

Drunken Sailor, The (sea chantey) — arr. Schumann-Erickson
Bourne No. C3004. *A cappella.* Medium.

Each Little Flower (Swedish folk melody) — arr. Lundquist
Elkan-Vogel No. 1150. *A cappella.* Easy.

Early One Morning (English folk song) — arr. Christy
Schmitt, Hall & McCreary No. 1115. *A cappella.* Moderately easy.

Elijah Rock (spiritual) — arr. Hairston
Bourne No. S 1017. Optional accompaniment. Medium.

Every Time I Feel de Spirit (Negro spiritual) — arr. Murray
Boosey & Hawkes No. 1737. Accompanied. Moderately easy.

Ezekiel Saw the Wheel (Negro spiritual) — arr. Simeone
Shawnee. Accompanied. Moderately difficult.

Farmer's Daughters, The (traditional English) — arr. Williams
G. Schirmer No. 8116. *A cappella.* Easy.

Fireflies (Russian) — arr. Clough-Leighter
E. C. Schirmer No. 1178. *A cappella.* Easy.

Gay Fiesta (Mexican folk song) — arr. Riegger
Flammer No. 81149. Accompanied. Moderately easy.

Gently, Johnny, My Jingalo (English folk song)—arr. Parker & Shaw
    Lawson-Gould No. 643. *A cappella.* Moderately easy.

Girl with the Buckles on Her Shoes, The (Irish traditional)—arr.
    Nelson. G. Schirmer No. 10968. Accompanied. Moderately easy.

Good Night (German folk song)—arr. Manney
    B. F. Wood No. 292. Accompanied. Moderately easy.

Great Angelic Host, The (Norwegian folk song)—arr. Grieg
    Carl Fischer No. CM530.*A cappella.* Medium.

Hawaiian Lullaby—arr. Sargent
    Oxford No. X85. *A cappella.* Medium.

Ho-La-Hi (German folk song)—arr. Fiske
    Oxford No. F53. *A cappella.* Easy.

I Know My Love (Irish folk song)—arr. Parker & Shaw
    Lawson-Gould No. 657. Accompanied. Moderately easy.

I Ride an Old Paint—arr. Bright
    Shawnee A-661. *A cappella.* Moderately easy.

I Sowed the Seeds of Love (Hampshire folk song)—arr. Holst
    G. Schirmer No. 11149. *A cappella.* Medium.

I Won't Kiss Katy (Yugoslavian folk song)—arr. Smith-Aschen-
    brenner.
    Carl Fischer No. CM4596. *A cappella.* Moderately difficult.

Ifca's Castle (Czechoslovakian folk song)—arr. Harley-Aschen-
    brenner. Carl Fischer No. CM 4708. *A cappella.* Easy.

I'm Goin' to Sing (spiritual)—arr. Parker-Shaw
    Lawson-Gould No. 51101. *A cappella.* Moderately easy.

Jacob's Ladder (spiritual)—arr. Wilson. Ricordi No. NY 1476.
    Optional accompaniment. Moderately easy.

Jesus on the Water Side (spiritual)—arr. Aschenbrenner
    Fitzsimons No. 1032. *A cappella.* Moderately difficult.

Just as the Tide Was Flowing (English folk song)—arr. Vaughan
    Williams. Galaxy No. 130. *A cappella.* Medium.

Keys of My Heart, The (North country traditional song)—arr. Warrell
    G. Schirmer No. 8474. *A cappella.* Moderately easy.

Lark on the Morn, The (folk song from *Sommersetshire*)—arr.
    Thompson. E. C. Schirmer No. 1782. *A cappella.* Easy.

Linden Lea (old English folk song)—Vaughan Williams, arr. Salter
    Boosey & Hawkes No. 1401. Accompanied. Moderately easy.

Little Duck in the Meadow (Russian folk song)—arr. Nikolsky
    G. Schirmer No. 6669. *A cappella.* Moderately easy.

Marching to Pretoria (South African Veld song) —arr. Marais-Abbott
G. Schirmer No. 10423. Four-hand piano accompaniment. Easy.

Matthew, Mark, Luke and John (West country folk song) —arr. G. T.
Holst. G. Schirmer No. 8548. *A cappella.* Moderately easy.

Mayday Carol (English folk song) —arr. Taylor
J. Fischer No. 4838. Accompanied. Moderately easy.

Moan to the Moon (Estonian folk song) —arr. Hunter
Lawson-Gould No. 954. Accompanied. Moderately easy.

Morning Now Beckons (Czechoslovakian folk song) —arr. Manney
Wood No. 355. Accompanied. Easy.

My Lord, What a Mornin' (spiritual) —arr. Burleigh
Ricordi No. 412. *A cappella.* Medium.

My Pretty Little Pink (American folk song) —arr. Barthelson
Lawson-Gould No. 792. Accompanied. Moderately easy.

Oh, Dear! What Can the Matter Be? (English folk song) —arr. Bantock.
Joseph Williams, Ltd. No. 19. *A cappella.* Moderately easy.

Old Woman and the Peddler, The (old English) —arr. Kinscella
G. Schirmer No. 7819. *A cappella.* Moderately easy.

Peasant and His Oxen (Yugoslavian folk song) —arr. Smith-Aschenbrenner. Carl Fischer No. 4595. *A cappella.* Medium.

Prince Charlie's Farewell (traditional English air) —arr. Roberton
G. Schirmer No. 8512. *A cappella.* Moderately easy.

Ride the Chariot (spiritual) —arr. Smith
Kjos No. 1015. Optional accompaniment. Medium.

Rock-a My Soul (spiritual) —arr. De Vaux
Bourne No. 667. Accompanied. Moderately easy.

Russian Picnic (Based on Russian folk tunes) —arr. Enders
G. Schirmer No. 9544. Accompanied. Moderately easy.

Sakura Sakura (Japanese folk song) —arr. Hairston
Bourne No. J1. Optional accompaniment. Moderately easy.

See the Gipsies (Hungarian folk song) —arr. Kodály
Oxford No. W61. *A cappella.* Medium.

She's Like the Swallow (Newfoundland folk song) —arr. Chapman
Oxford X64. *A cappella.* Moderately easy.

Silver Moon Is Shining, The (Italian folk song) —arr. Davis
E. C. Schirmer No. 1754. *A cappella.* Moderately easy.

Soon-Ah Will Be Done (spiritual) —Dawson
Tuskegee No. 101. Optional accompaniment. Medium.

Spring of the Year, The (English folk song)—arr. Vaughan Williams
Galaxy No. 129. *A cappella.* Moderately easy.

Swiss Skiing Song—arr. Krone
Kjos No. 1200. *A cappella.* Moderately easy.

There Is a Balm in Gilead (spiritual)—arr. Dawson
Tuskegee No. 105. *A cappella.* Sop. Solo. Medium.

Tomorrow Shall Be My Dancing Day (Traditional English carol)—
arr. Willcocks. Oxford No. 84.141. *A cappella.* Medium.

Turtle Dove, The (English folk song)—arr. Vaughan Williams
G. Schirmer No. 8105. *A cappella.* Baritone solo. Moderately
easy.

Twenty Eighteen (English folk song)—arr. Taylor
J. Fischer No. 4846. Accompanied. Easy.

Two Negro Spirituals (Deep River and Dig My Grave)—arr. Burleigh
G. Schirmer No. 5815. *A cappella.* Medium.

Waltzing Matilda (Australian song)—arr. Wood
Oxford No. OCS 790. *A cappella.* Medium.

Waters Ripple and Flow (Czechoslovakian folk song)—arr. Taylor
J. Fischer No. 5676. Accompanied. Sop. & bar. solos. Moderately
difficult.

Weep, O Willow (Mountain tune)—arr. Lekberg
Summy-Birchard No. 5009. *A cappella.* Sop. solo. Medium.

Well-Beloved, The (Armenian folk song)—arr. Taylor
J. Fischer No. 4844. Accompanied. Sop. solo. Moderately easy.

When Love Is Kind (English folk song)—arr. Terri
Lawson-Gould No. 843. *A cappella.* Moderately easy.

Yarmouth Fair (English folk song)—arr. Warlock
Oxford No. X37. *A cappella.* Moderately easy.

Special Occasions (Commencement, Thanksgiving, Patriotic)

Battle Hymn of the Republic (patriotic)—Steffe, arr. Ringwald
Shawnee. Accompanied. Moderately easy.

Battle Hymn of the Republic (patriotic)—Steffe, arr. Wilhousky
Carl Fischer No. CM 4743. Accompanied. Medium.

Come, Let Us Sing to the Lord (Thanksgiving)—Schvedov, arr. Cain
Boosey & Hawkes No. 1800. *A cappella.* Difficult.

Give Me Your Tired, Your Poor (patriotic or commencement) —Berlin, arr. Ringwald. Shawnee. Accompanied. Medium.

Give Thanks (Thanksgiving) —Williams
Flammer No. 84191. Accompanied. Sop. solo. Easy.

In Solemn Silence (a memorial anthem) —Ippolitov-Ivanov, arr. Wilhousky. Carl Fischer No. 635. *A cappella.* Medium.

Land of Hope and Glory (commencement) —Elgar
Boosey & Hawkes No. 1161. Accompanied. Moderately easy.

Let All Creatures of God His Praises Sing (Thanksgiving) —Kalinnikov, arr. Cain. Boosey & Hawkes No. 1801. *A cappella.* Medium.

Now Thank We All Our God (Thanksgiving) —Cruger, arr. Holst
Kjos No. 5138. Accompanied. Moderately easy.

Onward, Ye Peoples! (commencement) —Sibelius, arr. Lefebvre
Galaxy No. 938–10. Accompanied. Medium.

Prayer of Thanksgiving (Netherlands folk song; Thanksgiving) —arr. Kremser. G. Schirmer No. 4345. Accompanied. Easy.

Preludes to Eternity (commencement) —Liszt, arr. Reibold
Summy-Birchard No. 1442. Accompanied. Moderately difficult.

Recessional (Memorial Day) —DeKoven
Presser No. 322–35015. Accompanied. Moderately easy.

To Music (commencement) —Schubert, arr. Wilson
Schmitt, Hall & McCreary No. 1070. Accompanied. Moderately easy.

General: Sacred

Absalom—Tomkins
Chappell No. 6140. *A cappella.* Medium

Adoramus Te—Corsi, arr. Greyson
Bourne No. ES15. *A cappella.* Moderately easy.

Adoramus Te—Gasparini
Belwin No. 2148. *A cappella.* Medium.

Adoramus Te—Lassus
Music Press No. MP-76. *A cappella.* Medium.

Adoramus Te—Mozart
G. Schirmer No. 9932. Optional accompaniment. Moderately easy.

Adoramus Te, Christe—Palestrina
   Carl Fischer No. CM6578. *A cappella.* Easy.

Agnus Dei—Lotti
   Edw. B. Marks. No. 4365. *A cappella.* Moderately easy.

Agnus Dei—Morley, arr. Greyson
   Bourne No. ES36. *A cappella.* Medium.

Agnus Dei—Pergolesi
   Mercury No. MC 147. Accompanied. Medium.

Agnus Dei (from *Deutsche Messe*)—Schubert
   Piedmont No. 4449. Accompanied. Medium.

Agnus Dei—Victoria
   Lawson-Gould No. 925. *A cappella.* Medium.

All Breathing Life (from the motet *Sing Ye to the Lord*)—Bach
   G. Schirmer No. 7470. Optional accompaniment. Difficult.

All Glory Be to God on High (melody of Gregorian origin)—arr.
   Malin. Summy-Birchard No. 345. Accompanied. Moderately easy.

All Hail the Power—Vaughan Williams
   Oxford. Accompanied. Moderately difficult.

All the Earth Doth Worship Thee—Handel
   Ricordi No. NY2030. Accompanied. Moderately easy.

Alleluia (from the motet *Exultate, Jubilate*)—Mozart, arr. Rosen-
   berg. Carl Fischer No. 541. Accompanied. Medium. (Sop. solo,
   difficult.)

Alleluia—Thompson
   E. C. Schirmer No. 1786. *A cappella.* Moderately difficult.

Alleluja—J. S. Bach
   Peters No. 6106a. Accompanied. Medium.

Almighty and Everlasting God—Gibbons
   Bourne No. ES35. *A cappella.* Moderately easy.

Almighty God, Who Hast Me Brought—Ford
   C. F. Peters No. 1558. *A cappella.* Moderately easy.

Ave Maria—Bach & Gounod, arr. Tolmadge
   Staff No. 243. Accompanied. Easy.

Ave Maria—Brahms
   C. F. Peters No. 66136. Accompanied. Medium.

Ave Maria—Bruckner
   Marks No. 47. *A cappella.* Moderately easy.

Ave Maria—Franck, arr. Borucchia
McLaughlin & Reilly No. 1072. Organ accompaniment. Moderately easy.

Ave Maria—Mouton
Music Press No. DCS 40. *A cappella.* Moderately easy.

Ave Maria—Rachmaninoff
Ditson No. 332-14564. *A cappella.* Medium.

Ave Maria—Tchaikovsky
Boston Music Co. No. 1064. *A cappella.* Moderately easy.

Ave Maria—Verdi
Peters No. 4256a. *A cappella.* Moderately difficult.

Ave Maria—Victoria
Music Press No. MP-79. *A cappella.* Moderately easy.

Ave Maria No. 20—Villa-Lobos, new text by H. R. Wilson
Consolidated. *A cappella.* Medium.

Ave Maris Stella—Hassler
Kjos No. 5012. *A cappella.* Moderately easy.

Ave Regina Coelorum—Lassus
Associated No. A-406. *A cappella.* Medium.

Ave Regina Coelorum—Willaert
Ricordi No. NY 1887. *A cappella.* Medium.

Ave Verum Corpus—Byrd
Bourne No. ES44. *A cappella.* Moderately easy.

Ave Verum Corpus—Mozart
G. Schirmer No. 5471. Organ accompaniment. Moderately easy.

Beautiful Savior (Silesian folk tune)—arr. F. M. Christiansen
Augsburg No. 51. *A cappella.* Medium.

Be Joyful, Be Joyful—Homilius
Sam Fox No. MM 5. Accompanied. Moderately easy.

Behold a Hallowed Day—Handl
Concordia No. 98-1690. *A cappella.* Medium.

Benedixisti (Thou Hast Been Gracious, Lord)—G. Gabrieli
G. Schirmer No. 7625. *A cappella.* Medium.

Best of Rooms, The—Thompson
E. C. Schirmer No. 2672. *A cappella.* Medium.

Blessed Are the Faithful—Schütz, ed. Shaw & Speer
G. Schirmer No. 10114. *A cappella.* Moderately difficult.

Blessed Savior, Our Lord Jesus—Hassler
  G. Schirmer No. 7563. *A cappella.* Medium.

Blest Be the Lord—Haydn
  McLaughlin & Reilly Co. No. 2217. Accompanied. Medium.

Brother James' Air (Marosa)—Jacob
  Carl Fischer No. OCS763. *A cappella.* Easy.

Call to Remembrance—Farrant, arr. Greyson
  Bourne No. ES 17. *A cappella.* Moderately easy.

Cantantibus Organis—Marenzio
  Available—World Library. *A cappella.* Moderately easy.

Cantate Domino—Pitoni
  Bourne No. ES 5. *A cappella.* Moderately easy.

Cantate Domino—Schütz
  Bourne No. ES 33. *A cappella.* Moderately difficult.

Cantique de Jean Racine—Fauré
  Broude No. 801. Accompanied. Moderately easy.

Cherubic Hymn (Greek liturgy)—arr. Aliferis
  Witmark No. 5-W3063. *A cappella.* Moderately difficult.

Cherubim Song—Gretchaninov, arr. Cain
  Hoffman No. 46012A. *A cappella.* Medium.

Cherubim Song No. 3—Tchaikovsky
  G. Schirmer No. 2561. Piano or organ accompaniment. Moderately difficult.

Cherubim Song No. 7—Bortniansky, arr. Tchaikovsky
  G. Schirmer No. 2560. *A cappella.* Easy.

Come, Blessed Rest—Bach
  Kjos No. 2004. *A cappella.* Medium.

Come Let Us Start a Joyful Song—Hassler
  Bourne No. ES 74. *A cappella.* Moderately easy.

Come, Then, O Holy Breath of God—Palestrina
  Piedmont No. 4414. *A cappella.* Medium.

Come Thou, O Saviour—J. S. Bach
  Summy-Birchard No. 5203. *A cappella.* Moderately easy.

Contentment—Mozart
  Lawson-Gould No. 937. Accompanied. Sop. solo. Moderately easy.

Corporis Mysterium (Sacrament of Priceless Worth)—Palestrina
  Ricordi No. NY1852. *A cappella.* Moderately easy.

Create in Me, O God, a Pure Heart—Brahms, arr. Williamson
G. Schirmer No. 7504. *A cappella.* Moderately easy.

Day by Day We Magnify Thee—Handel
Lawson-Gould No. 797. Accompanied. Medium.

De Profundis (Out of the Deep)—Thompson
Weintraub. *A cappella.* Moderately difficult.

Dies Irae (from *Requiem*)—Mozart
G. Schirmer No. 10016. Accompanied. Medium.

Ehre sei dir, Christe (Christ, Be Thine the Glory!)—Schütz
G. Schirmer No. 10123. Optional accompaniment. Medium.

Every Thing You Do—Buxtehude
Sam Fox No. CM 19. Accompanied. Medium.

Exaltabo Te, Domine—Palestrina
G. Schirmer No. 7620. *A cappella.* Medium.

Exultate Deo (Sing and Praise Jehovah)—Palestrina
G. Schirmer No. 7672. *A cappella.* Medium.

Exultate Deo—Scarlatti
G. Schirmer No. 11001. *A cappella.* Medium.

Gloria in Excelsis—Mozart
G. Schirmer No. 3515. Accompanied. Medium.

Gloria–Only Begotten Son—Gretchaninov, arr. Tellep
Boosey & Hawkes No. 5097. *A cappella.* Medium.

Gloria Patri (Glory to God)—Palestrina, arr. Greyson
Bourne No. ES46. *A cappella.* Easy.

Glory—Lotti
Edw. B. Marks No. 4366. *A cappella.* Moderately easy.

Glory and Honor Are Before Him—J. S. Bach
Kjos No. 5150. *A cappella.* Medium.

Glory and Worship—Purcell
E. C. Schirmer No. 1108. Organ accompaniment. Moderately easy.

Glory Be to God—Rachmaninoff, arr. Tkach
Kjos No. 6528. *A cappella.* Medium.

Glory to God—Bach, ed. Wilson
Ricordi No. NY1397. Optional accompaniment. Moderately difficult.

Glory to God—Bortniansky
Witmark No. 5-W2743. *A cappella.* Moderately easy.

Glory to God—Handel
    Lawson-Gould No. 796. Accompanied. Medium.

Glory to God in the Highest—Thompson
    E. C. Schirmer No. 2470. *A cappella.* Medium.

Graduale—Sancta Maria—Mozart
    Broude Bros. No. 77. Accompanied. Medium.

Grant Unto Me the Joy of Thy Salvation—Brahms
    G. Schirmer No. 7506. *A cappella.* Moderately difficult.

Great and Glorious—Haydn
    Wood No. 316. Accompanied. Medium.

Haec Dies—Byrd
    Oxford No. TCM 50. Optional accompaniment. Moderately difficult.

Hail, Thou Gladdening Light—Gretchaninov
    Wood No. 594. *A cappella.* Moderately difficult.

Hail, Thou Holy One—Tchaikovsky, arr. Cain
    Boosey & Hawkes No. 1979. *A cappella.* Medium.

Hallelujah (from *Mount of Olives*)—Beethoven
    G. Schirmer No. 2215. Accompanied. Difficult.

Hallelujah, Amen (from *Judas Maccabaeus*)—Handel
    Witmark No. 5-W3026. Optional accompaniment. Medium.

He Shall Rule from Sea to Sea—Rorem
    Boosey and Hawkes No. 5651. Accompanied. Medium.

He Watching Over Israel (from *Elijah*)—Mendelssohn
    G. Schirmer No. 2498. Accompanied. Moderately difficult.

He Who with Weeping Soweth—Schütz
    G. Schirmer No. 10115. Optional accompaniment. Moderately difficult.

Hear My Prayer—Kopylov
    Boston Music No. 1294. *A cappella.* Medium.

Hear, O Lord, Hear My Prayer—Lasso, arr. Lundquist
    Elkan-Vogel No. 1110. *A cappella.* Moderately easy.

Heavenly Light—Kopylov, arr. Wilhousky
    Carl Fischer No. CM 497. *A cappella.* Moderately easy.

Heavens Are Declaring, The—Beethoven
    G. Schirmer No. 3032. Accompanied. Easy.

Heavens Are Telling, The (from *The Creation*) —Haydn, arr. Phillips
Carl Fischer No. CM 127. Organ accompaniment. Moderately difficult.

Here Is Thy Footstool—Creston
G. Schirmer No. 11146. *A cappella.* Medium.

Hide Not Thy Face, O My Savior (Finnish folk melody) —arr. Lundquist. Willis No. 8469. *A cappella.* Moderately easy.

Hodie Nobis Coelorum Rex—Bright
Shawnee Press No. A-812. Accompanied. Medium.

Holy, Holy, Holy (Sanctus) —Lotti
E. C. Schirmer No. 2216. *A cappella.* Medium.

Holy, Holy, Holy—Scarlatti
Chappell No. 6141. *A cappella.* Medium.

Holy Is the Lord—Schubert
Presser No. 312-21416. Accompanied. Easy.

Honor and Glory—J. S. Bach
Plymouth No. SC10. Accompanied. Moderately easy.

Hospodi Pomilui—von Lvov, ed. Wilhousky
Carl Fischer No. CM 6580. *A cappella.* Medium.

How Lovely Is Thy Dwelling Place—Brahms, ed. Wilson
Ricordi No. 1515. Accompanied. Moderately difficult.

Hymn to Saint Peter—Britten
Boosey & Hawkes. Organ accompaniment. Sop. solo. Moderately difficult.

Hymn to the Trinity—Kopylov
Kjos No. 5337. *A cappella.* Easy.

If Ye Love Me, Keep My Commandments—Tallis
E. C. Schirmer No. 2269. *A cappella.* Medium.

Incline Thine Ear, Oh Lord—Arkhangelsky.
Witmark No. 5-W2689. *A cappella.* Medium.

Iustorum Animae—Byrd
E. C. Schirmer No. 327. *A cappella.* Medium.

Jesu dulcis memoria—Victoria
G. Schirmer No. 5573. *A cappella.* Easy.

Jesu, Joy of Man's Desiring—J. S. Bach
E. C. Schirmer No. 317. Organ accompaniment. Moderately easy.

Jesus, Now to Thee I Turn Me—Cherubini, arr. Lundquist
Elkan-Vogel No. 1159. *A cappella.* Easy.

Jubilate Deo—Lassus
Mercury No. MP-80. *A cappella.* Moderately easy.

Jubilate Deo—Mozart
Pro-Art No. 1007. *A cappella.* Moderately easy.

Kyrie Eleison—Durante
Pro-Art No. 2279. *A cappella.* Moderately easy.

Lacrymosa (from *Requiem*)—Mozart
G. Schirmer No. 10017. Accompanied. Medium.

Lasciatemi morire—Monteverdi
Ricordi No. NY841. *A cappella.* Moderately easy.

Last Words of David, The—Thompson
E. C. Schirmer No. 2294. Accompanied. Medium.

Laudate Pueri—Mozart
Lawson-Gould No. 51166. Accompanied. Moderately difficult.

Lend Thine Ear to My Prayer—Arkhangelsky, arr. Wilhousky
Carl Fischer No. CM 613. *A cappella.* Moderately difficult.

Let All Mortal Flesh Keep Silence—Holst
Galaxy. Accompanied. Medium.

Let Every Nation His Praises Sing—Franck
Sam Fox No. CM 20. *A cappella.* Medium.

Let My Prayer Come Up (Offertorium)—Purcell
Gray No. 1527. Accompanied. Moderately easy.

Let Nothing Ever Grieve Thee—Brahms
C. F. Peters No. 6093. Accompanied. Moderately easy.

Let Their Celestial Concerts All Unite (from *Samson*)—Handel
E. C. Schirmer No. 312. Accompanied. Moderately difficult.

Let Thy Holy Presence—Tchesnokov, arr. Cain
Summy-Birchard No. 12. *A cappella.* Medium.

Libera Me—Fauré
Belwin No. 2032. Accompanied. Medium.

Like as the Hart—Palestrina
G. Schirmer No. 3509. *A cappella.* Moderately easy.

Lo, I Am the Voice of One Crying in the Wilderness—Schütz
G. Schirmer No. 10116. Optional accompaniment. Moderately difficult.

Lord Bless You and Keep You, The—Lutkin
Summy-Birchard No. 1089. *A cappella.* Easy.

Lord Christ, Son of God (Christe Dei Soboles)—Lasso
G. Schirmer No. 9414. *A cappella.* Medium.

Lord God, in Power and Glory—Haydn
J. Curwen No. 80782. Optional accompaniment. Moderately easy.

Lord, Have Mercy Upon Us—Beethoven
Chappell No. 6145. Accompanied. Moderately easy.

Lord, Hear Our Prayer (from *Otello*)—Verdi, arr. Huguelet
Carl Fischer No. CM 616. Optional accompaniment. Medium.

Lord Is My Shepherd, The—Thompson
E. C. Schirmer No. 2688. Accompanied. Moderately easy.

Lord, Remember Not—Mendelssohn
Walton No. 6010. Optional accompaniment. Medium.

Lord, We Love the Place—Graun
Sam Fox No. MM 6. Accompanied. Medium.

Lovely Appear (from *The Redemption*)—Gounod
G. Schirmer No. 2013. Accompanied. Medium.

Magnificat—Gabrieli
Curwen No. 10565. *A cappella.* Three choirs. Difficult.

Mighty Fortress Is Our God, A—Luther
Witmark No. 5W2835. Optional accompaniment. Moderately easy.

Miserere Mei—Lotti
Boosey & Hawkes No. 1938. *A cappella.* Easy.

Miserere Mei—Pergolesi
Walton No. 6011. Accompanied. Medium.

Now God Be Praised in Heav'n Above—Vulpius
E. C. Schirmer No. 1693. Optional accompaniment. Moderately easy.

Nunc Dimittis—Purcell
Summy-Birchard No. 5433. Accompanied. Moderately easy.

O Be Joyful! (Freut Euch, Freut Euch)—Mozart
Sam Fox No. MM 9. Accompanied. Medium.

O Bone Jesu—Palestrina
Oliver Ditson No. 332-03070. *A cappella.* Easy.

O Cast Me Not Away from Thy Countenance—Brahms
   G. Schirmer No. 7505. *A cappella.* Moderately difficult.

O Clap Your Hands—Vaughan Williams
   Galaxy No. 222. Organ accompaniment. Moderately difficult.

O Divine Redeemer—Gounod, arr. Cain
   Schmitt, Hall & McCreary No. 1602. Accompanied. Moderately
   easy.

O Glorious One—Gretchaninov, arr. Cain
   Hoffman No. 46,339. *A cappella.* Moderately easy.

O God, I Thank Thee—Schumann, arr. Lundquist
   Willis No. 8466. *A cappella.* Easy.

O Hear Me When I Call on Thee—Schubert
   E. C. Schirmer No. 2684. Accompanied. Medium.

O Lord, Have Mercy on Us (Kyrie Eleison)—Buxtehude
   Sam Fox No. CM 6. Optional accompaniment. Medium.

O, Lord, in Thee Have I Trusted—Handel
   Kjos No. 5481 C. Accompanied. Medium.

O Lord Most Holy (Panis Angelicus)—Franck
   Summy-Birchard No. 396. Accompanied. Medium.

O Rejoice, Ye Christians, Loudly—Bach
   Carl Fischer No. CM 6600. *A cappella.* Moderately easy.

O Savior, Throw the Heavens Wide (Motet, Op. 74, No. 2)—Brahms
   G. Schirmer No. 8545. *A cappella.* Moderately difficult.

O Sing Unto the Lord—Hassler
   G. Schirmer No. 10872. *A cappella.* Moderately easy.

O Sing Unto the Lord—Purcell
   E. C. Schirmer No. 1103. Organ accompaniment. Moderately
   easy.

O Vos Omnes—Victoria
   Ricordi No. NY1875. *A cappella.* Medium.

Oh, Blest Are They—Tschaikovsky, arr. Cain
   Remick No. 3024. *A cappella.* Moderately difficult.

Omnipotence, The—Schubert
   G. Schirmer No. 10146. Accompanied. Medium.

Once I Had Hoped from Thee—De Monte
   Piedmont No. 4427. *A cappella.* Medium.

Onward, Ye Peoples! Sibelius, arr. Lefebvre
Galaxy No. 938-10. Accompanied. Moderately easy.

Os Justi—Bruckner
G. Schirmer No. 8121. *A cappella.* Medium.

Our Father—Gretchaninov, English text by Kimball
Presser No. 332-13000. *A cappella.* Moderately difficult.

Pater Noster—Stravinsky
Boosey & Hawkes No. 1833. *A cappella.* Medium.

Pater Noster (Our Father)—Tchaikovsky
G. Schirmer No. 5475. *A cappella.* Moderately easy.

Plorate Filii Israel (Lament, Ye Children of Israel)—Carissimi
Bourne No. ES34. Accompanied. Medium.

Praise Be to Thee—Palestrina, arr. Lundquist
Willis No. 5678. *A cappella.* Easy.

Prayer and Chorale—Mendelssohn
Lawson-Gould No. 849. *A cappella.* Moderately easy.

Psallite—Praetorius, arr. Greyson
Bourne No. ES 21. *A cappella.* Easy.

Psalm 61—Hovhaness
Peters No. 6255. Organ accompaniment. Medium.

Psalm CL (Praise Ye the Lord)—Franck
Oliver Ditson No. 332-14082. Organ accompaniment. Medium.

Psalm 150 (Hallelujah, Praise Ye the Lord)—Lewandowski
Schmitt, Hall & McCreary No. 1640. Optional *a cappella*
Medium.

Rejoice in the Lord Alway—Purcell
Novello No. 1581. Accompanied. Moderately easy.

Requiescat—Schuman
G. Schirmer No. 8926. Accompanied. Medium.

Salvation Is Created—Tschesnokov, arr. Norden
J. Fischer No. 4129. *A cappella.* Medium.

Salve Regina—Lasso
Music Press No. MP-73. *A cappella.* Medium.

Sanctus (from *B minor Mass*)—Bach
G. Schirmer No. 5654. Accompanied. Difficult.

Sanctus (from *C Major Mass*)—Beethoven
Walton No. 6014. Accompanied. Medium.

Sanctus (from *Requiem*) —Fauré
    Fitzsimons No. 2119. Accompanied. Easy.

Sanctus (from *Mass VII*) —Lotti
    G. Schirmer No. 9407. *A cappella.* Moderately easy.

Send Out Thy Light (Emitte Spiritum Tuum) —Schuetky
    Carl Fischer No. CM 548. *A cappella.* Moderately easy.

Serve the Lord with Gladness—Handel
    Lawson-Gould No. 794. Accompanied. Medium.

Sicut Moses Serpentem—Schütz
    Associated No. A-412. Accompanied. Difficult.

Sing to the Lord (Gloria in excelsis Deo) —Haydn
    G. Schirmer No. 5414. Accompanied. Moderately easy.

Sing Unto the Lord Most High—Pergolesi
    Boosey & Hawkes. *A cappella.* Easy.

Sing We All Now with One Accord—Praetorius
    G. Schirmer No. 7543. Accompanied. Moderately easy.

Song of Galilee (El Yivneh Hagalil) —transcribed by Chajes
    Transcontinental No. TCL 214. Accompanied. Medium.

Song of Repentance—J. S. Bach
    Broude No. 65. *A cappella.* Medium.

Sound the Cymbal—Schubert
    Schmitt, Hall & McCreary No. 1745. Accompanied. Medium.

Stabat Mater—Schubert
    Belwin No. 2164. Accompanied. Moderately easy.

Te Deum—Schuman
    G. Schirmer No. 9453. *A cappella.* Medium.

This is the Record of John—Gibbons, ed. Parker & Shaw
    Lawson-Gould No. 550. Organ accompaniment. Ten. solo.
    Medium.

Thou Art the King of Glory—Handel
    Kjos No. 5481A. Accompanied. Moderately easy.

Thou Art Worthy of Praise—Haydn
    Sam Fox No. MM 13. *A cappella.* Moderately easy.

Thou Must Leave Thy Lowly Dwelling (from *Childhood of Christ*)
    —Berlioz. H. W. Gray No. 1898. Accompanied. Medium.

Tribulationes Civitatum—Thomson
    Weintraub. *A cappella.* Moderately difficult.

Tribus miraculis—Marenzio
Available—World Library. *A cappella.* Medium.

Turn Back, O Man—Holst
Galaxy No. 6. Accompanied. Medium.

Twenty-Third Psalm, The—Wilson
Bourne. *A cappella.* Medium.

Unto Thee I Lift My Spirit—Hiller
Sam Fox MM 7. Accompanied. Moderately easy.

Veni Jesu—Cherubini, arr. Riegger
Flammer No. 84189. Accompanied. Medium.

Venite, Exsultemus Domino (O Come Let Us Sing)—Sweelinck
Summy-Birchard No. 5517. Optional accompaniment. Medium.

Von Himmel Hoch (From Highest Heav'n)—J. S. Bach
Lawson-Gould No. 903. *A cappella.* Medium.

Vouchsafe, O Lord—Gretchaninov
Galaxy No. 1356. Optional accompaniment. Medium.

We Adore Thee (Adoramus Te)—Lotti
Chappell No. 6149. *A cappella.* Moderately easy.

We Have No Other Help—Arkhangelsky, arr. Gnotov
M. Witmark No. 5-W3005. *A cappella.* Moderately easy.

We Praise and Bless Thee (from *Messe Solennelle*)—Gounod, arr.
Witford. Oliver Ditson No. 332-40049. Accompanied. Moderately easy.

We Praise Thee—Gretchaninov, arr. Cain
Hoffman No. 46,335. *A cappella.* Easy.

Who With Grieving Soweth—Schein
Mercury No. 19. *A cappella.* Moderately difficult.

With a Voice of Singing—Shaw
G. Schirmer No. 8103. Accompanied. Moderately easy.

Ye Are Not of the Flesh (from the motet *Jesu meine Freude*)—Bach
Lawson-Gould No. 785. Accompanied. Difficult.

General: Secular

Anthony O Daly—Barber
G. Schirmer No. 8909. *A cappella.* Medium.

April Is in Her Lovely Face—Morley
Ricordi No. 1398. *A cappella.* Moderately easy.

As Long as Beauty Shall Remain—Brahms, arr. Christy
Schmitt, Hall & McCreary No. 1172. *A cappella.* Easy.

As Torrents in Summer—Elgar, arr. Cain
Flammer No. 81068. *A cappella.* Moderately easy.

Ballad of Green Broom—Britten
Boosey & Hawkes No. 1875. *A Cappella.* Moderately difficult.

Begger's Canon (from *The Brigands*)—Offenbach
Broude Brothers No. 117. Accompanied. Medium.

Choose Something Like a Star—Thompson
E. C. Schirmer No. 2487. Accompanied. Moderately easy.

Come and Sing (from *Die Fledermaus*)—Strauss
Carl Fischer No. CM 4628. Accompanied. Moderately difficult.

Coolin, The—Barber
G. Schirmer No. 8910. *A cappella.* Moderately difficult.

Come, Let Your Hearts Be Singing—Gastoldi, arr. Greyson
Bourne No. ES 26. *A cappella.* Moderately easy.

Dedication—Franz, arr. Riegger
Flammer No. 81043. *A cappella.* Medium.

Dirge for Two Veterans—Lockwood
Witmark No. 2879. *A cappella.* Sop. solo. Difficult.

Evening—Kodály
Boosey & Hawkes No. 1710. *A cappella.* Difficult.

Fable, A—Dello Joio
Carl Fischer No. CM 6299. Accompanied. Moderately easy.

Fair Is the Crystal—di Lasso
Piedmont No. 4384. *A cappella.* Medium.

Fall, Leaves, Fall—Bright
Shawnee Press No. A-945. *A cappella.* Medium.

Farewell, The (Horch, der Wind Klagt in den Zweigen)—Brahms
Sam Fox No. RC 2. Accompanied. Moderately easy.

Farmer's Wife Lost Her Cat—Mozart
Marks No. 1. *A cappella.* Moderately difficult.

Fa Una Canzone—Vecchi
Lawson-Gould No. 556. *A cappella.* Easy.

From Grief to Glory (Verse II–Love in Grief)—F. M. Christiansen
Augsburg No. 175. *A cappella.* Difficult.

Geographical Fugue (speaking chorus)—Toch
Mills No. 347. Difficult.

Glory (March from *Aida*)—Verdi
Willis No. 2892. Accompanied. Moderately difficult.

Hear Me Now, Beloved—Marenzio
Piedmont No. 4334. *A cappella.* Medium.

Hunting Song—Mendelssohn
Sam Fox No. RC 9. *A cappella.* Medium.

In Silent Night—Brahms
G. Schirmer No. 5848. *A cappella.* Easy.

In the Quiet Night—Mennin
Carl Fischer No. CM6417. *A cappella.* Medium.

In These Delightful, Pleasant Groves—Purcell
Novello No. M. T. 1. *A cappella.* Medium.

In Winter—Hindemith
Associated No. AS 19432V. *A cappella.* Medium.

It Is Good to Be Merry—Berger
Kjos No. 5293. *A cappella.* Medium.

Jig for Voices—Rowley
Boosey & Hawkes No. 1699. Optional accompaniment. Medium.

Lady, So Fair Thou Seemest—de Wert
Mills Music No. 60778. *A cappella.* Moderately easy.

Las Agachadas—Copland
Boosey & Hawkes. *A cappella.* For solo group and eight-part
chorus. Moderately difficult.

Lobster Quadrille, The—Fine
Witmark No. 5-W3180 I. Accompanied. Moderately easy.

Lotus Dust, The—Bright
Shawnee Press No. A-883. *A cappella.* Moderately easy.

Love Song—Brahms, arr. Wilson
Ricordi No. NY 1475. Optional accompaniment. Moderately
easy.

Lullaby (Wiegenlied)—Mozart
Associated No. A-84. Accompanied. Sop. solo. Moderately easy.

Madrigal—Gesualdo
E. B. Marks No. 52. *A cappella.* Medium.

Matona, Lovely Maiden—Lasso
Carl Fischer CM 4637. *A cappella.* Moderately easy.

Monotone—Lockwood
Kjos No. 8. *A cappella.* Medium.

Music the Comforter (Trösterin Music) —Bruckner
Sam Fox No. MM 12. Accompanied. Moderately easy.

My Love Dwelt in a Northern Land—Elgar
G. Schirmer No. 2366. *A cappella.* Moderately easy.

Neighbors' Chorus—Offenbach
Broude No. 130. Accompanied. Medium.

Old Abram Brown—Britten
Boosey & Hawkes No. 1786. Accompanied. Easy.

Old Joe Has Gone Fishing (from *Peter Grimes*) —Britten
Boosey & Hawkes No. 1784. Accompanied. Moderately difficult.

O Lovely Mai (O Sussex Mai) —Brahms
Belwin No. 2174. *A cappella.* Moderately easy.

Oh, When My Husband Comes Back Home—di Lasso
Pro Art No. 2365. *A cappella.* Moderately easy.

O Voi Che Sospirate a Migliore Note—Marenzio
Dartmouth Publications No. A-977. *A cappella.* Medium.

Pavane Pour une Infante Défunte—Ravel
Broude Bros. No. 100. Accompanied. Moderately difficult.

Placido e Il Mar (from *Idomeneo*) —Mozart
Lawson-Gould No. 841. Accompanied. Medium.

Prelude—Schuman
G. Schirmer No. 8929. *A cappella.* Sop. solo. Moderately difficult.

Promise of Living, The (from *The Tender Land*) —Copland
Boosey & Hawkes No. 5020. Piano duet accompaniment. Moderately difficult.

Rise Up, Oh Flame—Praetorius, arr. Harley & Aschenbrenner
Carl Fischer No. CM 4712. *A cappella.* Moderately easy.

Road Not Taken, The—Thompson
E. C. Schirmer No. 2485. Accompanied. Moderately easy.

Roses of the South—Strauss, arr. Gibb
Homeyer No. 437. Accompanied. Moderately easy.

See How Aurora Comes with Brow All Glowing—Marenzio
Piedmont No. 4438. *A cappella*. Medium.

Since All Is Passing—Hindemith
Associated. *A cappella*. Moderately easy.

Sing a Song of Sixpence—Bright
Shawnee Press No. A-851. *A cappella*. Medium.

Six Balletti—Gastoldi
C. F. Peters, Set I, No. 6877a. *A cappella*. Moderately easy. Set
II, No. 6877b. *A cappella*. Medium.

Six Love Songs—Brahms
Summy-Birchard. Four-hand accompaniment. Moderately difficult.

Skylark's Song, The—Mendelssohn
Belwin No. 2181. Optional accompaniment. Moderately easy.

Song of the Lark (Lerchengesang)—Mendelssohn
Sam Fox No. RC 11. *A cappella*. Moderately easy.

Springtime—Hindemith
Schott No. 19432 IV. *A cappella*. Moderately difficult.

Stomp Your Foot (from *The Tender Land*)—Copland
Boosey & Hawkes No. 5019. Piano duet accompaniment. Moderately difficult.

Sunrise—Taneyev
G. Schirmer No. 2623. *A cappella*. Difficult.

Sure on This Shining Night—Barber
G. Schirmer No. 10864. Accompanied. Moderately easy.

Swan, A—Hindemith
Schott No. 19432, II. *A cappella*. Medium.

Talk Not to Me—Kaderavek
Westwood Press No. ESE-1497-8. *A cappella*. Medium.

These Are My Heartfelt Tears (Madrigal)—Palestrina
Lawson-Gould No. 51029. *A cappella*. Moderately easy.

Thought Like Music, A—Brahms, arr. Suchoff
Plymouth No. A.S. 103. Accompanied. Moderately easy.

Three Nocturnes—Chávez
G. Schirmer No. 9522. *A cappella*. Moderately difficult.

To All, To Each—Schuman
    Presser No. 342-40013. *A cappella*. Medium.

Trysting Place, The—Brahms
    E. C. Schirmer No. 391. Accompanied. Moderately easy.

Under the Willow Tree (from *Vanessa*)—Barber
    G. Schirmer No. 10861. Accompanied. Sop. solo. Moderately difficult.

Voix Celestes (humming chorus)—Alcock
    Chappell No. 2055. *A cappella*. Medium.

We Are Brave Matadors (from *La Traviata*)—Verdi
    G. Schirmer No. 5435. Accompanied. Medium.

Welcome Sweet May (Wohl Kommt der Mai)—de Lasso
    Carl Fischer No. CM 7566. *A cappella*. Moderately easy.

When the Bright Sun—Byrd
    Mills Music No. A-202. *A cappella*. Moderately easy.

Whether Men Do Laugh or Weep—Vaughan Williams
    Oxford No. X66. Accompanied. Medium.

Woman Is a Worthy Thing, A—Chávez
    G. Schirmer No. 9611. *A cappella*. Medium.

Wonderful Life, A (Lebenslust)—Schubert
    Sam Fox No. MM 8. Accompanied. Medium.

Younger Generation—Copland, arr. Swift
    Boosey & Hawkes No. 1723. Accompanied. Moderately easy.

PUBLICATIONS FOR MIXED VOICES (SAB)

Sacred

Alleluja (from the motet *Exultate, Jubilate*)—Mozart, arr. Riegger
    Flammer No. 88522. Accompanied. Moderately difficult.

As Torrents in Summer—Elgar, arr. Cain
    Flammer No. 88046. Optional *A cappella*. Easy.

Ave Maria—Gounod, arr. Downing
    G. Schirmer No. 9450. Accompanied. Moderately easy.

Bless the Lord, O My Soul—Ippolitov-Ivanov, arr. Richardson
    Boston Music No. 2801. *A cappella*. Moderately easy.

Cherubic Hymn, The (Opus 29)—Gretchaninov, arr. Howorth
Pro Art No. 1031. *A cappella.* Moderately easy.

Cherubim Song No. 7—Bortniansky, arr. Tchaikovsky
G. Schirmer No. 9753. Accompanied. Moderately easy.

Christus Resurgens (Christ Being Raised)—Viadana
Leeds No. L-441. Organ accompaniment. Moderately easy.

Come, Souls, Behold Today—Bach, arr. Nelson
Augsburg No. 1171. *A cappella.* Moderately easy.

Dona Nobis Pacem (old German canon)—arr. Wilson
Schmitt, Hall & McCreary No. 5510. *A cappella.* Moderately
easy.

For the Beauty of the Earth—Kocher, arr. Davis
Remick No. 4-R3231. Accompanied. Easy.

God So Loved the World—Stainer, arr. Martin
Schmitt, Hall & McCreary No. 5509. *A cappella.* Easy.

Heavens Are Declaring, The—Beethoven, arr. Kountz
Witmark No. 2565. Accompanied. Easy.

Heavens Are Declaring, The—Beethoven, arr. Mueller
G. Schirmer No. 10670. Accompanied. Easy.

Heavens Are Telling, The—Haydn, arr. Wilson
Lorenz No. 7020. Accompanied. Moderately easy.

Jesu, Joy of Man's Desiring (from Cantata No. 147)—Bach
G. Schirmer No. 10023; Remick No. R3279. Accompanied.
Easy.

Jesu, Son of God (Ave Verum Corpus)—Mozart
Schmitt, Hall & McGreary 5502. Accompanied. Moderately easy.

Lead Me, O Lord—Wesley, arr. Pitcher
Willis No. 8493. Accompanied. Easy.

Legend, A (from the cycle *Songs for Young People*)—Tchaikovsky,
arr. Deis. G. Schirmer No. 10035. Accompanied. Medium.

Let Our Gladness Know No End (Old Bohemian Christmas Carol)
arr. Ryg. Belwin No. 1761. *A cappella.* Moderately easy.

Lift Thine Eyes (from *Elijah*)—Mendelssohn, arr. Luther
Kjos No. 5710. Optional accompaniment. Easy.

Lift Thine Eyes (from *Elijah*)—Mendelssohn, arr. Pitcher
Willis No. 8486. Optional accompaniment. Moderately easy.

Moon Shines Bright, The (Old English carol)—arr. Wilson
Bourne No. T8. Accompanied. Moderately easy.

O Little Jesus (16th Century German carol)—arr. Gordon
Belwin No. 1873. Accompanied. Easy.

O Lord Most Holy—Franck, arr. Pitcher
Willis No. 8489. Accompanied. Easy.

O Lord, Our God—Schvedov, arr. Wilson
Bourne No. T5. Optional accompaniment. Medium.

Praise the Almighty, My Soul, Adore Him—Zipp
Concordia No. CH 1086. *A cappella.* Moderately easy.

Praise Ye the Father—Gounod, arr. Pitcher
Willis No. 8482. Accompanied. Moderately easy.

Prayer for Peace, A (Panis Angelicus)—Franck, arr. Hoffman
Hoffman No. 46,107. Accompanied. Moderately easy.

Rocking (Czech carol)—arr. Ehret
Scholin No. 1076. Accompanied. Moderately easy.

Send Out Thy Light—Gounod, arr. Mueller
G. Schirmer No. 8695. Accompanied. Medium.

Shepherd of Eager Youth—Roff
Elkan-Vogel No. 507. Accompanied. Moderately easy.

To Realms of Glory—Schein, arr. Nelson
Augsburg No. 1169. *A cappella.* Easy.

Turn Thy Face from My Sins—Attwood, arr. Pitcher
Willis No. 8487. Accompanied. Easy.

Secular

Bells of St. Mary's—Adams, arr. Stickles
Chappell No. 7006. Accompanied. Easy.

Bells of the Sea—Solman, arr. Wilson
Sam Fox No. 542. Accompanied. Moderately easy.

Carol of the Bells (Ukrainian carol)—Leontovich, arr. Wilhousky
Carl Fischer No. 4747. Optional *a cappella.* Easy.

Danse Macabre—Saint-Saëns, arr. Lorenz
Lorenz No. 7098. Accompanied. Moderately difficult.

Dedication—Franz, arr. Wilson
Paull-Pioneer. Accompanied. Moderately easy.

Down South—Myddleton, arr. High
Marks No. 403. Accompanied. Easy.

Green Cathedral—Hahn, arr Montrose.
    Presser No. 322-35447. Accompanied. Easy.

Homing—Del Riego, arr. Stickles
    Chappell No. 7007. Accompanied. Easy.

Kentucky Babe—Giebel, arr. Stickles
    Edwin H. Morris No. 8003. Accompanied. Easy.

Ol' Man River—Kern, arr. Stickles
    Chappell No. CR77. Accompanied. Moderately easy.

Pines of Home—Luvaas
    Carl Fischer No. 6452. Optional *a cappella.* Moderately easy.

Prayer from *Hansel and Gretel*—Humperdinck, arr. Riegger
    Flammer No. 88019. Accompanied. Easy.

Shortnin' Bread—Wolfe, arr. Riegger
    Flammer No. 88008. Accompanied. Moderately easy.

Sing, Sing a Song for Me—Vecchi, arr. Greyson
    Bourne No. ES 53C. Optional accompaniment. Moderately easy.

Three Madrigals from the XVIIth Century:
    1. Your Shining Eyes—Bateson
    2. As Late in My Accounting—Weelkes
    3. Follow Me, Sweet Love—East
    J. Fischer No. 9455. *A cappella.* Medium.

Tickling Trio (Vadasi Via di Qua)—Martini
    Witmark No. 4-W2750. *A cappella.* Moderately easy.

To Music—Schubert, arr. Wilson
    Schmitt, Hall & McCreary No. 5011. Accompanied. Moderately easy.

Turn Ye to Me—Wilson, arr. Churchill
    Belwin No. 1619. Accompanied. Moderately easy.

When Day Is Done—Katcher, arr. Koshetz
    Harms, Inc. No. 614. Accompanied. Moderately easy.

Folk Songs and Spirituals

Certainly, Lord (Negro spiritual)—arr. Kirk
    Pro Art No. 1834. Accompanied. Moderately easy.

Cindy (American folk song)—arr. Barthelson
    Belwin No. 1984. Accompanied. Moderately easy.

Cindy (mountain dance song)—arr. Wilson
Schmitt, Hall & McCreary No. 5012. Optional *a cappella.* Moderately easy.

Cowboy's Meditation, The (American folk song)—arr. Wilson
Paull-Pioneer. Accompanied. Moderately easy.

Ezekiel Saw De Wheel (Spiritual)—arr. Cain
Belwin No. 1131. Accompanied. Medium.

From Lucerne to Weggis Fair (Swiss folk song)—arr. Harris
Pro Art No. 2369. Accompanied. Medium.

Go Down, Moses (Negro spiritual)—arr. Lorenz
Lorenz No. 7096. Accompanied. Easy.

He Never Said a Mumbalin' Word (spiritual)—arr. Wilson
Paull-Pioneer. Optional accompaniment. Moderately easy.

Hi, Ho, Sing Gaily! (Swiss folk tune)—arr. Luvaas
Summy-Birchard No. B1637. Accompanied. Moderately easy.

Ho La Li (Bavarian melody)—arr. Luvaas
Summy-Birchard No. B1613. Accompanied. Moderately easy.

I Ain't Gonna Grieve My Lord No More (Negro spiritual)—arr. Ehret
Belwin No. 1661. Accompanied. Medium.

I Got Shoes (Negro spiritual)—arr. Cain
Flammer No. 88047. Accompanied. Easy.

Jennie Jenkins (American dialogue song)—arr. Churchill
Belwin No. 1893. Accompanied. Easy.

John Anderson, My Jo (Scottish folk song)—arr. Gordon
Belwin No. 1494. Accompanied. Moderately easy.

Little David, Play on Your Harp (Negro spiritual)—arr. Cain
Flammer No. 88054. Accompanied. Moderately easy.

Night Herding Song (country folk ballad)—arr. Barker
Belwin No. 1828. Optional accompaniment. Moderately easy.

Oh, Vreneli (Swiss folk song)—arr. Larson
Summy-Birchard No. B1594. Accompanied. Moderately easy.

Rock-a My Soul (spiritual)—arr. Wilson
Bourne No. T 11. Accompanied. Moderately easy.

Russian Picnic (based on Russian folk tunes)—arr. Enders
G. Schirmer No. 9632. Accompanied. Medium.

Stodola Pumpa (Czech folk song)—arr. Wilson
Bourne No. T 12. Accompanied. Medium.

Water Boy (Negro work song)—arr. Pitcher
  Boston Music No. 2359. Accompanied. Bar. solo—melody in baritone. Easy.

Were You There (spiritual)—arr. Wilson
  Bourne No. T 2. Accompanied. Medium.

PUBLICATIONS FOR TREBLE VOICES (SSA)

Sacred

Alleluia—Mozart, arr. Riegger
  Flammer No. 89024. Accompanied. Medium.

All Ye That Cried Unto the Lord—Mendelssohn, arr. Gray
  Pro-Art No. 1839. Accompanied. Easy.

Angel Ever Bright—Handel, arr. Overby
  Augsburg No. 1013. Optional accompaniment. Moderately easy.

Angels and the Shepherds—Kodály
  Universal No. 312-40593. *A cappella.* Medium

At the Gate of Heaven (Spanish folk song)—arr. Allen
  Summy-Birchard No. 1570. Accompanied. Moderately easy.

Ave Maria—Arcadelt
  Bourne No. ES 3. *A cappella.* Moderately easy.

Away In a Manger (traditional carol)—arr. Terri
  Lawson-Gould No. 666. *A cappella.* Moderately easy.

Bless Ye the Lord—Ippolitov-Ivanov, arr. Wilhousky
  Carl Fischer No. 639. *A cappella.* Moderately easy.

Blest is the Man—Lasso
  Augsburg No. PS603. *A cappella.* Moderately easy.

Bring a Torch, Jeannette, Isabella (old French carol)—arr. Nunn
  E. C. Schirmer No. 496. *A cappella.* Moderately easy.

Call of the Shepherds, The (French Noël)—arr. Malin
  B. F. Wood No. 826. *A cappella.* Moderately easy.

Cantate Domino—Pitoni
  Flammer No. 89181. *A cappella.* Moderately easy.

Cherubic Hymn—Musitcheskoo
  Boosey & Hawkes No. 5026. Accompanied. Medium.

Christ Is Born (Ukrainian carol)—arr. Boberg
    Carl Fischer No. 7455. *A cappella.* Moderately easy.

Christ Is Born in a Manger Bed (17th century melody)
    World Library No. AC-596-3. *A cappella.* Easy.

Christmas Hymn (17th century)—arr. Jüngst
    G. Schirmer No. 9890. *A cappella.* Moderately easy.

Come to Me—Beethoven, arr. Aslanoff
    G. Schirmer No. 7811. Accompanied. Easy.

Come, Ye Lofty, Come, Ye Lowly (Breton carol)—arr. Malin
    Summy-Birchard No. 1419. Accompanied. Moderately easy.

Coventry Carol (English carol)—arr. Stone
    Belwin No. 2070. Accompanied. Moderately easy.

Glory to God in the Highest!—Pergolesi, arr. Riegger
    Flammer No. 89041. Accompanied. Medium.

God of Abraham Praise, The (traditional Hebrew melody)—arr.
    Malmin. Augsburg No. 1238. Accompanied. Easy.

God Rest You Merry, Gentlemen (English carol)—arr. Scholin
    Belwin No. 1625. Accompanied. Moderately easy.

Holy Infant's Lullaby, The—Dello Joio
    Edw. B. Marks No. 4392. Accompanied. Moderately easy.

How Far Is It to Bethlehem?—Chesterton
    World Library No. AC-595-3.*A cappella.* Easy.

Hush My Babe—Rousseau-Stone
    Belwin No. 2067. Accompanied. Easy.

Incline Thine Ear, O Lord—Arkhangelsky, arr. Krone
    Witmark No. 3220. *A cappella.* Medium.

Jesu, Joy of Man's Desiring—Bach, arr. Treharne
    G. Schirmer No. 8388. Accompanied. Easy.

Jesu, Priceless Treasure (from the motet *Jesu, Meine Freude*)—Bach
    Summy-Birchard No. 4204. Optional accompaniment. Easy.

Lacrymosa—Mozart
    Carl Fischer No. CM 6945. Accompanied. Medium.

Legend, A—Tschaikovsky
    Carl Fischer No. CM 6325. Accompanied. Moderately easy.

Lift Thine Eyes (from *Elijah*)—Mendelssohn
    Willis No. 698. *A cappella.* Moderately easy.

Lo, A Voice to Heaven Sounding—Bortniansky, arr. Davis
  E. C. Schirmer No. 1079. *A cappella.* Moderately easy.

Lord Is My Shepherd, The—Schubert, arr. Watson
  Remick No. 2-G1646. Accompanied. Moderately difficult.

O Little Jesus (16th-century German carol)—arr. Gordon
  Belwin No. 1874. Accompanied. Moderately easy.

Once in Royal David's City (Finnish folk melody)—arr. Lundquist
  Elkan-Vogel No. 3079. *A cappella.* Easy.

Praise to the Lord (17th-century German tune)—arr. Whitehead
  Gray No. 2095. Organ accompaniment. Moderately easy.

Praise Ye the Lord of Hosts—Saint-Saens
  Mills Music No. 698. Accompanied. Easy.

Prayer of Thanksgiving (old Dutch melody)—arr. Kremser
  G. Schirmer No. 6812. Accompanied. Easy.

Puer Natus Est—Morales
  Bourne No. ES 73. Optional accompaniment. Medium.

Rejoice All Men—Niles-Ross
  Carl Fischer No. CM 6462. Accompanied. Medium.

Rejoice, Holy Mary (French carol)—arr. Malin
  Mills Music No. 693. Accompanied. Moderately easy.

Send Out Thy Light—Balakirev
  Boosey & Hawkes No. 1924. *A cappella.* Medium.

Shepherd's Carol—Billings
  H. W. Gray No. 3024. Accompanied. Moderately easy.

Sing a Gay Noel (Basque melody)—arr. Glaser
  B. F. Wood No. 816. *A cappella.* Moderately easy.

Slumber of the Infant Jesus—Gevaert, arr. Davis
  E. C. Schirmer No. 1088. *A cappella.* Medium.

This Little Babe (from *A Ceremony of Carols*)—Britten
  Boosey & Hawkes No. 5138. Accompanied. Moderately easy.

To Our Little Town (French carol)—arr. Malin
  Mills Music No. 692. *A cappella.* Moderately easy.

To Us There Comes a Little Child (German melody)—arr. Malin
  Mills Music No. 704. Accompanied. Moderately easy.

Two Czech Carols—arr. Peloguin
  McLaughlin & Reilly No. 2047. *A cappella.* Moderately easy.

Vere Languores Nostros—Lotti
> Bourne No. ES 22. *A cappella.* Moderately easy.

While Shepherds Watched (17-century melody)—arr. Tkach
> Kjos No. 6044. Accompanied. Easy.

Whither Going, Shepherd? (Hungarian folk song)—arr. Taylor
> J. Fischer No. 5054. Accompanied. Moderately easy.

Wolcum Yole! (from *A Ceremony of Carols*)—Britten
> Boosey & Hawkes No. 1755B. Accompanied. Medium.

Secular

Adelaide—Beethoven
> Boston Music No. 3045. Accompanied. Moderately easy.

Adieu, Mignonne, When You Are Gone—Dello Joio
> Carl Fischer No. 6784. Accompanied. Moderately difficult.

Amarilli, Mia Bella—Caccini, arr. Taylor
> J. Fischer No. 4375. Accompanied. Medium.

An Offering—Baldwin, arr. Watson
> Witmark No. 5W3362. *A cappella.* Moderately easy.

As Fair as Morn—Wilbye
> Marks No. 4331. *A cappella.* Moderately easy.

As from the Earth a Flower Grows—Monteverdi
> Marks No. 45. *A cappella.* Moderately easy.

Bird Flew, A—Clokey
> J. Fischer No. 5506. Accompanied. Medium.

Bois Epais—Lully, arr. Taylor
> J. Fischer No. 4562. Accompanied. Moderately easy.

Calm as the Night—Boehm, arr. Cain
> Schmitt, Hall & McCreary No. 2016. Accompanied. Moderately easy.

Carol of the Bells (Christmas)—Leontovich, arr. Wilhousky
> Carl Fischer No. 5276. Optional accompaniment. Medium.

Come, Let Us Start a Joyful Song—Hassler
> Bourne No. ES 31. Optional accompaniment. Moderately easy.

Come, Sirrah Jack Ho—Weelkes
> E. C. Schirmer No. 840. *A cappella.* Medium.

Come, You Maidens—Tschaikovsky
Boosey & Hawkes No. 5031. Accompanied. Moderately easy.

Danza, Danza—Durante, arr. Taylor
J. Fischer No. 4378. Accompanied. Medium.

Dreams—Wagner, arr. Shelley
Presser No. 10687. Accompanied. Medium.

Go 'Way from My Window—Niles, arr. Ross
G. Schirmer No. 9805. Accompanied. Sop. Solo. Medium.

Happiness—Schubert, arr. Frank
Galaxy. Accompanied. Moderately easy.

Hark! Hark! the Lark—Schubert, arr. Bliss
Willis No. 2338. Accompanied. Easy.

He Came to Me—Franz
Schmitt, Hall and McCreary No. 2127. Accompanied. Easy.

In Summer Fields—Brahms
Boston Music Co. No. 3044. Accompanied. Moderately easy.

In the Mill—Rebikoff, arr. Sammond
J. Fischer No. 5689. *A cappella.* Medium.

In These Delightful Pleasant Groves—Purcell
Bourne No. ES 28. Optional accompaniment. Medium.

Invocation of Orpheus—Peri
Witmark No. W 2728. Accompanied. Medium.

Let Us Sing—Rameau
Witmark No. 2-W 2988. Accompanied. Medium.

Love Song—Brahms, arr. Gibb
Boston No. 3046. Accompanied. Moderately easy.

Marienwürmehen (My Lady Bird)—Schumann, arr. Robinson
G. Schirmer No. 10743. Accompanied. Medium.

Mocking of Youth—Bartók
Boosey & Hawkes No. 1955. *A cappella.* Medium.

Mother, I Will Have a Husband—Vautor
Bourne No. ES 11. Optional accompaniment. Moderately easy.

Musetta's Waltz Song (from *La Bohème*)—Puccini
Boosey & Hawkes No. 5120. Accompanied. Moderately easy.

Music When Soft Voices Die—Clokey, arr. Cain
Flammer No. 83121. *A cappella.* Easy.

Nightingale, The—Weelkes, arr. Leslie
    E. C. Schirmer No. 1008. *A cappella.* Moderately difficult.

O Lovely Spring—Brahms, arr. Grant
    Belwin No. 1839. Accompanied. Medium.

Pat-a-Pan (Burgundian carol; Christmas)—arr. Davis
    E. C. Schirmer No. 1052. *A cappella.* Medium.

Prayer from *Hansel and Gretel*—Humperdinck, arr. Riegger
    Flammer No. 83087. Accompanied. Easy.

Pretense—Clokey
    J. Fischer No. 7361. Accompanied. Moderately easy.

Robin Loves Me—De La Halle
    Edition Musicus No. 014. Optional accompaniment. Easy.

Silent Strings—Bantock, arr. O'Shea
    Boosey & Hawkes No. 1467. Accompanied. Moderately easy.

Slumber, Beloved One—Ravel, arr. Douty
    Presser No. 21434. Accompanied. Moderately difficult.

Slumber Song—Gretchaninoff
    G. Schirmer No. 7510. Accompanied. Moderately easy.

Smith, The—Brahms
    Presser No. 312–40053. Accompanied. Easy.

Song of Sorrow—Schumann
    Leeds Music No. L-423. Optional accompaniment. Moderately
    easy.

Songs My Mother Taught Me—Dvořák, arr. Cain
    Flammer No. 83097. Accompanied. Moderately easy.

Spanish Serenata—Granados, arr. Harris
    G. Schirmer No. 7814. Accompanied. Moderately difficult.

Tambourine, The—Schumann
    Leeds Music No. L-428. Optional accompaniment. Medium.

Weep, O Mine Eyes—Wilbye
    E. C. Schirmer No. 841. *A cappella.* Moderately easy.

While the Birds Are Singing—Boccherini, arr. Ambrose
    Schmidt No. 747. Accompanied. Moderately difficult.

Who Is Sylvia?—Schubert
    G. Schirmer No. 733. Accompanied. Moderately easy.

Within My Heart Breathes Music—Brahms, arr. Gibb
    J. Fischer No. 9158. Accompanied. Moderately easy.

Younger Generation—Copland, arr. Swift
  Boosey & Hawkes No. 1722. Accompanied. Medium.

Folk Songs and Spirituals

Ay, Ay, Ay!—Freire-Malin
  Piedmont No. 4372. Accompanied. Moderately easy.

Charlottown—Bryan
  J. Fischer No. 7993. *A cappella.* Medium.

Chiapanecas (Mexican dance song)—arr. Marlowe
  Huntzinger No. 2039. Accompanied. Moderately easy.

Czechoslovakian Dance Song—arr. Row
  R. D. Row No. 234. *A cappella.* Easy.

Dove on the Lily Tree, The (Swedish folk song)—arr. Vené
  Carl Fischer No. CM 6280. Accompanied. Easy.

Down by the Sally Gardens (Old Irish Air)—arr. Donovan
  Galaxy No. 555. Accompanied. Moderately easy.

Early One Morning (old English folk song)—arr. Scott
  Shawnee. Accompanied. Medium.

Farewell (Austrian folk song)—arr. Kanitz
  Carl Fischer No. CM 6397. Accompanied. Easy.

Goin' to Boston (Kentucky folk song)—arr. Davis
  Summy-Birchard No. 1573. Accompanied. Medium.

Good Night (German folk song)—arr. Malin
  B. F. Wood No. 830. Accompanied. Moderately easy.

Gute Nacht (German folk song)—arr. G. W. W.
  E. C. Schirmer No. 819. Accompanied. Medium.

He's Gone Away (American folk song)—arr. Seigmeister-Ehret
  Bourne No. 203. Accompanied. Moderately easy.

Hi, Ho, Sing Gaily (Swiss folk tune)—arr. Luvaas
  Summy-Birchard No. 1505. Accompanied. Easy.

Ifca's Castle (Czechoslovakian folk song)—arr. Harley &
  Aschenbrenner.
  Carl Fischer No. 5323. *A cappella.* Moderately easy.

I Got Shoes (Spiritual)—arr. Cain
  Flammer No. 83206. Accompanied. Moderately easy.

I Live Not Where I Love (traditional English tune)—arr. Parry
Oxford No. W45. Accompanied. Easy.

Keel Row, The (Tyneside air)—arr. Fletcher
Curwen No. 71227. Optional accompaniment. Medium.

Linden Lea—Vaughan Williams
Boosey & Hawkes No. MFS 219. Accompanied. Moderately
easy.

Little Bird (Mexican folk song)—arr. Grant
Belwin No. 1723. Accompanied. Moderately easy.

Little David, Play on Your Harp (spiritual)—arr. Cain
Flammer No. 83178. Accompanied. Easy.

Little Sandman, The (German folk song)—arr. Harley &
Aschenbrenner. Carl Fischer No. CM 5280. *A cappella.* Easy.

Lollytoodum (American folk song)—arr. Bell
Shawnee. Accompanied. Medium.

May Day Carol (English folk song)—arr. Taylor
J. Fischer No. 4872. Accompanied. Moderately easy.

Meadows, Grow Ye Greene (Austrian folk song)—arr. Kanitz
Carl Fischer No. CM 6395. Accompanied. Easy.

Memories (Irish folk tune)—arr. Luvaas
Summy-Birchard No. 374. *A cappella.* Easy.

Meneate, Buena Moza (Spanish folk song)—arr. Malin
Piedmont No. 4374. Accompanied. Moderately easy.

My Desert Flower (North African folk song)—arr. Marshall
Belwin No. 1821. Accompanied. Moderately easy.

O Can Ye Sew Cushions? (old Scottish cradle song)— arr. Mansfield
Mills No. 711. Accompanied. Moderately easy.

O Little Star in the Sky (Swedish folk tune)—arr. Davis
E. C. Schirmer No. 1065. Accompanied. Medium.

O Mary, Don't You Weep (Spiritual)—arr. Siegmaster & Ehret
Bourne No. 25. Accompanied. Medium.

Old Woman and the Pedlar, The (English air)—arr. Davis
E. C. Schirmer No. 1060. *A cappella.* Medium.

Rock-a My Soul (Spiritual)—arr. De Vaux
Bourne No. 195. Accompanied. Medium.

Shy Love (Ukrainian folk song)—arr. Boberg
Kjos No. 6088. Accompanied. Easy.

Song of a Happy Heart (Ukrainian folk song)—arr. Boberg
Kjos No. 6091. Accompanied. Easy.

Swallow's Wooing, The (Hungarian children's song)—arr. Kodály
Oxford No. 542. *A cappella.* Medium.

Swing Low, Sweet Chariot (Spiritual)—arr. Burleigh
Ricordi No. 116469. Accompanied. Moderately easy.

Three Highland Airs (traditional Scotch melodies)—arr. Best
Shawnee No. B-158. Accompanied. Moderately easy.

Three Hungarian Folks Songs—Bartok
Boosey & Hawkes No. 5488. Accompanied. Moderately easy.

Vreneli (Swiss folk song)—arr. Lester
Belwin No. 1830. Accompanied. Moderately easy.

Wandering River (Korean folk song)—arr. Ritz
Westwood Press No. ESE-1432-3. Accompanied. Moderately
easy.

Waters Ripple and Flow (Czechoslovak folk song)—arr. Taylor
J. Fischer No. 5065. Accompanied. Moderately difficult.

We Wish You a Merry Christmas (English folk song)—arr. Krone
Kjos No. 1211. Optional accompaniment. Medium.

When Love Is Kind (traditional English or Austrian)—arr. Trinkaus
Carl Fischer No. 6139. Accompanied. Moderately easy.

PUBLICATIONS FOR MALE VOICES (TTBB)

Sacred

Adoramus Te—Palestrina, arr. Greyson
Bourne No. ES 16. *A cappella.* Easy.

Adoramus Te, Christe—Corsi, arr. Cain
Choral Art No. R180. *A cappella.* Moderately easy.

All Glory Be to God on High (chorale melody of Gregorian origin)—
arr. Malin. Summy-Birchard No. 1538. Accompanied. Moderately easy.

Alleluia—Handel, arr. Dawe
G. Schirmer No. 9412. Accompanied. Tenor solo. Moderately
difficult.

At Sunset—Schubert, arr. Ringwald
 Shawnee. Accompanied. Medium.

Ave Maria (Give Ear Unto my Prayer)—Arcadelt, arr. Greyson
 Bourne No. ES 4. Optional accompaniment. Moderately difficult.

Ave, Maria—Vittoria, arr. Cain
 Choral Art No. R174. *A cappella.* Moderately easy.

Ave, Maris Stella (Hail, O Star; Christmas)—Grieg, arr. Pitcher
 Summy-Birchard No. 881. *A cappella.* Moderately difficult.

Babe, So Tender, A (old Flemish carol)—arr. Manton
 E. C. Schirmer No. 543. *A cappella.* Medium.

Beautiful Savior (Silesian folk tune)—arr. F. M. Christiansen &
 Wycisk. Augsburg No. 263. *A cappella.* Moderately easy.

Behold That Star (Spiritual-Christmas)—arr. Cunkle
 Shawnee No. 10. *A cappella.* Bass solo. Medium.

Carol of the Russian Children (White Russian carol)—arr. Gaul
 G. Schirmer No. 7363. Optional accompaniment. Medium.

Christ Is Born of Maiden Fair (ancient carol)—ed. H. Clough-
 Leighter. E. C. Schirmer No. 515. *A cappella.* Medium.

Christmas Hymn (17th century)—arr. Jüngst
 G. Schirmer No. 1414. *A cappella.* Moderately easy.

Come, Sweet Death—Bach, arr. Reed
 G. Schirmer No. 8956. *A cappella.* Moderately easy.

God Rest You Merry, Gentlemen (English carol)—arr. the Krones
 Kjos No. 1117. Optional accompaniment. Moderately easy.

Hallelujah (from *Mount of Olives*)—Beethoven
 G. Schirmer No. 10774. Accompanied. Moderately difficult.

Hallelujah, Amen—Handel, arr. Davison
 E. C. Schirmer No. 38. Accompanied. Moderately difficult.

Heart Worships, The—Holst, arr. Duey
 Boston Music No. 2952. Accompanied. Medium.

Heavenly Light—Kopylov, arr. Wilhousky
 Carl Fischer No. CM 611. *A cappella.* Moderately difficult.

I Wonder as I Wander (Appalachian carol)—arr. Niles & Horton
 G. Schirmer No. 9292. *A cappella.* Medium.

Jacob's Ladder (Spiritual)—arr. Wilson
 Ricordi No. NY1680. Optional accompaniment. Medium.

Jesus, Joy of My Endeavor (chorale from *Cantata No. 147*) —Bach, arr. Scott. Shawnee. Accompanied. Moderately easy.

Joyous Christmas Song, A (Norwegian carol) —arr. Hokanson Summy-Birchard No. 3142. *A cappella.* Moderately easy.

Let All Give Thanks to Thee—Bach, arr. Treharne G. Schirmer No. 8342. *A cappella.* Moderately easy.

Let Nothing Ever Grieve Thee—Brahms C. F. Peters No. 6009. Accompanied. Medium.

Let Thy Holy Presence—Tschesnokov, arr. Ehret Boosey & Hawkes No. 5022. *A cappella.* Moderately easy.

Lullaby of the Christ Child (old French carol) —arr. Scott Shawnee. *A cappella.* Incidental ten. solo. Medium.

Matthew, Mark, Luke, and John (West Country folk song) —arr. Holst. Curwen No. 50616. *A cappella.* Ten. solo. Moderately easy.

May Now Thy Spirit—Schuetky, arr. Treharne Willis No. 5641. *A cappella.* Medium.

May Thy Blessed Spirit—Tschesnokov, arr. Cookson Fitzsimons No. 4062. *A cappella.* Medium.

My Gracious Lord and Master—Schubert Piedmont No. 4450. *A cappella.* Medium.

Nature's Praise of God—Beethoven G. Schirmer No. 6566. Optional accompaniment. Moderately easy.

Noel, Noel—Gevaert, arr. Grayson Kjos No. 5513. Accompanied. Easy.

Now Thank We All Our God—Cruger, harmonized by Mendelssohn Boston Music No. 471. Organ accompaniment. Easy.

O Bone Jesu—Palestrina Bourne No. ES 45. *A cappella.* Easy.

O Light Divine—Arkhangelsky, arr. Bement Oliver Ditson No. 15182. *A cappella.* Medium.

O Lovely, Holy Night (Christmas) —Kremser, arr. Biedermann J. Fischer No. 3344. *A cappella.* Medium.

Praise the Name of the Lord—Ivanoff, arr. McKinney J. Fischer No. 9166. *A cappella.* Medium.

Requiem Aeternam—Cherubini
  Edition Musicus No. 1013. *A cappella.* Moderately easy.

Sleep of the Child Jesus—Gevaert, arr. Lefebvre
  Franco Colombo No. NY773. *A cappella.* Easy.

Stars, The—Schubert, arr. Larson
  Summy-Birchard No. 5021. *A cappella.* Tenor solo. Medium.

Tell Me, Shepherds, Dear (Polish carol)—arr. H. G. M.
  E. C. Schirmer No. 2105. *A cappella.* Medium.

Thanks Be to Thee—Handel, arr. Lefebvre
  Galaxy No. 1222. Accompanied. Tenor solo. Easy.

They Sang that Night in Bethlehem—Schubert, arr. Deis
  G. Schirmer No. 8292. *A cappella.* Medium.

Thou Must Leave Thy Lowly Dwelling—Berlioz
  Galaxy No. 2065. Accompanied. Medium.

Who Ne'er His Bread with Tears Did Eat—Schubert
  Lawson-Gould No. 876. Accompanied. Medium.

With a Voice of Singing—Shaw
  G. Schirmer No. 10454. Piano or organ accompaniment. Medium.

Ye Watchers and Ye Holy Ones (17th-century German melody)—arr.
  Davison. E. C. Schirmer No. 65. Piano or organ accompaniment.
  Medium.

Secular

Aura Lee—Poulton, arr. Hunter-Parker-Shaw
  Lawson-Gould No. 527. *A cappella.* Moderately easy.

Battle Hymn of the Republic—Steffe, arr. Ringwald
  Shawnee. Four-hand piano accompaniment. Bar. solo. Medium.

Brothers, Sing On!—Grieg, arr. McKinney
  J. Fischer No. 6927. *A cappella.* Medium.

By the Sea—Schubert, arr. Bantock
  Mills Music No. 1145. *A cappella.* Moderately easy.

Crown of Roses, The—Tchaikovsky, arr. Bell
  Mills Music No. 1085. *A cappella.* Medium.

Death Came Knocking—Floyd
  Boosey & Hawkes No. 5368. Accompanied. Moderately difficult.

Dreams—Wagner, arr. Scherer
Gray No. 436. Accompanied. Medium.

Gambler's Lament, The—Niles
G. Schirmer No. 10305. Accompanied. Medium.

Good Fellows Be Merry—Bach, arr. Duey
Boston Music No. 2944. Accompanied. Difficult.

Holiday Song—Schuman
G. Schirmer No. 9866. Accompanied. Moderately easy.

In the Doorways I Will Linger—Schubert, arr. Rider
Lawson-Gould No. 875. Accompanied. Medium.

Laura Lee—Foster, arr. Parker-Shaw
Lawson-Gould No. 874. *A cappella.* Moderately easy.

Musical Trust, The—Hadley
G. Schirmer No. 5800. *A cappella.* Medium.

Night, The (Die Nacht)—Schubert
Lawson-Gould No. 786. *A cappella.* Medium.

Nocturne—Mendelssohn, arr. Treharne
Boston Music No. 2987. Accompanied. Moderately difficult.

Passing By—Purcell, arr. Parker-Shaw
Lawson-Gould No. 967. *A cappella.* Moderately easy.

Pilgrims' Chorus (from *Tannhauser*)—Wagner
Kjos No. 5490. *A cappella.* Medium.

Pilgrim's Song—Tchaikovsky, arr. Treharne
G. Schirmer No. 8802. Accompanied. Moderately difficult.

Rain Has Kissed the Rose, The—Schumann
G. Schirmer No. 412. *A cappella.* Moderately easy.

Rest (Du Bist Die Ruh)—Schubert, arr. Bantock
Mills Music No. 1146. *A cappella.* Medium.

Rhapsodie—Brahms
Boston Music No. 229. Accompanied. Alto solo. Moderately difficult.

Serenade—Haydn, arr. Schultz
G. Schirmer No. 1087. *A cappella.* Easy.

Sophomoric Philosophy—Dvorak
Remick No. 9G 1108. *A cappella.* Moderately easy.

Stopwatch and an Ordinance Map, A—Barber
G. Schirmer No. 8799. Kettledrum accompaniment. Moderately difficult.

Stouthearted Men—Romberg, arr. Scotson
Harms, Inc., No. 9–H1184. Accompanied. Moderately easy.

Swan, The—Saint-Saëns, arr. Boyce
G. Schirmer No. 10527. Humming chorus with violin solo and piano accompaniment. Medium.

Sweet Love Doth Now Invite—Dowland
Bourne No. ES7. Optional accompaniment. Moderately easy.

To All You Ladies Now on Land—Callcott
E. C. Schirmer No. 533. *A cappella.* Moderately easy.

When Allen-A-Dale Went A-Hunting—Pearsall, arr. Shepherd
Modern Music Press No. 4152. *A cappella.* Medium.

Winter Song—Bullard
Oliver Ditson No. 10160. Accompanied. Moderately easy.

Woods So Dense—Lully, arr. Sodero
G. Schirmer No. 8568. *A cappella.* Moderately easy.

Folk Songs and Spirituals

All Through the Night (old Welsh song)—arr. Ringwald
Shawnee Press No. C-21. Optional accompaniment. Medium.

A-Roving (sea chantey)—arr. Wagner
Lawson-Gould No. 791. *A cappella.* Baritone solo. Medium.

Believe Me, If All Those Endearing Young Charms (old Irish air)—
arr. Hunter, Parker & Shaw. Lawson-Gould No. 528. *A cappella.* Medium.

Blow the Man Down (English sea chantey)—arr. Parker-Shaw
Lawson-Gould No. 51055. *A cappella.* Bass solo. Moderately difficult.

Boar's Head Carol, The (English secular carol)—arr. Parker-Shaw
G. Schirmer No. 10179. *A cappella.* Easy.

Carol of the Bells (Ukrainian carol; Christmas)—Leontovich, arr. Wilhousky. Carl Fischer No. CM 2270. *A cappella.* Moderately easy.

Climbin' Up the Mountain (Negro spiritual)—arr. Smith
Kjos No. 1101. *A cappella.* Medium.

De Animals a-Comin' (Negro spiritual) —arr. Bartholomew
G. Schirmer No. 8046. *A cappella*. Medium.

Down Among the Dead Men (old English air) —arr. Vaughan
Williams. Mills Music No. 1142. *A cappella*. Medium.

Down in the Valley (Kentucky folk tune) —arr. Mead
Galaxy No. 1716. Accompanied. Moderately easy.

Drink to Me Only with Thine Eyes (old English air) —arr. Hunter,
Parker & Shaw. Lawson-Gould No. 530. *A cappella*. Moderately
easy.

Gloustershire Wassail (traditional old English yule song) —arr. Scott
Words & Music. Accompanied. Baritone solo. Moderately difficult.

Go Tell It on the Mountain (Negro spiritual) —arr. Huntley
Fitzsimons No. 4067. *A cappella*. Easy.

Green Grow the Rushes O! (Scottish folk song) —arr. Roberton
R. D. Row No. 519. *A cappella*. Medium.

Hickory Stick, The (American folk song) —arr. Sheppard
Boston Music No. 13042. Optional accompaniment. Medium.

I Got Shoes (Negro spiritual) —arr. Bartholomew
G. Schirmer No. 7144. *A cappella*. Moderately easy.

John Peel (old English hunting song) —arr. Andrews
Gray No. 31. *A cappella*. Moderately easy.

Lincolnshire Poacher, The (English folk song) —arr. Bantock
Mills Music. *A cappella*. Medium.

Little Innocent Lamb (Negro spiritual) —arr. Bartholomew
G. Schirmer. No. 9907. *A cappella*. Moderately easy.

Lord Randall (British folk song) —arr. Duey
Boston Music No. 2954. *A cappella*. Baritone or tenor solo.
Medium.

Marianina (Italian folk song) —arr. Parker-Shaw
Lawson-Gould No. 974. *A cappella*. Tenor solo. Medium.

My Johnny Was a Shoemaker (English folk song) —arr. Taylor
J. Fischer No. 4834. Accompanied. Medium.

My Lord, What a Mornin' (Negro spiritual) —arr. Burleigh
Franco Colombo No. NY1713. *A cappella*. Moderately easy.

Night Herding Song (cowboy song) —arr. Luboff
Walton No. 1006. Accompanied. Easy.

O Tannenbaum (traditional German)—arr. Parker & Shaw
G. Schirmer No. 10195. *A cappella.* Moderately easy.

Old Chisholm Trail, The (Western folk song)—arr. Cain
Pro Art No. 1483. Accompanied. Easy.

On Top of Old Smoky (American folk song)—arr. Stone
Pro Art No. 1347. Accompanied. Easy.

Over Here (Irish folk song)—arr. Roberton
Boosey & Hawkes No. 1987. *A cappella.* Moderately easy.

Poor Lonesome Cowboy (cowboy song)—arr. Luboff
Walton No. 1007. *A cappella.* Moderately easy.

Poor Man Lazrus (Negro spiritual)—arr. Hairston
Bourne No. S1022. *A cappella.* Medium.

Rantin' Rovin' Robin (Scottish folk song)—arr. Davison
E. C. Schirmer No. 84. Accompanied. Baritone solo. Moderately
easy.

Rebel Soldier, The (American folk song)—arr. Sheppard
Boston Music No. 3081. *A cappella.* Moderately easy.

Ride the Chariot (Negro spiritual)—arr. Smith
Kjos No. 1102. *A cappella.* Tenor solo. Moderately easy.

Rio Grande (sea chantey)—arr. Dougherty
G. Schirmer No. 10414. Accompanied. Moderately easy.

Scissors-Grinder, The (Flemish folk song)—arr. Jungst
G. Schirmer No. 10414. Accompanied. Moderately easy.

Sippin' Cider (American folk song)—arr. Sheppard
Summy-Birchard No. 1588. *A cappella.* Moderately easy.

Sister Mary Wore Three Lengths of Chain (Negro spiritual)—arr.
Bartholomew. G. Schirmer No. 10243. *A cappella.* Medium.

Soon-Ah Will Be Done—Dawson
Tuskegee No. 101. *A cappella.* Moderately difficult.

Sourwood Mountain (Kentucky mountain song)—arr. Hall
G. Schirmer No. 8140. *A cappella.* Medium.

Swansea Town (Hampshire folk song)—arr. Holst
Curwen No. 50615. *A cappella.* Medium.

Turtle Dove, The (folk song)—arr. Vaughan Williams
Curwen No. 50570. Accompanied. Baritone or tenor solo.
Medium.

We Wish You a Merry Christmas (English folk song; secular) —arr. the Krones. Kjos No. 1114. Optional accompaniment. Moderately easy.

What Shall We Do with a Drunken Sailor? (traditional sea chantey) —arr. Bartholomew. G. Schirmer No. 7422. Accompanied. Easy.

PUBLICATIONS FOR TWO PARTS (SA OR TB)

Achieved Is the Glorious Work—Haydn-Davies
 Oxford No. E111. Accompanied. Medium.

Ah, Lovely Meadows (Czech folk song) —arr. Kjelson
 Belwin No. 1901. Accompanied. Easy.

Ash Grove, The (Welsh folk song) —arr. Stone
 Belwin No. 2199. Accompanied. Moderately easy.

At the Gates of Heaven (Basque folk song) —arr. Kjelson
 Belwin No. 1903. Accompanied. Moderately easy.

Bright Star (Polish carol) —arr. Ehret
 Edw. B. Marks No. 4407. Accompanied. Moderately easy.

Christ Is Born to You Today (German folk song) —arr. Ehret
 Edw. B. Marks. No. 4408. Accompanied. Moderately easy.

Cielito Lindo (Mexican folk song) —arr. Tate
 Oxford No. T72. Accompanied. Medium.

Cindy (American folk song) —arr. Barthelson
 Belwin No. 1746. Moderately easy.

Come, All Ye Lads and Lassies (old English melody) —arr. Howorth
 Belwin No. 1847. Medium.

Coventry Carol (English carol) —arr. Stone
 Belwin No. 2142. Accompanied. Moderately easy.

Cuckoo Song (German folk song) —arr. Keldermans
 Greenwood Press No. ESE-1059-2. Accompanied. Easy.

Cuckoo, the Nightingale, and the Donkey, The—Mahler
 Oxford No. T75. Accompanied. Medium.

De Gospel Train (spiritual), and There's Music in the Air (G. F. Root) —arr. Rhea. Bourne No. MD2. Easy.

Drill, Ye Tarriers, Drill (American ballad) —arr. Kjelson
Belwin No. 1904. Moderately easy.

Go Tell it on the Mountain (Christmas spiritual) —arr. Barthelson
Belwin No. 1833. Moderately easy.

He's Goin' Away (American folk song) —arr. Howorth
Belwin No. 1848. Moderately easy.

He's Got the Whole World in His Hands (spiritual) —arr. Howorth
Belwin No. 1777. Optional solo. Moderately easy.

I Love Little Willie (Southern mountain song) —arr. Barthelson
Belwin No. 1748. Easy.

I'm Goin' Leave Old Texas Now (cowboy song) —arr. Pitcher
Belwin No. 1835. Easy.

Jesus Christ Our Savior is Born (Lithuanian carol) —arr. Gordon
Belwin No. 1844. Moderately easy.

Kentucky Babe—Giebel, arr. Churchill
Belwin No. 1836. Easy.

Let Us Cheer the Weary Traveller (Spiritual) —arr. Howorth
Belwin No. 1846. Medium.

Loch Lomond (old Scotch air) —arr. Kirk
Belwin No. 1605. Easy.

Lolly Tu-Dum (American folk song) —arr. Churchill
Belwin No. 1630. Moderately easy.

O Come, all Ye Children (German Christmas carol) —arr. Gordon
Belwin No. 1720. Easy.

Patapan (Burgundian carol) —arr. Jacques
Oxford No. T86. Accompanied. Easy.

Rocking (Christmas carol) —arr. Ehret
Scholin No. 2012. Medium.

Shenandoah (sea chantey) —arr. Stone
Belwin No. 2141. Accompanied. Moderately easy.

Sing Hallelujah, Praise the Lord (Moravian melody) —arr. Mueller
G. Schirmer No. 10754. Moderately easy.

Standin' in the Need of Prayer (Negro spiritual) —arr. Kjelson
Belwin No. 1902. With solo voice. Moderately easy.

Still, Still (German carol) —arr. Sumner
Scholin No. 2021. Easy.

Sweet Betsy From Pike (American folk song) —arr. Swift
Belwin No. 1622. Moderately easy.

The Cuckoo Cries—Möller, arr. Swift
Belwin No. 1436. With solo voices. Medium.

The Elephant and the Flea (nonsense song) —arr. Barthelson
Belwin No. 1747. Moderately easy.

There's a Little Wheel a-Turnin' (Negro spiritual)—arr. Vance
Belwin No. 1898. Optional third voice and solo. Medium.

Today with Loud Rejoicing—Mozart, arr. Heinrich
Boston No. 3117. Easy.

Viennese Lullaby (Viennese popular song) —arr. Wilson
Bourne No. HL 12. Easy.

Wandering River (Korean folk song) —arr. Papale
Westwood Press No. ESE-1413-2. Accompanied. Easy.

Wild Wind (Korean folk song) —arr. Papale
Westwood Press ESE-1415-2. Percussion accompaniment. Easy.

PUBLICATIONS FOR COMBINED CHORUS AND BAND AND/OR ORCHESTRA

All Glory, Laud and Honor—Teschner, arr. Cain
Flammer. SATB—For chorus and band; chorus and orchestra.

America—E. Williams
Morris. SSAATTBB—For chorus and band; chorus and orchestra; chorus, band, and orchestra.

Ave Maria—Bach-Gounod, arr. Tolmadge
Staff. SATB—For chorus and band.

Battle Hymn of the Republic—Steffe, arr. Ringwald
Shawnee. SATB; TTBB—For chorus and band; chorus and orchestra.

Battle Hymn of the Republic—Steffe, arr. Wilhousky
Carl Fischer. SSATTBB—For chorus and band; chorus and orchestra.

Beautiful Dreamer—Foster, arr. Frangkiser
Boosey & Hawkes. SATB; TTBB—For chorus and band.

Bells of St. Mary's—Adams, arr. Lucas & Clark
   Chappell. SATB—For chorus and band.

Break Forth, O Beauteous Heavenly Light—Bach
   G. Schirmer. SATB—For chorus and orchestra (orchestra parts
   available from publisher on rental only).

Brigadoon (choral selection)—Loewe, arr. Leidzen
   Sam Fox. SATB—For chorus and band; chorus and orchestra.

Choral Prelude on Dundee—Whitney
   Sam Fox. SATB—For chorus and band.

Choral Procession (Finale to Cantata *The Song of Man*)—Kountz,
   arr. Campbell-Watson. Witmark, SATB—For chorus and band.

Chorale: St. Antoni—Haydn-Brahms, arr. Tolmadge.
   Staff. SATB—For chorus and band.

Christmas Day—Holst
   Gray. SATB—For chorus and orchestra (orchestral parts available from publisher on rental only).

Christmas Story, The—Yoder
   Kjos. SATB—For chorus and band.

Come Let Us Sing (95th Psalm)—Mendelssohn
   G. Schirmer. SATB—For chorus and orchestra (orchestral parts
   available from publisher on rental only).

Elsa Entering the Cathedral (from *Lohengrin*)—Wagner, arr. Duelz-
   man. Carl Fischer. SSAATTBB—For chorus and orchestra
   (orchestral parts available from publisher on rental only).

Emperor Waltz—Strauss
   Sam Fox. SATB—For chorus and orchestra (orchestral parts
   available in Fox Festival Series for Orchestra, Book 3 by
   Dykema and Reibold).

Fantasie on Christmas Carols—Vaughan Williams
   Galaxy. SATB, with bar, solo—For chorus and orchestra
   (orchestral parts available from publisher on rental only).

Festival Finale—Maddy
   Kjos. SATB—For chorus and band; chorus and orchestra;
   chorus, band and orchestra.

Festival Song of Praise—Mendelssohn, arr. Wilson & Harris
   Bourne. SATB—For chorus and orchestra.

Gloria in Excelsis (from *Twelfth Mass*)—Mozart
   Presser. SATB—For chorus and orchestra.

Glory—Rimsky-Korsakov
    Witmark. SSAATTBB—For chorus and orchestra.

Glory and Honor—J. S. Bach, arr. Klein
    Schmitt, Hall & McCreary. SATB—For chorus and band.

Glory and Triumph—Berlioz
    Mercury. SATB—For chorus and band; chorus and orchestra.

Glory to God in the Highest—Pergolesi, arr. Houseknecht
    Kjos. SATB—For chorus and band.

God of Our Fathers—arr. Gearhart
    Shawnee. SATB—For chorus, with three trumpets, percussion,
    four-hand piano and organ accompaniment.

Gypsy Songs (Zigeunerlieder)—Brahms
    Carl Fischer. SATB; SSA; TTBB—For chorus and orchestra
    (orchestral score and parts available from publisher on rental
    only).

Hail, Glorious Day—Elgar, arr. Schaefer
    Boosey & Hawkes. SATB—For chorus and band.

Hallelujah Chorus (from *Messiah*)—Handel
    Carl Fischer. SATB—For chorus and orchestra; chorus and
    band.

Heavens Are Telling, The—Haydn
    Carl Fischer. SATB—For chorus and orchestra.

Holy, Holy, Holy—arr. Ledizén
    Bourne. SATB—For chorus and band.

How Lovely Is Thy Dwelling (from *Requiem*)—Brahms
    G. Schirmer. SATB—For chorus and orchestra (orchestral parts
    available from publisher on rental only).

Hymn of Freedom—Brahms, arr. Tolmadge
    Staff. SATB—For chorus and band.

Hymn of Praise—Mozart, arr. Tolmadge
    Staff. SATB—For chorus and band.

Hymn to America—McKay
    Schmitt, Hall & McCreary. SATB—For chorus and band.

Joshua—Moussorgsky
    G. Schirmer. SAATTBB—For chorus and orchestra (orchestral
    parts available from publisher on rental only).

Joshua (a rhythmic novelty)—arr. Yoder
    Kjos. SATB—For chorus and band.

Land of Hope and Glory—Elgar
> Boosey & Hawkes. SATB; SSA—For chorus and band; chorus and orchestra.

Land of Our Fathers (ode to America)—Lavalle
> Sam Fox. SATB—For chorus and band.

Land-Sighting—Grieg
> G. Schirmer. SATB—For chorus and orchestra (orchestral parts available from publisher on rental only).

Largo from *New World Symphony* (choral parts: "Behold Our God")—Dvořák. Belwin. SATB—For chorus and band.

Let All Mortal Flesh Keep Silence—Holst
> Galaxy. SATB—For chorus and orchestra.

Lift Up Your Heads—Coleridge-Taylor, arr. Buchtel
> Kjos. SATB—For chorus and band.

Magnificat—Vaughan Williams
> Oxford. SSA, with contr. solo—For chorus and orchestra (orchestral parts available from publisher on rental only).

Mannin Veen (Dear Isle of Man)—Wood
> Boosey & Hawkes. SATB; SAB; SSA—For chorus and orchestra; chorus and band.

Message of the Bells (Prelude in C♯ Minor)—Rachmaninoff, arr. Lester. Remick. SATB—For chorus and orchestra.

Mighty Fortress Is Our God, A—Luther, arr. Caillet
> Boosey & Hawkes. SATB; TTBB—For chorus and band; chorus and orchestra.

Nation's Creed, The—Williams
> Schmitt, Hall & McCreary. SATB—For chorus and band.

Nation's Prayer, The (Panis Angelicus)—Franck
> Belwin. SATB; SSA; TTBB—For chorus and band; chorus and orchestra; chorus, band and orchestra.

O Clap Your Hands—Vaughan Williams
> Galaxy. SATB—For chorus, brass choir and percussion.

Ode to America—Cain
> Flammer. SATB; SAB; SSA—For chorus and band; chorus and orchestra; chorus, band and orchestra.

Old Black Joe—Foster, arr. Frangkiser
> Boosey & Hawkes. SATB; TTBB—For chorus and band.

Omnipotence, The—Franz Schubert
 G. Schirmer. SSAATTBB; TTBB; SSA—For chorus and orchestra (orchestral parts available from publisher on rental only).

One World—O'Hara, arr. Wilson & Leidzen
 Bourne. SATB; TTBB; SSA—For chorus and band; chorus and orchestra.

Onward, Christian Soldiers—arr. Simeone
 Shawnee. SATB; TTBB—For chorus and band; chorus and orchestra.

Onward, Ye Peoples—Sibelius, arr. Lefebvre
 Galaxy. SATB; SSA; TTBB—For chorus and band; chorus and orchestra.

Pilgrims' Chorus, The (from *Tannhäuser*) —Wagner
 G. Schirmer. SATB—For chorus and orchestra (orchestral parts available from publisher on rental only).

Prayer for United Nations—Moore.
 Gray. SATB—For chorus and orchestra (orchestral parts available from publisher on rental only).

Rhapsody in Blue (choral finale) —Gershwin, arr. Warnick
 Harms, Inc. SSATTBB—For chorus and band; chorus and orchestra.

Romany Life—Herbert
 Witmark, SATB; SA; SSA; SSAA; TTBB; with sop. solo—For chorus and orchestra; chorus and band.

Rose Marie (choral selections) —Friml and Stothart, arr. MacLean-Schoenfeld. Witmark. SATB—For chorus and band.

Soldiers' Chorus (from *Faust*) —Gounod
 G. Schirmer. TTBB; SATB—For chorus and orchestra (orchestration available for either arrangement from publisher on rental only).

Spirit of Music—Bennett
 Carl Fischer. SATB divided—For chorus and band; chorus and orchestra; chorus, band and orchestra).

To Music—Schubert, arr. Wilson
 Schmitt, Hall & McCreary. SATB; SAB; SSA—For chorus and orchestra.

Turn Back, O Man—Holst
 Galaxy. SATB—For chorus and orchestra (orchestral parts available from publisher on rental only).

Victor Herbert Favorites—arr. MacLean
  Witmark. SATB; SSA; TTBB—For chorus and orchestra; chorus and band.

Voice of Freedom—Rubinstein, arr. Caillet
  Boosey & Hawkes. SATB; TTBB—For chorus and band; chorus and orchestra.

With a Voice of Singing—Shaw
  G. Schirmer. SATB—For chorus and orchestra (orchestral accompaniment available from publisher on rental only).

Yuletide Overture—Lang
  Mills. SATB—For chorus and band.

CHORAL COLLECTIONS

Whether or not to use choral collections has been a subject of some concern to conductors. One's criterion in arriving at a decision should simply be: Is it possible to use the majority of the selections in the collection? If so, then the use of a collection may be a saving to the budget. When it is not feasible to use most of the selections, then it is a better practice to utilize separate octavo publications. Following are particular collections that the author has found useful, and that the conductor will want to examine to see if they meet the particular needs of his groups.

Collections for mixed voices (SATB, SAB) [2]

A Cappella Singer, The—edited by Clough-Leighter. E. C. Schirmer 1682. A collection of 30 secular selections, primarily madrigals, from the choral literature of the sixteenth and early seventeenth centuries. An excellent basic book for madrigal groups.

Carols for Choirs—edited and arranged by Reginald Jacques and David Willcocks. Oxford University Press. A collection of 50 Christmas carols, arranged mostly for mixed voices.

Choral Program Series (Books Four, Five, and Six)— Harry R. Wilson. Silver Burdett. Each book contains representative numbers from various styles of choral literature. Book Four contains 17 easy, three-part selections (SAB) for junior high school choirs.

---

[2] All collections are for SATB unless otherwise indicated.

Book Five contains 15 numbers for mixed groups (SATB). Optional descants and solos are included for several selections. Book Six contains 12 more advanced selections for mixed voices (SATB). Some numbers have divided parts.

Concord Anthem Book, The—compiled and edited by Archibald T. Davison and Henry Wilder Foote. E. C. Schirmer No. 13. (Cloth bound.) Contains 40 anthems selected from the choral literature of the sixteenth through the nineteenth centuries. Music varies in difficulty from easy to moderately difficult.

First Motet Book, A—compiled and edited by Paul Thomas, Concordia Publishing House. Contains 17 motets in a variety of styles from the Renaissance to the twentieth century.

Five Centuries of Choral Music—compiled by a committee of teachers in the Los Angeles City High Schools, William C. Hartshorn, Supervisor in charge. G. Schirmer, Inc. A collection of 30 compositions representing various types and styles from the Renaissance to the present.

Golden Age of the Madrigal, The—edited by Alfred Einstein. G. Schirmer, Inc. Twelve Italian madrigals for five-part chorus of mixed voices.

Renaissance to Baroque—edited by Lehman Engel. Harold Flammer. A collection, in seven volumes, of choral music from the Renaissance and Baroque periods. Volume I, French-Netherland Music; Volume II, Italian Music; Volume III, English Music; Volume IV, German Music; Volume V, Spanish Music; Volume VI; English Music; Volume VII, French Music.

Second Concord Anthem Book, The—compiled and edited by Archibald T. Davison and Henry Wilder Foote. E. C. Schirmer No. 1200. (Cloth bound.) Contains 40 additional anthems selected from the choral literature of the sixteenth through the nineteenth centuries. Music varies in difficulty from easy to moderately difficult.

3 to Make Music—Hawley Ades, and edited by Lara Hoggard. Shawnee Press. "Three part songs for girls and boys." A collection of 32 songs—folk songs, spirituals, patriotic, faith and brotherhood, Christmas and general secular. Difficulty: easy to medium.

Collections for Treble Voices (SA, SSA, SSAA)

Choral Program Series (Books One and Two)—Harry R. Wilson. Silver Burdett. Each book contains representative selections from various styles of choral literature. Book One contains 17 two-part songs (SA) for girls' voices. Book Two contains 17 three- and four-part selections for girls' glee clubs (SSA and SSAA).

Christmas Carols for Treble Choirs—arranged and edited by Florence M. Martin. Schmitt, Hall & McCreary, Auditorium Series No. 56. (SA and SSA.) A collection of 15 Christmas carols. Difficulty: easy to medium.

Concert Songs for Girls—edited by M. Therese Armitage. Summy-Birchard. A collection of 106 selections in two, three, and four parts (SA, SSA, SSAA). Folk songs, songs by master composers as well as contemporary writers. For high school girls' glee clubs.

Glenn Glee Club Book for Girls—edited by Mabelle Glenn and Virginia French. Oliver Ditson. A collection of 42 songs for use in junior and senior high schools.

Presser Choral Collection: Sacred and Secular Literature—Past and Present—general editors, Geraldine Healy and William C. Hartshorn. Theodore Presser Company. A collection of 40 compositions for treble voices, representing various types and styles of choral music, compiled by a committee of choral music teachers in the Los Angeles City Public Schools.

Collections for Male Voices (TB, TTB, TTBB)

Birchard Choral Collections No. 1 (TTBB)—edited by J. Lilian Vandevere and Stuart B. Hoppin. Summy-Birchard. Fifty songs of various types—work songs, patriotic songs, classics, hymns, spirituals, and nonsense songs. Difficulty: easy to medium.

Choral Program Series (Book Three)—Harry R. Wilson. Silver Burdett. Contains a variety of types and styles of music. Seventeen selections for boys' glee clubs in two, three, and four parts (TB, TTB, and TTBB).

Christmas Carols for Male Voices—arranged and edited by George F. Strickling. Schmitt, Hall & McCreary, Auditorium Series No. 43. (TTBB.) Collection of 45 Christmas carols, some familiar, and other lesser-known carols from many countries. Difficulty: easy to medium.

Gentlemen Songsters—Livingston Gearhart, edited by Lara Hoggard. Shawnee Press. A collection of 42 songs for boys' glee clubs in two, three, and four parts TB, TTB, and TTBB). Sea chanties, songs of the American Revolution, ballads, folk songs, classics, songs for Christmas and other special occasions, college songs and novelties, songs of faith and brotherhood, spirituals, and patriotic songs. Difficulty: easy to medium.

EXTENDED CHORAL WORKS

All choral conductors should familiarize themselves with the extended choral works of various composers, for if a conductor is not familiar with major choral works, which in certain instances represent the crowning achievement of a composer, he has only an incomplete picture or concept of choral literature. Although the advanced high school choir could perform some of these works in their entirety, even an advanced choir could not perform certain others, because of their over-all difficulty. Conductors of college, university, and adult community choruses should examine all of these works for possible use by their groups.

Ahle, Joann Rudolf	
Be Not Afraid	Concordia
Antheil, George	
Cabeza de Vaca	Templeton Pub. Co.
Bach, Carl Philip Emanuel	
Holy Is God	Concordia;
Magnificat	G. Schirmer
Bach, Johann Christoph	
The Childhood of Christ	J. Fischer
Bach, Johann Sebastian	
Be Not Afraid (Motet IV)	C. F. Peters
Beautify Thyself, My Spirit	
(Cantata No. 180)	G. Schirmer
Christ Lay in Death's Dark Prison	Breitkopf & Härtel;
(Cantata No. 4)	G. Schirmer
Christmas Oratorio	G. Schirmer
The Coffee Cantata (3-part chorus)	G. Schirmer
Come, Jesus, Come (Motet V)	H. W. Gray;
	C. F. Peters
Come, My Spirit, Come Exalt	
(Cantata No. 189)	Breitkopf & Härtel
Come, Thou Lovely Hour	
(Cantata No. 161)	E. C. Schirmer

Deck Thyself, My Soul, With Gladness (Cantata No. 180)	E. C. Schirmer
Dem Gerechten muss das Licht (Cantata No. 195)	Breitkopf & Härtel
For as the Rain and Snow from Heaven Fall (Cantata No. 18)	G. Schirmer
For the Righteous, Wedding Cantata (No. 195)	Breitkopf & Härtel
For Us a Child Is Born (Cantata No. 142)	Galaxy
From Depths of Woe (Cantata No. 38)	E. C. Schirmer
Gloria in Excelsis Deo (Cantata No. 191)	G. Schirmer
God Is My King (Cantata No. 71)	Breitkopf & Härtel
God, the Lord Is Sun and Shield (Cantata No. 79)	G. Schirmer
God's Time Is the Best (Cantata No. 106)	G. Schirmer
Great David's Lord and Greater Son (Cantata No. 23)	E. C. Schirmer
The Heavens Declare the Glory of God (Cantata No. 76)	Breitkopf & Härtel
The Heavens Laugh, the Earth Exults (Cantata No. 31)	G. Schirmer
How Brightly Shines Yon Morning Star (Cantata No. 1)	E. C. Schirmer
I Suffered with Great Heaviness (Cantata No. 21)	G. Schirmer
If Thou wilt Suffer God to Guide Thee (Cantata No. 93)	G. Schirmer
In God I Place My Faith and Trust (Cantata No. 188)	G. Schirmer
It Is Enough (Cantata No. 82)	Breitkopf & Härtel
Jesus, My Great Pleasure (Motet III)	C. F. Peters
Jesus, Thou My Constant Gladness (Cantata No. 147)	H. W. Gray
Jesus, Thou My Wearied Spirit (Cantata No. 78)	G. Schirmer
Kantate	Breitkopf & Härtel
King of Heaven, Come in Triumph (Cantata No. 182)	E. C. Schirmer
Kyrie in D minor	G. Schirmer
Let Songs of Rejoicing Be Raised (Cantata No. 149)	H. W. Gray
Lord, Enter Not Into Wrath (Cantata No. 105)	E. C. Schirmer
Magnificat	Breitkopf & Härtel; C. F. Peters; G. Schirmer

Mass in B minor	G. Schirmer
Messe No. 4 in G Major	C. F. Peters
Missa Brevis in G	H. W. Gray
My Soul Doth Magnify the Lord (Cantata No. 10)	G. Schirmer
My Soul Exalts the Lord (Cantata No. 10)	E. C. Schirmer
New-Born Babe, The (Cantata No. 122)	G. Schirmer
Now Thank We All Our God (Cantata No. 192)	G. Schirmer
Nun ist das Heil und die Kraft (Cantata No. 50)	Breitkopf & Härtel
O Christ, My All in Living (Cantata No. 95)	Novello
O God, How Grievous (Cantata No. 3)	E. C. Schirmer
O Jesus Christ, My Life and Light (Cantata No. 118)	G. Schirmer
O Light Everlasting (Cantata No. 34)	E. C. Schirmer
O Lord, Relent, I Pray (Cantata No. 135)	E. C. Schirmer
O Lord, This Grieving Spirit (Cantata No. 135)	G. Schirmer
Ode of Mourning (Cantata No. 198)	G. Schirmer
Out of Darkness Call I Lord to Thee (Cantata No. 131)	Breitkopf & Härtel
O Praise the Lord for All His Mercies (Cantata No. 28)	H. W. Gray
Passion According to St. John, The	Breitkopf & Härtel; G. Schirmer
Passion According to St. Matthew, The	Breitkopf & Härtel; G. Schirmer
Peasant Cantata, The	Paterson's Pub. Ltd.
Praise Him, the Lord, the Almighty King (Cantata No. 137)	Breitkopf & Härtel
Praise Our God in All His Splendor (Cantata No. 11)	G. Schirmer
Praise the Lord, All ye Nations (Motet VI)	C. F. Peters
Sheep May Safely Graze (Cantata No. 208)	G. Schirmer
Sing Ye to the Lord (Motet I)	C. F. Peters
Sleepers, Wake! (Cantata No. 140)	H. W. Gray
The Spirit Also Helpeth Us (Motet II)	H. W. Gray; C. F. Peters
Stronghold Sure, A (Cantata No. 80)	G. Schirmer
There Uprose a Great Strife (Cantata No. 19)	G. Schirmer
Thou Guide of Israel (Cantata No. 104)	H. W. Gray

Thou Very God and David's Son
    (Cantata No. 23)   G. Schirmer
To Us a Child Is Given
    (Cantata No. 142)   G. Schirmer
We Must Through Great Tribulation
    (Cantata No. 146)   G. Schirmer
Weeping, Crying, Sorrow, Sighing
    (Cantata No. 12)   G. Schirmer
When Will God Recall My Spirit?
    (Cantata No. 8)   E. C. Schirmer
Barber, Samuel
    Prayers of Kierkegaard   G. Schirmer
Bartók, Béla
    Cantata Profana   Boosey & Hawkes
    Shepherd's Christmas Songs   Boosey & Hawkes
Beethoven, Ludwig van
    Cantata on the Death of
        Emperor Joseph II   G. Schirmer
    Choral Fantasia   Edwin F. Kalmus
    Choral Finale to the Ninth Symphony H. W. Gray;
                                     G. Schirmer
    Christ on the Mount of Olives   Edwin F. Kalmus
    Mass in C Major   Edwin F. Kalmus
    Mass in D   Novello
    Missa Solemnis, Op. 123   G. Schirmer
Berger, Jean
    Brazilian Psalm   G. Schirmer
    The Fiery Furnace   G. Schirmer
    Psalm 57   Theodore Presser
    Vision of Peace   Broude Bros.
Berlioz, Hector
    Childhood of Christ   G. Schirmer
    Childhood of Christ (abridged version) H. W. Gray
    Choral Suite from *Benvenuto Cellini* Oxford
    Grand Death Mass, Op. 5   Breitkopf & Härtel
    Requiem   G. Schirmer
    Te Deum   G. Schirmer
Bernstein, Leonard
    Chichester Psalms   G. Schirmer
    Choruses from *The Lark*   G. Schirmer
    Kaddish   G. Schirmer
Blitzstein, Marc
    The Airborne (cantata)   Chappell
Bloch, Ernest
    Sacred Service   Broude Bros.

Boito, Arrigo
    Prologue in Heaven (from *Mefistofele*)   G. Schirmer
Borodin, Alex
    Polovetzian Dance and Chorus
      (from *Prince Igor*)   G. Schirmer
Brahms, Johannes
    Love-Song Waltzes (Liebeslieder Walzer) Associated
    Marienlieder   Breitkopf & Härtel;
                              C. F. Peters;
                              E. C. Schirmer
    Motet from Psalm LI Op. 29, No. 2   G. Schirmer
    Nänie   G. Schirmer;
                              E. C. Schirmer
    Neue Liebeslieder   Lawson-Gould
    Requiem, Op. 45   Edwin F. Kalmus;
                              G. Schirmer
    Schicksalslied (Song of Destiny)   H. W. Gray;
                              E. C. Schirmer
    Triumphal Hymn   G. Schirmer
Britten, Benjamin
    Ballad of Heroes   Boosey & Hawkes
    Cantata Misericordium   Boosey & Hawkcs
    Ceremony of Carols, A (SATB; SSA) Boosey & Hawkes
    Festival Te Deum   Boosey & Hawkes
    Hymn to St. Cecilia   Boosey & Hawkes
    Rejoice in the Lamb   Boosey & Hawkes
    Saint Nicolas   Boosey & Hawkes
    Spring Symphony   Boosey & Hawkes
    Voices for Today   G. Schirmer
    War Requiem   Boosey & Hawkes
    Wedding Anthem, A (Amo ergo Sum) Boosey & Hawkes
Bruckner, Anton
    Mass No. 1 in D minor   C. F. Peters
    Mass No. 3 in F minor   C. F. Peters
    Mass in E minor   Broude Bros.
    Te Deum Laudamus   G. Schirmer
Buxtehude, Dietrich
    Aperite Mihi Portas Justitiae   C. F. Peters
      (Open to Me Gates of Justice)
    Good Christian Men, With Joy Draw
      Near   Concordia
    Jesu, Joy and Treasure   C. F. Peters
    Lauda Sion Salvatorem   Chantry Music Press
    Missa Brevis   Mercury
    Open to Me Gates of Justice   C. F. Peters

Rejoice, Earth and Heaven ... C. F. Peters
Sing to God the Lord ... Concordia
What Is the World to Me ... Concordia
Byrd, William
  Mass for 4 Voices ... Galaxy; Stainer & Bell
  Mass for 5 Voices ... Galaxy; Stainer & Bell
Carissimi, Giacomo
  Jephte ... Ricordi
Charpentier, Marc-Antoine
  Midnight Mass for Christmas ... Elkan-Vogel
  Venite ad me ... G. Schirmer
Cherubini, Luigi
  Requiem Mass in C minor ... G. Schirmer
  Requiem in D minor ... C. F. Peters
Coleridge-Taylor, Samuel
  Hiawatha's Wedding Feast ... G. Schirmer
Comes, Juan Bautista
  Beatus Vir ... G. Schirmer
  Lamentacion ... G. Schirmer
  Magnificat ... G. Schirmer
Copland, Aaron
  In the Beginning ... Boosey & Hawkes
Creston, Paul
  Celestial Vision, The ... Shawnee Press
  Isaiah's Phophecy ... Franco Colombo
  Missa Solemnis, Op. 44 ... Mills Music
Debussy, Claude
  Blessed Damoiselle, The ... G. Schirmer
  L'Enfant Prodigue ... Elkan-Vogel
  Ode à la France ... Elkan-Vogel
Delius, Frederick
  A Mass of Life ... Universal
  Appalachia ... Boosey & Hawkes
  Sea Drift ... Boosey & Hawkes
  Songs of Farewell ... Boosey & Hawkes
Dello Joio, Norman
  The Mystic Trumpeter ... G. Schirmer
  Psalm of David, A ... Carl Fischer
  Song of Affirmation ... Carl Fischer
  Song of the Open Road ... Carl Fischer
  To St. Cecilia ... Carl Fischer
  Years of the Modern ... Edward B. Marks
Diamond, David
  This Sacred Ground ... Southern Music
Dorati, Antal
  Missa Brevis ... Mills Music

Dubois, Theodore
    Seven Last Words of Christ, The   G. Schirmer
Duruflé, Maurice
    Requiem   Durand
Dvořák, Anton
    Stabat Mater, Op. 58   G. Schirmer
Effinger, Cecil
    Invisible Fire, The   H. W. Gray
    St. Luke Christmas Story, The   G. Schirmer
    Set of Three   Elkan-Vogel
Elgar, Edward
    Dream of Gerontius   Novello
    29th Psalm   Novello
    48th Psalm   Novello
Etler, Alvin
    Ode to Pothos   Associated
Fauré, Gabriel
    Requiem   H. T. Fitzsimons
Fetler, Paul
    Now This Is the Story (SSA)   Carl Fischer
    Te Deum   Augsburg
Foss, Lukas
    A Parable of Death   Carl Fischer
    Prairie, The   G. Schirmer
    Psalms   Carl Fischer
Franck, César
    The Beatitudes (an oratorio)   G. Schirmer
    Communion Service in A Major, Op. 12   E. C. Schirmer
Gabrieli, Giovanni
    Jubilate Deo   Bourne; G. Schirmer
    Timor et Tremor   Annie Banks
Gesualdo, Carlo
    Illumina Nos   Boosey & Hawkes
    Tres Sacrae Cantiones   Boosey & Hawkes
Gounod, Charles
    Gallia   G. Schirmer
    Mass in C   G. Schirmer
    Messe Solennelle (St. Cecilia)   G. Schirmer
    Missa Choralis   E. C. Schirmer
    Missa Paschalis   E. C. Schirmer
Grieg, Edvard
    Choral Suite   Hinrichsen & Peters
    Psalms for Mixed Chorus   C. F. Peters
Hammerschmidt, Andreas
    Holy Is the Lord   Concordia
    How Then Shall We Find Bread?   Concordia

Now Death Is Devoured	Concordia
Handel, George Frederick	
Acis and Galatea	Novello
Alceste	Novello
An Autumn Day	Oxford
Belshazzar	Associated
Canticle of Praise	G. Schirmer
Dettingen Te Deum	H. W. Gray
Foundling Hospital Anthem	C. F. Peters
Israel in Egypt	G. Schirmer
Joshua	Novello
Judas Maccabaeus	G. Schirmer
King Shall Rejoice, The	Novello
Laudate Pueri Dominum (Psalm 112)	C. F. Peters
Messiah	G. Schirmer
O Sing Unto the Lord (Psalm 96)	G. Schirmer
Samson	G. Schirmer
Saul	H. W. Gray
Sixth Chandos Anthem	G. Schirmer
Solomon	Breitkopf & Härtel; H. W. Gray
Te Deum Laudamus	Verlag Merseburger
Hanson, Howard	
Beat! Beat! Drums!	J. Fischer
Cherubic Hymn, The	Carl Fischer
Song of Democracy	Carl Fischer
Song of Human Rights	Carl Fischer
Songs from *Drum Taps*	J. Fischer
Harris, Roy	
Mass in C (for Male Voices and Organ)	Carl Fischer
Hassler, Hans Leo	
Mass No. 5	Concordia
Haydn, Joseph	
Creation, The	G. Schirmer
Mass in Time of War	G. Schirmer
Missa Brevis in F	Doblinger
Missa Solemnis	C. F. Peters
Seasons, The	G. Schirmer
Seven Last Words of Christ, The	G. Schirmer
Sixteenth Mass	H. W. Gray
Third Mass (The Imperial or Lord Nelson)	G. Schirmer
Haydn, Michael	
Timete Dominum (O Fear the Lord)	G. Schirmer
Hindemith, Paul	
Apparebit Repentina Dies	Schott

Four Songs	Schott
Messe	Schott
When Lilacs Last in the Door-yard Bloom'd	Schott
Holst, Gustav	
The Coming of Christ	G. Schirmer
Honegger, Arthur	
Cantate de Noël	Editions Salabert
Danse des Morts, La	Editions Salabert
King David	E. C. Schirmer
Nicholas de Flue	E. C. Schirmer
Hovhaness, Alan	
Glory to God	C. F. Peters
In the Beginning Was the Word	C. F. Peters
Look Toward the Sea	C. F. Peters
Make a Joyful Noise	C. F. Peters
30th Ode of Solomon	C. F. Peters
Kodály, Zoltán	
Missa Brevis	Boosey & Hawkes
Psalmus Hungaricus	Universal
Te Deum	Universal
Kubik, Gail	
Litany and Prayer (TTBB)	Southern Music
Lasso, Orlando di	
Missa *Puisque j'ay Perdu*	J. Fischer
Lockwood, Normand	
A Ballad of the North and South	Associated
Carol Fantasy	Associated
The Holy Birth	Choral Services
Lotti, Antonio	
Mass VII in the Doric Mode	E. C. Schirmer
Liszt, Franz	
The XIIIth Psalm	G. Schirmer
Lully, Jean Baptiste	
Te Deum	Schott
Martirano, Salvatore	
O O O O That Shakespearian Rag	Schott
McDonald, Harl	
Pioneers, O Pioneers	Elkan-Vogel
Songs of Conquest	Elkan-Vogel
McKay, George F.	
Choral Rhapsody	J. Fischer
Mendelssohn, Felix	
As the Hart Pants (42nd Psalm)	G. Schirmer
Christus	G. Schirmer
Come Let Us Sing (95th Psalm)	G. Schirmer

Elijah (oratorio)	G. Schirmer
First Walpurgis Night, The Op. 60	G. Schirmer
Hear My Prayer	G. Schirmer
Hymn of Praise	G. Schirmer
Kyrie	Oxford
114th Psalm	Novello
St. Paul (oratorio)	G. Schirmer
Mennin, Peter	
Christmas Story, The	Carl Fischer
The Cycle (Symphony No. 4)	Carl Fischer
Menotti, Gian Carlo	
Death of the Bishop of Brindisi, The	G. Schirmer
Milhaud, Darius	
Cantate pour louer le Seigneur	Universal
Cantique du Rhone	Elkan-Vogel
Château du Feu, Le	Associated
Miracles of Faith	G. Schirmer
Naissance de Vénus	Heugel
Pan et Syrinx	Editions Salabert
Three Psalms of David	Associated
Monteverdi, Claudio	
Lagrime d'Amante al Sepolcro dill'Amata	Lawson-Gould
Magnificat Primo	Lawson-Gould
Mozart, Wolfgang A.	
Coronation Mass	G. Schirmer
Davidde Penitente (K. 469)	Broude Bros.
Glory, Praise and Power	H. W. Gray
Grand Mass in C minor	G. Schirmer
Litania in E flat (K. 243)	Edwin F. Kalmus
Mass in C (K. 317, "Coronation")	Breitkopf & Härtel; G. Schirmer
Misericordias Offertorium de Tempore	G. Schirmer
Missa Brevis in C (K. 220)	Associated
Missa Brevis in D (K. 194)	Edward B. Marks
Missa Brevis in F Major (K. 192)	G. Schirmer
Regina Coeli	G. Schirmer
Requiem Mass	H. W. Gray; C. F. Peters; G. Schirmer
Orff, Carl	
Carmina Burana	Schott
Catulli Carmina	Schott
Trionfo di Afrodite	Schott
Pachelbel, Johann	
Der Herr ist König	Concordia

Jauchzet dem Herrn (Shout Forth to the Lord)	Concordia
Magnificat in C	Summy-Birchard
Palestrina, Giovanni	
Assumpta est Maria	Breitkopf & Härtel
Leichte Chore	Breitkopf & Härtel
Missa Iste Confessor	Breitkopf & Härtel; Edward B. Marks
Missa Brevis	Breitkopf & Härtel; G. Schirmer
Missa Papae Marcelli	J. Fischer; G. Schirmer
Missa Tu es Petrus	Breitkopf & Härtel
Pater Noster	Breitkopf & Härtel
Stabat Mater	Mills; G. Schirmer
Pergolesi, Giovanni	
Magnificat, The	Walton Music
Persichetti, Vincent	
Mass	Elkan-Vogel
Pierné, Gabriel	
Children at Bethlehem, The	G. Schirmer
Pinkham, Daniel	
Canticle of Praise	E. C. Schirmer
Easter Cantata	C. F. Peters
Emily Dickinson Mosaic, An (SSAA)	C. F. Peters
Jonah	E. C. Schirmer
Jubilate Deo	E. C. Schirmer
Mass of the Word of God	E. C. Schirmer
Requiem	C. F. Peters
Saint Mark Passion	C. F. Peters
Wedding Cantata	C. F. Peters
Poulenc, Francis	
Gloria	Editions Salabert
Stabat Mater	Editions Salabert
Praetorius, Michael	
Canticum Trium Puerorum	Sam Fox
Prokofieff, Serge	
Alexander Nevsky	Leeds Music
Purcell, Henry	
Te Deum Laudamus and Jubilate Deo	G. Schirmer
Rachmaninoff, Sergei	
Springtide	G. Schirmer
Reizenstein, Franz	
Voices of Night	H. W. Gray
Respighi, Ottorino	
Laud to the Nativity	Franco Colombo

Rimsky-Korsakov, Nikolai
    Polonaise with Chorus   Boosey & Hawkes
Rogers, Bernard
    A Letter from Pete   Southern Music
    Prophet Isaiah, The   Southern Music
Rorem, Ned
    From an Unknown Past   Southern Music
    Two Psalms and a Proverb   E. C. Schirmer
Rossini, Gioacchino
    Stabat Mater   G. Schirmer
Rozsa, Miklos
    To Everything There Is a Season   Broude Bros.
Saint-Saëns, Camille
    Christmas Oratorio   G. Schirmer
Scarlatti, Alessandro
    Salve Regina   Walton
    Te Deum Laudamus   Theodore Presser
Schoenberg, Arnold
    De Profundis (Psalm 150)   Leeds Music
    Gurre-Lieder   Universal
    Kol Nidre   Boelke-Bomart
    Ode to Napoleon (for Speaker and String
        Orchestra)   G. Schirmer
    Peace on Earth   Schott
    Survivor of Warsaw, A   Boelke-Bomart
Schubert, Franz
    Gesang der Geister über den Wassern
        (for male voices)   Carl Fischer
    Mass in A♭   Breitkopf & Härtel;
                                          Novello
    Mass in F   G. Schirmer
    Mass in G   H. W. Gray;
                                          G. Schirmer
    Miriam's Song of Triumph   G. Schirmer
    Rosamunde   G. Schirmer
Schuman, William
    A Free Song   G. Schirmer
    This Is Our Time   Boosey & Hawkes
Schütz, Heinrich
    Annunciation According to St. Luke, The J. Fischer;
                                          G. Schirmer
    Christmas Story, The   G. Schirmer
    Deutsches Magnificat   Bärenreiter-Ausgabe
    84th Psalm   G. Schirmer
    German Requiem, A   G. Schirmer
    Magnificat   Breitkopf & Härtel

Mein Sohn, warum hast du uns das getan? Oxford
Nativity   Bärenreiter
Passion According to St. John, The   Oxford
Seven Last Words, The   Oxford; G. Schirmer
St. Luke Passion, The   Oxford
St. Matthew Passion, The   Augsburg; Breitkopf
      & Härtel; Oxford

Symphonia Sacra No. 4   Oxford

Senfl, Ludwig
    Ich stund an einem Morgen   Lawson-Gould

Shostakovich, Dimitri
    Song of the Forests (cantata)   Leeds

Sowerby, Leo
    The Ark of the Covenant   H. W. Gray
    The Canticle of the Sun   H. W. Gray
    Christ Reborn   H. W. Gray
    Forsaken of Man   H. W. Gray
    Great Is the Lord   H. W. Gray
    The Throne of God   H. W. Gray

Stainer, John
    Crucifixion, The   G. Schirmer
    Daughter of Jairus, The (cantata)   G. Schirmer

Stravinsky, Igor
    Cantata   Boosey & Hawkes
    Flood, The   Boosey & Hawkes
    Les Noces   Boosey & Hawkes
    Mass   Boosey & Hawkes
    Oedipus Rex   Boosey & Hawkes
    Perséphone (ballet with chorus)   Boosey & Hawkes
    Symphony of Psalms   Boosey & Hawkes
    Threni   Boosey & Hawkes

Surinach, Carlos
    Cantata of St. John   Associated

Tallis, Thomas
    Lamentations (Parts I and II)   Oxford

Thompson, Randall
    Americana   E. C. Schirmer
    A Feast of Praise   E. C. Schirmer
    Mass of the Holy Spirit   E. C. Schirmer
    Nativity According to St. Luke   E. C. Schirmer
    Ode to the Virginian Voyage   E. C. Schirmer
    Passion According to St. Luke   E. C. Schirmer
    Peaceable Kingdom, The   E. C. Schirmer
    Requiem   E. C. Schirmer
    Testament of Freedom   E. C. Schirmer

Thomson, Virgil
    Mass (unison)   G. Schirmer
    Missa pro Defunctis   H. W. Gray
Vaughan Williams, Ralph
    Dona Nobis Pacem   Oxford
    Epithalamion   Oxford
    First Nowell, The   Oxford
    Five Tudor Portraits   Oxford
    Four Songs of the Four Seasons   Oxford
    Mass in G minor   G. Schirmer
    Pilgrim's Journey   Oxford
    Sancta Civitas   Oxford; G. Schirmer
    Sea Symphony, A   Galaxy; Oxford;
                                      Stainer & Bell
    Serenade to Music   Oxford
    Song of Thinksgiving, A   Oxford
    Thanksgiving for Victory   Oxford
    This Day   Oxford
    Vision of Aeroplanes (Motet), A   Oxford
Verdi, Guiseppe
    Four Sacred Pieces   Franco Colombo
    Requiem   G. Schirmer
    Te Deum   C. F. Peters
Victoria, Tomas Luis de
    O Magnum Mysterium   Associated; J. Fischer
                                      & Bros.
Vivaldi, Antonio
    Chamber Mass   Lawson-Gould
    Gloria   Ricordi
Walton, William
    Belshazzar's Feast   Oxford
    Coronation Te Deum   Oxford
    Gloria   Oxford
    In Honor of the City of London   Oxford
Weber, Carl Maria von
    Mass No. 1 in G   Lawson-Gould

MUSIC PUBLISHERS

Alfred Music Co., Inc. 75 Channel Drive, Port Washington, N.Y. 11050

Annie Banks (order from World Library Publications)

Associated Music Publishers, Inc., 609 Fifth Ave., New York, N.Y. 10017

Augsburg Publishing House, 426 S. Fifth St., Minneapolis, Minn. 55415

Bärenreiter Music Publishers, Inc., 250 West 57th St., New York, N.Y. 10019

Belwin, Inc., 250 Maple Ave., Rockville Center, L.I., N.Y. 11571

Boelke-Bomart (order from Associated Music Publishers, Inc.)

Boosey & Hawkes, Inc., Oceanside, N.Y. 11572

Boston Music Co., 116 Boylston St., Boston, Mass. 02116

Bourne, Inc., 136 W. 52nd St., New York, N.Y. 10019

Breitkopf & Härtel (order from Associated Music Publishers, Inc.)

Broude Bros., 56 W. 45th St., New York, N.Y. 10036

Chantry Music Press, Box 1101, Springfield, Ohio 45501

Chappell & Co., Inc., 609 Fifth Ave., New York, N.Y. 10017

Choral Art Publications (order from Sam Fox Publishing Co.)

Choral Press, 1311 N. Highland, Hollywood, Calif. 90028

Franco Colombo, Inc. (order from Belwin, Inc.)

Concordia Publishing House, 3558 S. Jefferson Ave., St. Louis, Mo. 63118

Consolidated Music Publishers, Inc. (order from Ashley Music Press, 39 W. 60th St., New York, N.Y. 10023)

Crawford Music Corp. (order from Chappell & Co., Inc) .

J. Curwen & Sons (order from G. Schirmer, Inc.)

Dartmouth Publications (order from Shawnee Press, Inc.)

De Sylva, Brown & Henderson, Inc. (order from Chappell & Co., Inc.)

Oliver Ditson (order from Theodore Presser Co.)

Edition Musicus, 333 W. 52nd St., New York, N.Y. 10019

Editions Salabert (order from Belwin, Inc.)

Elkan-Vogel Co., Inc., 1716 Sansom St., Philadelphia, Pa. 19103

Carl Fischer, Inc., 62 Cooper Square, New York, N.Y. 10003

J. Fischer & Bro., Harristown Rd., Glen Rock, N.J. 07452

H. T. Fitzsimons Co., Inc., 615 N. LaSalle St., Chicago, Ill. 60610

Harold Flammer, Inc., 251 W. 19th St., New York, N.Y. 10011

Mark Foster Music Co., P.O. Box 783, Marquette, Michigan 49855

Sam Fox Publishing Co., 11 West 60th St., New York, N.Y. 10023

Galaxy Music Corp., 2121 Broadway, New York, N.Y. 10023

Garland Music Corp. (order from Hansen Publications, Inc.)

H. W. Gray Co., Inc., 159 E. 48th St., New York, N.Y. 10017

Greenwood Press (see World Library Publications)

Hansen Publications, Inc., 1824 West Ave., Miami Beach, Fla. 33139

T. B. Harms Co. (order from Chappell & Co., Inc.)

Harms, Inc. (see Warner Bros.—Seven Arts Music)

Heugel and Cie (order from Theodore Presser Co.)

Hinrichsen & Peters (order from C. F. Peters Corp.)

Raymond A. Hoffman, 1615 Briggs, Wichita, Kansas 67203

Charles W. Homeyer & Co. (order from Carl Fischer, Inc.)

R. L. Huntzinger (order from Willis Music Co.)

Neil A. Kjos Music Co., 525 Busse, Park Ridge, Ill. 60028

Lawson-Gould Music Publishers, Inc. (order from G. Schirmer, Inc.)

Leeds Music (order from MCA Music)

Lorenz Publishing Co., 501 E. 3rd St., Dayton, Ohio 45401

Ludwig Doblinger Verlag (order from Associated Music Publishers, Inc.)

MCA Music, 543 West 43rd St., New York, N.Y. 10036

McLaughlin & Reilly Co., 67 Kingston St., Boston, Mass. 02111

Edward B. Marks Music Corp., 136 W. 52nd St., New York, N.Y. 10019

Mercury Music Corp., 47 W. 63rd St., New York, N.Y. 10023

Mills Music, Inc., 1790 Broadway, New York, N.Y. 10019

Edwin H. Morris & Co., Inc., 31 W. 54th St., New York, N.Y. 10019

Music Press (order from Century Music Co., 39 W. 60th St., New York, N.Y. 10023)

Music Publishers Holding Corp. (see Warner Bros.—Seven Arts Music)

Novello (order from H. W. Gray Co., Inc.)

Oxford University Press, 1600 Pollitt Drive, Fair Lawn, N.J. 07410

Paterson's Pub., Ltd. (order from Carl Fischer, Inc.)

Paull-Pioneer Music Corp., 1657 Broadway, New York, N.Y. 10019 (order from Shawnee Press, Inc.)

C. F. Peters Corp., 373 Park Ave. South, New York, N.Y. 10016

Piedmont Music Company, Inc. (order from Edward B. Marks Music Corp.)

Plymouth Music Co., Inc., 1841 Broadway, New York, N.Y. 10023

Theodore Presser Co., Presser Place, Bryn Mawr, Pa. 19010

Pro-Art Publications, 469 Union Ave., Westbury, L.I., N.Y. 11590

Remick Music Corp. (see Warner Bros.—Seven Arts Music)

G. Ricordi & Co. (order from Belwin, Inc.)

J. J. Robbins (Consolidated Music Publishers), 240 W. 55th St., New York, N.Y. 10019

R. D. Row Music Co. (order from Carl Fischer, Inc.)

E. C. Schirmer Music Co., 600 Washington St., Boston, Mass. 02111

G. Schirmer, Inc., 609 Fifth Ave., New York, N.Y. 10017

Arthur P. Schmidt Co. (order from Summy-Birchard Co.)

Paul A. Schmitt (see Schmitt, Hall & McCreary Co.)

Schmitt, Hall & McCreary Co., 527 Park Ave., Minneapolis, Minn. 55415

Schott & Co., Ltd. (order from Associated Music Publishers, Inc.)

Shattinger (order from Hansen Publications, Inc.)

Shawnee Press, Inc., Delaware Water Gap, Pa. 18327

Southern Music Publishing Co., Inc., 619 Broadway, New York, N.Y. 10019

Staff Music Co., 374 Great Neck Rd., Great Neck, L.I., N.Y. 10023

Summy-Birchard Co., 1834 Ridge Ave., Evanston, Ill. 60204

Transcontinental Music Publications, 1674 Broadway, New York, N.Y. 10019

Tuskegee Institute, Music Press, P.O. Box 1052, Tuskegee, Ala. 36088

Universal Editions (order from Theodore Presser Co.)

Verlag Merseberger (order from C. F. Peters Corp.)

Volkwein Bros., Inc., 117 Sandusky St., Pittsburgh, Pa. 15212

Walton Music Corp., 1841 Broadway, New York, N.Y. 10023

Warner Bros.—Seven Arts Music (Music Publishers' Holding Corp.; Harms, Inc.; Witmark; Remick). 619 West 54th St., New York, N.Y. 10017

Weintraub Music Co. (order Consolidated Music Publishers, Inc.)

Westwood Press (see World Library Publications)

Joseph Williams, Ltd. (order from Mills Music, Inc.)

Williamson Music, Inc. (order from Chappell & Co., Inc.)

Willis Music Co., 440 Main St., Cincinnati, Ohio 45201

M. Witmark & Sons (see Warner Bros.—Seven Arts Music)

B. F. Wood Music, Inc. (order from Mills Music Co.)

Words and Music, 1841 Broadway and 60th, New York, N.Y. 10023

World Library Publications (Greenwood Press; Westwood Press; World Library of Sacred Music), 2145 Central Parkway, Cincinnati, Ohio 45214

World Library of Sacred Music (see World Library Publications)

EDUCATIONAL FILMS

Choral directors will find educational sound films to be of considerable value in broadening their singers' musical backgrounds, and increasing motivation and the effectiveness of their teaching. Specific films are included in this Appendix to aid the director in the following ways:

1. to provide information about fundamental vocal techniques;
2. to broaden and clarify the singers' concept of artistic choral singing;
3. to develop an understanding of historical eras, and the musical styles of various composers;
4. to increase the singers' understanding of the theoretical aspects of music;
5. to assist young singers in their exploration of music as a possible career.

Obtaining Films

Films are available from a variety of sources: (*a*) city libraries, audio-visual departments; (*b*) university audio-visual departments; (*c*) film producers; (*d*) regional and national film distributors. School music teachers should work through the visual-aids representative of their schools. This person usually has an adequate supply of visual-aids catalogs, and will be able to provide valuable information and assistance in securing appropriate films. It is suggested that in seeking films, teachers explore the sources in the order suggested above. If films are not available through local city libraries, then directors should study carefully the catalogs of the nearest state university, or a university that distributes films for educational purposes. As a final resort, one should inquire directly of the producer, or the national or regional distributor, for information concerning the availability and location of specifically desired films. Addresses of the latter firms are included at the end of this Appendix.

Following each film title in this listing is an abbreviation of the producer's name. For the complete name and address see the listing at the end of this Appendix. Also following the film title is the length of the film in minutes, the year of the film's release, and a key to the age level for which the film would be most appropriate. This key is as follows:

el—elementary school (grades 4-6)
jh—junior high school (grades 7-9)
sh—senior high school (grades 10-12)
 c—college or university level
ad—adult level.

Unless otherwise indicated, films are available in black and white only. Films available in color, or in either black and white (b & w) or color are also indicated by each title. Rental prices are not listed because they vary slightly with various film outlets. For specific price information, refer to the catalogs of film distributors in your area.

Procedure in Using Films

Three distinct steps are necessary in the successful use of films for instructional purposes:

1. Preparation
  If the group is to be adequately motivated to learn, and if it is to gain the maximum benefit from viewing the film, it is essential that the group be prepared for what it is going to see and hear. Before he shows the film, the instructor should preview it in order to have sufficient knowledge and understanding of its content to focus and direct the class discussion.

2. Presentation
  In presenting the film, the instructor should pay careful attention to the focus of the projector lens and the volume of the sound. Attention to these important factors is vital and permits the group to gain maximum benefit from the film. Attention to adequate ventilation and lighting and the elimination of outside disrupting sounds are also essential.

3. Follow-up
  Following the showing, a discussion should be held and the group should review the essential points illustrated in the film. The subject matter of the film should then be specifically related to the problems and subject-matter content with which the group has been working.

Choral Groups

A Time for Bach (AFFilms) 26 min. sh-c-ad. 1950.
  Includes a rehearsal of the Bach Aria Group, organized for the purpose of preforming arias from little-known Bach cantatas. The music of Bach is integrated into the various inconsistent patterns of contemporary life.

Anthems of the Church (Cathedral) 3 parts. 10 min. each. el-jh-sh-c-ad. 1945. The St. Luke Choristers sing: "The Cherubic Host"; Father of Mercies"; and "The Lord is Exalted." The text of these anthems is superimposed upon backgrounds to allow for audience participation.

Choral Concert (CanNFB) 10 min. sh-c-ad. 1948.
A choral concert by the "Leslie Bell Singers," a girl's choir. The following selections are included: "Ay-Ay-Ay," "Echo Song," "Ouard J'etau Chez Mon Père," "I Couldn't Hear Nobody Pray, "I'se De Boy Dat Builds De Boat," and "Ave Maria."

Christmas Carols (UW-Castle) 10 min. el-jh-sh-ad. 1945.
The Castle Choir sings "The First Noel," "Hark the Herald Angels Sing," and "Adeste Fideles." Words appear on the screen for the purpose of community singing.

Christmas Music for the Southwest (Ariz U.) 14 min. el-jh-sh-c-ad. 1955.
A traditional Mexican carol, a cowboy Christmas song, and a Latin hymn are sung by the University of Arizona Symphonic Choir.

Glasgow Orpheus Choir (BIS) 12 min. jh-sh-c-ad. 1953.
The Glasgow Orpheus Choir sings: Scots Psalm Tune—"Kedron"; Scottish song—"Mice and Men"; Highland Song—"The Isle of Mull"; Faery Chorus from "The Immortal Hour"; Choral Dance—"The Dashing White Sergeant".

Glee Club (Brown U.) 5 min. b & w or color. sh-c-ad. 1956.
The Brown University Glee Club sings the spiritual "Rock-a My Soul," and the Brown song. "God Bless this University."

Hail Alma Mater (US Army) 6 min. sh-c-ad. 1951. (Free loan.)
The West Point Glee Club sings "Army Blue" and "Hail Alma Mater." Scenes of the U.S. Military Academy at West Point are utilized as pictorial background.

Heart That Sings (Broadman) 20 min. c-ad. 1957.
Relates the role of music in the church and the importance of a graded choir program.

It's Fun to Sing (Sterling) 11 min. sh-c-ad. 1948.
A chorus of 60 Toronto business girls, under the direction of Leslie Bell, sings "Greensleeves," "Long Beach Sea," "Ah, Si Mon Moine," and Palestrina's "Sanctus." The selection "Dry Bones" is sung informally.

Let My People Live (Nat TB) 15 min. jh-sh-c-ad. 1938.
The Tuskegee Institute Choir sings three Negro spirituals and a portion of the "Hallelujah Chorus" from *Messiah* as a musical background to a film dealing primarily with the problem of tuberculosis.

Lord's Prayer, The (UW-Govt.) 4 min. el-jh-sh-c. 1950.
The U.S. Air Force Singing Sergeants sing "The Lord's Prayer."

Merry Christmas (Sterling) 12 min. el-jh-sh. 1949.
The Vienna Boys' Choir sings the traditional carols in preparation for an annual Christmas festival.

On Wings of Song (Brandon) 15 min. el-jh-sh-c-ad. 1955.
The Vienna Boys' Choir sings Schubert's "Horch, Horch" and "Serenade," Mozart's "Minuet in E Flat," Brahms' "Lullaby," and Herbeck's "Pueri Concinite." A description of the singers' daily lives is also included.

Selections from the Christmas Oratorio by J. S. Bach (Brandon) 14 min. jh-sh-c-ad. 1965.
Selections from J. S. Bach's *Christmas Oratorio* are performed by the Montreal Bach Choir, under the direction of George Little.

Singing Champions (Can NFB) 10 min. jh-sh-c-ad. 1952.
The Boys' Choir of St. Joseph's University, under the direction of Father Leandre Brault, sings "V'la l'bon vent," "Alouette," a Gregorian version of "Alleluia," and "La vie etudiante." Scenes are shown of the singers at work, at play, during rehearsals, and on the concert stage.

Songs of Christmas (Portafilms) 18½ min. Color. el-jh-sh-c-ad. 1957.
A presentation of Roy Ringwald's "The Song of Christmas," in which the story of the Nativity is related in songs, carols, and selections from the Bible.

Songs of the Campus (McGraw-Hill) 15 min. jh-sh-c-ad. 1952.
The University of Michigan Men's Glee Club sings familiar college songs representing various sections of the country. Activities at various colleges provide a visual background.

Voice of a Choir (UW-Govt.) 24 min. sh-c-ad. 1952.
A performance of the Bach Choir is included in this film produced for the U.S. Department of State.

Youth and Music in Detroit (Wayne U.) 24 min. Color. el-jh-sh-c-ad. 1956. Includes choral, instrumental, and modern dance numbers of the Detroit Cooley High School's annual spring festival.

Composers

Beethoven and His Music (Coronet) 13½ min. Color or b & w. jh. 1954. Relates how the social upheavals of the latter part of the eighteenth century are reflected in the music of Beethoven. Describes the unique qualities of Beethoven's music, and how it served as a bridge of transition from the Classical to the Romantic era.

Brahms and His Music (Coronet) 13 min. Color or b & w. el-jh-sh. 1957. The ideas of Brahms, where he lived, and the persons who influenced him are related within a framework of his selected compositions.

Finlandia (Sterling) 10 min. jh-sh-c-ad. 1947.
Pictures Sibelius at work and at leisure about his home. *Finlandia* and his *Second Symphony* are played by the Helsinki Philharmonic.

George Fredrick Handel (UW-Religious) 10 min. jh-sh-c-ad. 1947.
Scenes depicting Handel's early life are shown. The "Hallelujah Chorus," "Largo," and other selections are performed.

Great Waltz (TFC) 17 min. jh-sh-c-ad.
Scenes from the life of Johann Strauss, the "Waltz King," are depicted and some of his music is heard. Adapted from the MGM feature film produced in 1938, and prepared in collaboration with the Music Educators National Conference.

Immortal Bizet (Almanac Films) 20 min. jh-sh-c-ad. 1950.
Scenes depicting the life of Georges Bizet are shown against a background of European cities. Music is performed by the Concerts du Conservatoire, an outstanding French orchestra.

Liszt and His Music (Coronet) 13 min. Color and b & w. el-jh-sh. 1957. Relates portions of the life of Franz Liszt, cities where he composed and performed, and incidents that inspired him.

Mozart (NET) Two films. c-ad. 1956.
Part 1. 28 min. Relates the early life and music of Mozart. The humanistic qualities of Mozart's operas are described.
Part 2. 29 min. Mozart's mature operas and their background are listed and discussed.

Mozart and His Music (Coronet) 13½ min. Color or b & w. jh. 1954.
Selections composed by Mozart are performed, and the elegant, formal life of the eighteenth century is re-created.

Norman Dello Joio (Artists Films) 12½ min. el-jh-sh-c-ad. 1951.
Scenes from the life of the American contemporary composer, Norman Dello Joio.

One Life for Music, Richard Strauss (Mills) 26 min. el-jh-sh-c-ad. 1955. A documentary film on the life of Richard Strauss. Includes scenes in the composer's villa, as he composes and performs at the piano. Filmed during the last year of his life. Background music for these scenes includes excerpts from his operas *Salome* and *Der Rosenkavalier,* and from various symphonic poems.

Schubert and His Music (Coronet) 13½ min. Color or b & w. jh. 1954. Through various scenes, the film depicts the tempo of early nineteenth century Vienna, which is reflected in the music of Schubert. The Romantic aspects of Schubert's music are also stressed.

Schumann Story (TFC) 30 min. jh-sh-c.
Adapted from the feature film *Song of Love,* produced in 1947 by MGM. Scenes are shown depicting the life of the composer Robert Schumann and his music.

Verdi (NET) Two films: 30 min. each. c-ad. 1956.
Part 1. A background of Verdi's life is presented. The composer's early operatic productions, the characteristics of the Italian opera, and Verdi's contribution to his country are described. Part 2. The mature works of Verdi in his later years are discussed.

Music Theory[3]

"Music as a Language" (NET) 13 films. 29 min. each. sh-c-ad. 1955. Produced by the University of Rochester. Individual titles are:

1. *Music and Emotion.* Illustrates how composers have used rhythm, harmony, tonal quality, volume, and dissonance as a means of evoking emotion in music.

2. *Music as Sound.* Discusses the "chord of nature" as it is used in the composition of certain types of music.

3. *Alphabet in Black.* Illustrates how the use of black keys of the piano are characteristic of a great deal of primitive music, and describes how this device has been used by certain modern composers.

4. *Alphabet in White.* The different colors and tonal qualities of the various white key scales are illustrated as a part of the composer's musical vocabulary.

---

[3] Choral conductors will find particular films on music theory more adaptable for use with choral groups than others. However, since the conductor's ultimate use may extend to a theory class, a listing of the entire series on this topic has been included.

5. *Musical Words.* The use of various words is illustrated as a part of the composer's musical vocabulary.

6. *Modern Music.* Illustrates the difference between the white key scale and the scales used by such composers as Debussy.

7. *Six Basic Categories.* The theory that most music may be placed into one of six different categories is discussed.

8. *Meter and Rhythm.* Tempo, pulse, rhythm, meter, and accent are discussed and illustrated with various musical examples.

9. *Narrative Music.* Dicusses the similarity among various composers' uses of certain chords to describe specific moods in music.

10. *Romantic Symphony.* Analyzes the structure of a symphony and compares form to the form or structure or other related arts.

11. *Merry Mount.* Describes the techniques and devices that a composer uses to convey the mood of the music, and the characterizations of certain roles in an opera, to an audience.

12. *Colors in Music.* Describes the use of instrumental tone colors and groups of instruments as a means of achieving varied musical effects.

13. *Essay in Sound.* A symphonic score is analyzed and explained.

"Passing Notes on Music" (NET) 26 films. 29 min. each. c-ad. 1956. Produced by WKAR-TV. Individual titles are:

Set 1

1. *Passing Notes on Music: Introduction.* Discusses the importance of passing notes in music.

2. *Time in Music.* Discusses the importance of musical timing. Existing differences of opinion on the subject are also discussed.

3. *Aural Memory.* Discusses the importance of aural memory as a means of increasing one's understanding and enjoyment of music.

4. *Rhythm.* The importance of rhythm in music is explained and the three aspects of rhythm are illustrated.

5. *Musical Phrase.* The "onward surge" of the musical phrase is discussed and illustrated. Examples are drawn primarily from the Baroque period.

6. *Rhythmic Extensions.* The postponement of cadences and the extension of musical phrases are discussed as devices for "stretching time" in music.

7. *Elements of Tone.* Qualities of musical tone, such as pitch, loudness, timbre, and duration, are discussed and illustrated.

8. *Tonality.* The psychological effects of various tonal patterns are discussed and illustrated.

9. *Major and Minor Tonalities.* The relationship of various tones and chords to the keynote is discussed. The influence of major and minor tonalities upon mood is explored as it occurs in music from 1600 to 1900.

10. *Tonalities Old and New.* Discusses tonalities from the major and minor interrelationships used by Beethoven to the more modern tonal systems used today. A continuation of the film, *Major and Minor Tonalities.*

11. *Key-Feeling.* Differentiates between the terms "key" and "tonality." The subject of "key colors" is also discussed.

12. *Color Variation.* Color variation is defined as modulation or change of key, and its use as a means of adding to the total effect of the music is discussed.

13. *Expressive Modulation.* Excerpts from the music of Beethoven and Schubert illustrate the dramatic effect of sudden key changes and the expressive characteristics of modulation in music.

Set 2

1. *Passing Notes on Music II—Introduction.* The scope of this film series is outlined and the nature and function of passing notes in music is discussed. Music is compared with architecture.

2. *Texture.* Homophony and polyphony are compared as ways for combining voices in music.

3. *Polyphony.* The sixteenth-century motet and the fugue are used to illustrate two types of imitative polyphony.

4. *Motivic Repetition.* The motive is defined as the "core" or "kernel" of music and its repetition is necessary and essential until the music becomes meaningful.

5. *Sectional and Thematic Repetition.* Compares sectional repetition to forms existing in architecture. The uses of thematic repetition are also explained.

6. *Ternary Form.* Ternary form is defined and the relationship between the opening theme and the repetition is explained.

7. *Motivic and Thematic Variation.* The development of tonal and rhythmic change from the basic motive is explained, and the music of Beethoven is used to illustrate thematic variation.

8. *Thematic Development.* The expansion of the basic ternary form into the sonata form is discussed and illustrated.

9. *Variation Form.* The theme and variation form is discussed and a set of variations by Beethoven is used for illustrations.

10. *Tonal Contrast.* Describes the differences between tonal contrast and harmonic contrast. A portion of a Bach cantata is used as an illustration.

11. *Textural and Thematic Contrast.* Music by Palestrina, Bach, and Handel is used to illustrate thematic contrast.

12. *Character Contrast and the Episodic Principle.* Music by Beethoven is used to illustrate tempo and character contrast. Music by Mozart and Chopin is used to illustrate the episodic principal.

13. *Episodic Forms.* The episodic principle is defined and illustrated with music by Beethoven and Haydn.

Personality of Music (NET) 29 min. jh-sh-c-ad. 1957.
Discusses and illustrates the idea that the personality of music is determined by the composer's musical style and his use of particular musical effects.

Vocal Techniques

Changing Voice, The (Florida) 29 min. jh-c-ad. 1959.
A demonstration showing that boys can continue to sing throughout adolescence.

Human Throat (Bray) 12 min. sh-c-ad. 1947.
The function of the pharynx and larynx is described from the anatomical viewpoint.

Improving Your Posture (Coronet) 10 min. Color. el-jh-sh. 1949.
Good posture is explained and demonstrated. Certain posture difficulties are demonstrated, and exercises for their improvement are discussed.

Mechanisms of Breathing (EBF) 11 min. sh-c-ad. 1954.
Illustrates the various components of the body involved in the breathing process.

Vocal Music (EFB) 10 min. jh-sh. 1950.
The structure of the human vocal instrument and some of the

basic techniques of singing are described, such as correct posture, breath control, relaxation, use of chest and head resonators, and clarity of diction. Certain faults common to inexperienced singers are included. Filmed at the Carl Schurz High School in Chicago, Illinois.

Your Posture (Young America) 10 min. el-jh-sh. 1953.
The importance of good posture to health and appearance is discussed and demonstrated.

Your Voice (EBF) 11 min. jh-sh-c-ad. 1949.
The four phases of voice production—respiration, phonation, resonance, and articulation—are explained. Photography of the vocal cords or folds shows them in operation. Examples of solo and group singing are included, and the importance of proper exercises for vocal improvement is stressed.

Miscellaneous Films

Methods of Ensemble Singing (NET) 29 min. sh-c-ad. 1958.
Various staging techniques used in effective ensemble singing in opera are demonstrated.

Music: Career or Hobby? (Coronet) 11 min. Color or b & w. sh. 1953. A boy interested in the possibilities of music as a career is assisted by a music teacher, a guidance counselor, and professional musicians. The advantages and the disadvantages of a musical career are emphasized. The importance of exploring the variety of possible vocations in music and determining one's basic musical aptitude is presented.

Music Reading (Johnson Hunt) 20 min. el-c. 1953.
A film designed to demonstrate the teaching of music reading in the classroom. For elementary school children and classroom teachers.

Operetta (NET) 29 min. c-ad. 1956.
The characteristics of operetta and its emergence from various eighteenth-century opera styles are discussed. A summary of some of the better-known and more established operettas is presented.

Recording with Magnetic Tape (Minnesota U.) 8 min. el-jh-sh-c-ad. 1954. Instructions are provided for the operation of tape recorders. The varied uses of the tape recorder, including the correction of choir mistakes, is demonstrated.

Science of Musical Sound, The (Academy) 11 min. el-jh-sh. 1964.
An introduction to basic principles of musical sound through animation, oscilloscope patterns, and motion-picture techniques.

Singer and the Opera (NET) 29 min. c-ad. 1956.
An interview with Madame Lotte Lehmann, in which she relates the requirements of an opera singer and demonstrates her technique for teaching students how to sing with better musical expression.

Sound and the Story (Inst. Visual Tng.) 22 min. Color. jh-sh-c. 1956.
Illustrates the various procedures involved in the production of a high-fidelity recording.

Two-Part Singing (Johnson Hunt) 20 min. 31-jh. 1952.
Illustrates procedures for teaching two-part singing.

PRODUCERS AND DISTRIBUTORS OF EDUCATIONAL FILMS[4]

Academy	Academy Films, 748 N. Seward St., Los Angeles, Calif. 90028
AFFilms	A. F. Films, Inc., Rm. 1001, 1600 Broadway, New York, N.Y. 10019
Almanac Films	Almanac Films, Inc., 516 Fifth Ave., New York, N.Y. 10018
Ariz. U.	University of Arizona, Visual Aids Bureau, Tucson, Ariz. 85702
Artists Films	Artists Films, Inc., 8 W. 45th St., New York, N.Y. 10017
BIS	Contemporary Films, Inc., 267 W. 25th St., New York, N.Y.
Brandon	Brandon Films, Inc., 200 W. 57th St., New York, N.Y. 10019
Bray	Bray Studios, Inc., 729 Seventh Ave., New York, N.Y. 10019
Broadman	Broadman Films, 127 Ninth Ave. N., Nashville, Tenn. 37203
Brown U.	Brown University, Brown Photo Lab., Providence, R.I. 02912
CanNFB	National Film Board of Canada, 1270 Ave. of the Americas, New York, N.Y. 10020 (or 400 W. Madison St., Chicago, Ill. 60606)
Cathedral	Cathedral Films, 140 N. Hollywood Way, Burbank, Calif. 91503

---

[4] This list is limited only to the producers and distributors of films included in this publication. For addresses of firms not included in this Appendix, see the *Educational Film Guide*. New York: H. W. Wilson Co.

Coronet	Coronet Instructional Films, 65 E. South Water St., Chicago, Ill. 60601
EBF	Encyclopaedia Britannica Films, Inc., 1150 Wilmette Ave., Wilmette, Ill. 60091
Florida	Florida State University, University Broadcasting Services, Tallahasse, Fla. 32306
Inst. Visual Tng.	Institute of Visual Training, Inc., 40 E. 49th St., New York, N.Y. 10017
Johnson Hunt	Johnson Hunt Productions, 6509 De Longpre Ave., Hollywood, Calif. 90028
McGraw-Hill	McGraw-Hill Book Co., Text-Film Dept., 330 W. 42nd St., New York, N.Y. 10036
Mills	Mills Picture Corp., 6533 Hollywood Blvd., Hollywood, Calif. 90028
Minn. U.	University of Minnesota, Audio-Visual Education Service, Westbrook Hall, Minneapolis, Minn. 55414
Nat TB	National Tuberculosis Assoc., 1790 Broadway, New York, N.Y. 10019
NET	NET Film Service, Indiana University, Audio-Visual Center, Bloomington, Ind. 47401
Portafilms	Portafilms, Orchard Lake, Mich.
Sterling	Sterling Films, Inc., 316 W. 57th St., New York, N.Y. 10019
TFC	Teaching Film Custodians, Inc., 25 W. 43rd St., New York, N.Y. 10036
US Army	Army Pictorial Service Division, Motion Picture Branch, Washington, D.C. 20013
UW-Govt.	Government Films Dept., United World Films, Inc., 1445 Park Ave., New York, N.Y. 10029
UW-Religious	Religious Film Dept., United World Films, Inc., 1445 Park Ave., New York, N.Y. 10029
Wayne U.	Wayne State University, Audio-Visual Materials Construction Bureau, 438 Ferry St., Detroit, Mich. 48202
Young America	McGraw-Hill Book Co., Text-Film Dept., 330 W. 42nd St., New York, N.Y. 10036

MANUFACTURERS OF MUSIC EQUIPMENT

In general, choral directors will find that local music dealers can meet their particular music equipment needs, especially as they pertain to audio-visual equipment, pianos, and storage cabinets. In the event that certain equipment is not available through local firms, directors should contact the manufacturer directly for general information, including exact specifications and prices, as well as the name and address of the nearest dealer or company representative. Upon request, most companies will send catalogs as well as other pertinent information. Manufacturers of choir apparel, in addition, will send swatches of materials. The names of various companies and their addresses are as follows:

Audio-Visual Equipment

Microphones

Altec Lansing Corp., 1515 S. Manchester Ave., Anaheim, Calif. 92800
Electro-Voice, Inc., Buchanan, Mich. 49107
Telefunken—Gotham Audio Development Corp., 2 W. 46th St., New York, N.Y. 10036

Motion Picture Projectors (16mm)

Bell & Howell Co., 710 McCormick Rd., Chicago, Ill. 60645
Eastman Kodak Co., Rochester, N.Y. 14604
RCA Victor Div., Radio Corp. of America, Camden, N.J. 08100

Record Players

Califone Corp., 1041 N. Sycamore, Hollywood, Calif. 90038
Fairchild Recording Equipment Co., 10–40 45th St., Long Island City, N.Y. 11100
Garrard Sales Corp., 80 Shore Rd., Ft. Washington, L.I., N.Y. 10032
Rek-O-Kut Co., 38–19 108th St., Corona, N.Y. 11368

Tape Recorders

Ampex Audio, Inc., 1020 Kifer Rd., Sunnyvale, Calif. 94086
Bell Sound Systems, 555 Marion Rd., Columbus, Ohio 43207
Magnecord Div. of Mid-Western Instruments, Inc., Box 7186, Tulsa, Okla. 74100
Tanberg of America, Inc., 8 Third Ave., Pelham, N.Y. 10803

Acoustical Shells

Stagecraft Corp., 25 Belden Ave., Norwalk, Conn. 06850
Wenger Music Equipment Co., 90 Park Drive, Owatonna, Minn. 55060

Choir Apparel

Blazers

Academic Church & Choir Gowns, 1125 N. Highland Ave., Hollywood, Calif. 90038

Eastwood Apparel, Ltd., Staten Island, N.Y. 10314

Fechheimer Bros. Co., 400 Pike St., Cincinnati, Ohio 45202

Robert Rollins Blazers, Inc., 242 Park Ave. South, New York, N.Y. 10003

Stanbury & Company, 7233 Troost Ave., Kansas City, Missouri 64131

Choir Robes

Academic Church & Choir Gowns, 1125 N. Highland Ave., Hollywood, Calif. 90038

Collegiate Cap & Gown Co., 1000 N. Market St., Champaign, Ill. 61820

DeMoulin Bros. & Co., 1083 S. Fourth St., Greenville, Ill. 62246

Ireland Needlecraft, 3661 San Fernando Rd., Glendale, Calif. 91204

E. R. Moore Co., 932 Dakin St., Chicago, Ill. 60613

Thomas A. Peterson Co., 501 E. 33rd, Kansas City, Mo. 64109

The C. E. Ward Co., New London, Ohio 44851

Choir Risers

Berntsen Brass & Aluminum Foundry, 2334 Pennsylvania Ave., Madison, Wisc. 53700

Humes & Berg Mfg. Co., Inc., 4801 Railroad Ave., East Chicago, Ind. 46312

Mitchell Manufacturing Co., 2744 S. 34th St., Milwaukee, Wisc. 53246

The Monroe Co., 351 Church St., Colfax, Iowa 50054

Paysen Manufacturing Co., Box 136, Fairbury, Neb. 68352

Perry Products Co., Box 8156, Portland, Ore. 97207

Wenger Music Equipment Co., 90 Park Drive, Owatonna, Minn. 55060

Music Stands

Krauth & Benninghofen, Hamilton, Ohio 45011

Manhasset Specialty Co., Yakima, Wash. 98901

H. & A. Selmer, Inc., Selmer Building, Elkhart, Ind. 46514

Wenger Music Equipment Co., 13 Wenger Bldg., Owatonna, Minn. 55060

Pianos

Baldwin Piano Co., 1801 Gilbert Ave., Cincinnati, Ohio 45202
Everett Piano Co., South Haven, Mich. 49090
Steinway & Sons, Steinway Place, Long Island City, N.Y. 11105
Story & Clark Piano Co., 28 E. Jackson Blvd., Chicago, Ill. 60604
Rudolph Wurlitzer Co., De Kalb, Ill. 60115

Safety Candles (battery operated)

Gamble Hinged Music Co., Inc., 312 S. Wabash, Chicago, Ill. 60604
HAR-TEE, Inc., Box 3101, Cleveland, Ohio 44117

Storage Cabinets

All-Steel Equipment, Inc., 26 John St., Aurora, Ill. 60504
Art Metal Construction Co., Jones & Gifford Aves., Jamestown, N.Y.
   14701
Deluxe Metal Furniture Co., 22 Struthers St., Warren, Pa. 16365
Globe-Wernicke Co., Ross & Carthage Aves., Norwood, Ohio 45212
Lyon Metal Products, Inc., 1934 Madison Ave., Aurora, Ill. 60504
Norren Mfg. Co., 2220 E. Foothill Blvd., Pasadena, Calif. 91108
Remington Rand, Div. of Sperry Rand Corp., 3 Rockefeller Plaza,
   New York, N.Y. 10020

HAND SIGNALS FOR TV[5]

Stand by. *Arm bent. Hand up and open.*

Cue for "on the air." *Arm bent. Full arm motion with forefinger pointing to speaker.*

 Time signals: 1. One minute. *Upright extended forefinger.*

2. One-half minute. *Crooked forefinger.*

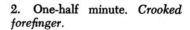
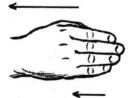 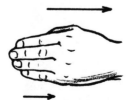

3. Stretch. *Motion of hands pulled apart.*

[5] As used by the Radio-TV Department, University of Cincinnati, Cincinnati, Ohio. Used by permission.

4. Speed up. *Extended fore-finger, spun around . . . slow or fast, accordingly.*

5. Time is up. *Clenched fist. Given at 10 seconds, to allow speaker to complete thought.*

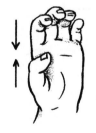

Cut. *Slashing motion of hand across throat.*

"On the air" camera. *Arm fully extended, forefinger pointing to camera.*

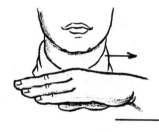

Speak louder. *"Donald Duck" motion with hand being raised.*

Speak softer. *"Donald Duck" motion with hand being low-ered.*

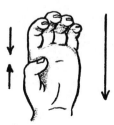

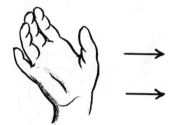

Move. *Hand motion in direction to move.*

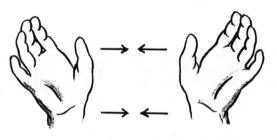

Move closer together. *Both hands moved toward each other.*

Move closer to microphone. *Hand moved toward mouth. Space being indicated.*

Rise. *Hand, palm up, being raised.*

Sit down. *Hand, palm down, being lowered.*

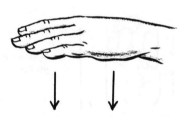

On time. *Forefinger touched to tip of nose.*

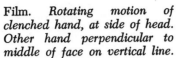

Film. *Rotating motion of clenched hand, at side of head. Other hand perpendicular to middle of face on vertical line.*

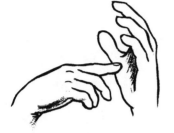

Spot signal. *Forefinger pointed to palm of other hand.*

Station break. *Both hands clenched, with breaking motion.*

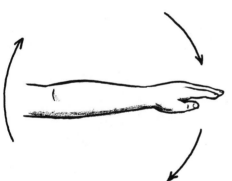

Repeat. *Windmill movement of entire arm. Used only for musical numbers.*

(*Note:* All time signals are indicated with the right hand. All other movements, etc., are indicated with the left hand.)

Index

Columbia College Library
Columbia, Missouri